AND ALL IS SAID

AND ALL IS SAID

MEMOIR OF A HOME DIVIDED

Zareer Masani

PENGUIN BOOKS

PENGUIN BOOKS

USA | Canada | UK | Ireland | Australia
New Zealand | India | South Africa | China

Penguin Books is part of the Penguin Random House group of companies whose addresses can be found at global.penguinrandomhouse.com

Published by Penguin Random House India Pvt Ltd
7th Floor, Infinity Tower C, DLF Cyber City,
Gurgaon 122 002, Haryana, India

Penguin
Random House
India

First published by Penguin Books India 2012

Copyright © Zareer Masani 2012

Photograph of 'Kailash', the Srivastava home in Kanpur, courtesy of
Vijay K. Srivastava
All other photographs courtesy of Zareer Masani

All rights reserved

10 9 8 7 6 5 4 3 2

The views and opinions expressed in this book are the author's own and the facts are as reported by him which have been verified to the extent possible, and the publishers are not in any way liable for the same.

ISBN 9780143417606

Typeset in Garamond by R. Ajith Kumar, New Delhi
Printed at Repro Knowledgecast Limited, India

This book is sold subject to the condition that it shall not, by way of trade or otherwise, be lent, resold, hired out, or otherwise circulated without the publisher's prior consent in any form of binding or cover other than that in which it is published and without a similar condition including this condition being imposed on the subsequent purchaser.

www.penguin.co.in

*To my
parents and
grandparents*

'Shakuntala, and all at once is said!'
—Kalidasa

CONTENTS

Introduction   x

1. Ashes of Roses   1
2. Lost Battles   11
3. A Daughter of Empire   29
4. Against the Tide   35
5. Officers and Gentlemen   59
6. Weddings and Divorces   70
7. An Only Child   91
8. Tough Love   107
9. A Political Wife   128
10. The Indira Wave   146
11. Emergency   179
12. Loose Ends   196
13. Little Problems   224

INTRODUCTION

This is the story of a controversial love marriage across India's communal divide, which ended tragically in seventeen-year-long divorce proceedings. I was the only child of that marriage and, to my continuing regret, played a crucial part in its breakdown. The half-century during which our triangular relationship was played out was also a period of dramatic political conflict and change in the subcontinent, a history in which both my parents and grandparents played a prominent part.

The Masani and the Srivastava families were as divided by temperament, lifestyle and political affiliation as the Montagues and Capulets of Shakespeare's Verona; and their mutual battles often reached the same intensity. But, for all their differences, they shared a passionate belief in the value of Western education, modernization, secularism and women's emancipation.

My paternal grandfather, Sir Rustom Masani, was a scholar and man of letters who scorned wealth and the comforts it could buy. He began his long career as a journalist at the turn of the nineteenth century, became the first 'native' Indian Municipal Commissioner of Bombay, then Rector and Vice Chancellor of Bombay University in the 1930s, and Leader of the National War Front in the 1940s. He spent the rest of his life, well into his nineties, writing scholarly historical books on subjects as wide-ranging as Persian court poets and British colonial rule.

My father Minoo rebelled against his own pro-British father in the 1930s, when he was one of the founder-leaders of the Congress Socialist Party. Later, in the 1940s, he was among the first left-wing intellectuals to see through the betrayal of socialism by Soviet Communism and by its Indian fellow travellers, among whom he numbered his former friend and colleague, Jawaharlal Nehru. His role as founder-leader of the pro-Western, free-market Swatantra Party, India's first serious parliamentary

Opposition, is well known; and it is ironical that our present Prime Minister from the Congress Party, Dr Manmohan Singh, acknowledges Minoo Masani as his main ideological inspiration, rather than Pandit Nehru.

My mother's family, Kayasths of Uttar Pradesh, could not have been more different from the Parsi Masanis. My maternal grandfather, Sir J.P. Srivastava, made a fortune as a textile mill owner, and his children grew up in the lap of hedonistic luxury with British and French governesses. Sir J.P. was an arch Empire loyalist and prominent in the viceregal cabinet through the 1940s as the right-hand man of two successive viceroys, Lords Linlithgow and Wavell. My mother rebelled, joined the Quit India movement and absconded from her parental home to work as a journalist in Bombay.

Neither family was pleased when my parents fell in love and eloped, especially as my father was fifteen years older than his bride and had been married and divorced twice before. Growing up in the 1950s and '60s, I was torn between the rival influences and attractions of my Parsi and Hindu grandparents. Later, in 1970, I rebelled politically against my father; and in a dramatic public defection that made press headlines, my mother and I joined Indira Gandhi and rejoiced in her landslide victory of 1971. Unfortunately, their political differences marked the end of my parents' marriage; and I paid the price for encouraging the break when I had to cope with my mother's loneliness, unhappiness and general decline in the decades that followed. Our disillusionment with Mrs Gandhi, especially when she imposed her state of Emergency, made the whole domestic rift seem even more futile.

My parents were remarkable individuals with considerable talents. In telling their story I have drawn heavily on their personal and very eloquent letters and diaries, especially as they both wrote extremely well. As far as possible, I have been candid about their flaws and my own, in the belief that the truth, warts and all, will do more justice to their memory than the usual Indian fashion for family hagiography. I have also been frank about my own sexuality and the trials and tribulations of growing up in the homophobic world of 1950s Bombay.

My father was vindicated in his lifetime by the collapse of socialism both globally and in India; but my mother departed with no such sense of achievement. I have tried to offer her in death some of the dignity that adverse circumstances denied her in later life. As a historian, I believe that this family memoir might also have some value as a record of three generations who bridged and contributed to India's evolution from nineteenth-century British colonial rule to the status of an emerging, twenty-first-century superpower.

ONE

ASHES OF ROSES

My mother's ashes are in a black cardboard box, about the size of a large shoebox. It is sealed with Sellotape when I collect it from the funeral parlour, and I don't dare open it for a closer look. It feels surprisingly light, about a kilo, which is fortunate, because I've been told by the funeral director that I have to carry it in my hand baggage. Customs might need to check that I'm not smuggling forbidden substances.

In life, she travelled anything but light, especially as her summer migrations to London grew longer with the advancing years. Regardless of local availability or airline baggage restrictions, she came with half a dozen suitcases full of everything she might conceivably need for several months, ranging from clothes for every season and occasion to towels and medication. To be fair, she also loved giving presents; and she came bearing gifts for me, my partner Dave and our friends, and for the north London house that was becoming her second home.

The pattern was established three decades ago, when it became clear that, after several years as a student, I would inevitably stay on abroad, first as a freelance journalist and, when that proved too uncertain, as a more secure BBC current affairs producer. Underlying my reluctance to return to India, where family connections would certainly have brightened my career prospects, lurked my sexuality, for which permissive 1970s London looked a great deal more promising. But there was also an instinctive need, not yet consciously articulated, to escape the domination of an overbearing father, the dependence of an overindulgent mother and their internecine warfare, which focused as much on the upbringing of an only child as on their own incompatibility.

Having tried and failed to entice me home from migrant mediocrity, my mother gave up and decided to join me for as long as she could each year. Dave welcomed her warmly, fascinated by tales of her exotic and gilded youth in viceregal India, a world away from his own Methodist childhood in rural Leicestershire. They became firm allies in a campaign to resist my bossy ways. When, after fifteen years, Dave finally gave up and left me, our parting was amicable: and my mother, without invitation, filled the vacuum.

More surely than any swallow ever made a summer, her arrivals and departures came to mark the seasons for me, and increasingly for the neighbours, local shopkeepers and dog-walkers she befriended. She had a natural charm which somehow enabled her to bridge class divisions in ways I couldn't. She made friends in the most unexpected places: like the Nag's Head flea market, where she browsed for bargains, or the local parks, where she regaled working-class Londoners with childhood memories of viceregal tiger-shoots and banquets in her parental home.

And then, suddenly one autumn it was clear that she was too frail for her usual winter migration back to India. Through another year of decline, delayed by dialysis, she fantasized about an Indian homecoming when she was 'better'. And now she is going back for good, with the remains of her seventy-nine years reduced to the contents of one shoebox.

During the final months she was unusually stoical, overlooking the impatience and irritation with which I tended her and appearing to understand intuitively that they were born of fear and exhaustion. Dave, though happily resettled with a Cuban refugee, also rose loyally to the occasion, helping me with the nursing and eventually the funeral arrangements. Then, it took me a month to sort through my mother's enormous wardrobe, distributing mementoes to friends and carers, and carting off the rest to Animal Aid, a choice of charity suggested by her own unabashed preference for animals over humans. All that remained now was to organize her return to India.

I have always been a nervous traveller, arriving at airports and railway stations far too early for fear of being late. At the Heathrow check-in, I am happy to see a familiar, smiling face. It is a duty officer who knew Mother from her many trips back and forth. She was adept at charming officials like him who could smooth her path with free excess baggage and upgrades to First Class. No sooner do I mention that she has died and that I am taking her remains back to India than he squeezes my hand and solemnly announces: 'I'm upgrading you to Business Class. I can't let Mrs Masani travel Economy on her last journey home.'

For the next ten hours, with her ashes nestling gratefully in a zip-bag under my comfortably extended long legs, I have plenty of opportunity to reflect on Mother's turbulent, often unhappy, but never dull, existence. While I knew her as a deeply needy and emotionally deprived individual, frightening in her unspoken demands for reassurance from me in particular, the outside world barely glimpsed the tip of the iceberg. To casual acquaintances, especially male, she projected feminine elegance and sensuality, along with an irresistibly seductive vulnerability. It was an aura which helped her, and incidentally me, to overcome many of the practical hurdles and vicissitudes of everyday life. For the first time, I shall be landing in India without that reassurance awaiting me.

It is three o'clock in the morning, Indian time, when we circle over Delhi, preparing to land. There are few lights at this hour, and the shapes of the city seem ghostly and forbidding. I emerge with growing apprehension from the baggage hall into a chaotic sea of faces outside. It takes me several minutes, wheeling my trolley nervously back and forth, before I spot cousin Meera leaning patiently against a pillar, her warm smile and ample shape as solid and welcoming as a stone *yakshi* at a temple gate. 'I couldn't *not* come when you were bringing Mausi's ashes,' she announces, with unusual solemnity, when I thank her. Half an hour later I am home, or rather at my mother's home. It is a moment I have dreaded, for the memories and ghosts that have still to be laid to rest. I am greeted by Mother's two trusted menservants and by the two mongrel dogs she rescued from the streets and turned into pampered pets. Their presence is reassuring as I walk with some trepidation to Mother's bedroom, now to be mine.

I wake late the morning after my return: it is the crack of dawn, London time. According to the usual custom of my mother's home, I ask Shanta, Mother's elderly maidservant, for a pot of tea in the bright, elegant drawing room, hung with antique Mughal miniature paintings, Tibetan *thangka*s and Rajasthani *pichwai*s. It all looks so normal that I almost expect Mother to walk in, fussing about whether I've had enough sleep and whether I want eggs for breakfast.

I have only two weeks in Delhi to deal with the bureaucratic intricacies of transferring various securities from my mother's name to mine, to sort through her personal effects and papers, to pack away fragile antiques and valuable silver, and generally leave the flat and other affairs in the kind of order that will enable Satish Babu, Mother's part-time secretary, to manage things in my absence. In addition to the practical demands of securing my inheritance, there are the emotional pressures of dealing with Mother's various siblings, with all of whom she had tempestuous relations. Their feelings now range from remorse and guilt about how little they had done for her during her long, final illness, to annoyance and resentment about how much she expected from them, not least financially, in her later years; it is as though by dying she has dealt them the ultimate blow, one to which there can be no comeback.

Since none of them attended her cremation on a cold autumn day in dismal Golders Green, the family now wants to organize a memorial puja for her; but they can't agree about where and when. They all agree that the ashes I had brought home with me must be immersed in the Ganges, but can't decide whether this should be before or after the puja, which bit of the sacred river is most suitable, how long a journey this might involve away from Delhi and who should go. Those who urge that the ashes should be dispersed in the farthest and cleanest reaches of the river do so safe in the knowledge that age, ill health or even gender will spare them the long journey: a convenient family tradition excludes women from such ceremonies.

My mother's sisters bear an uncanny resemblance to her, which I find both familiar and disconcerting, as though they are reflections of her distorted by trick mirrors. One is a leaner, elongated version, with an acerbic temper to match. The other is round, malleable and wreathed in smiles. The third and youngest, with whom she quarrelled for most of her life, lives in Bombay, so is out of the picture for the time being.

The two Delhi sisters, who live in large adjacent mansions, finally agree on a mutually convenient date to hold the memorial puja in their shared back garden. But when they inform cousin Meera, who has not been consulted, she says that she has other commitments that day. The more bossy of the two aunts, lean Sarala Mausi, promptly phones me in high dudgeon, to say that Meera is being ever so petty in threatening to boycott the puja; I must phone her at once to tell her off. Meera assures me that she has every intention of attending; all she said was that, not having been consulted about the date, she can't be expected to take on the religious and catering arrangements. When I pass this back to my aunt, she exclaims: 'What cheek! As though we can't make the arrangements ourselves. All we have to do is hire the pandit, and he'll do the rest.'

But on the day, Meera has the last word. The priest my aunts have booked arrives just before midday, when the ceremony is due to begin. About a hundred guests, mostly relatives, have already assembled in a large semicircle of chairs laid out on the back lawn, facing the large paved veranda where the havan is to take place. The priest is a middle-aged man with greedy eyes and a long, drooping moustache dyed jet black. He looks around, then asks my aunt: 'But Behenji, where are all the provisions I need for the puja? Sandalwood and ghee for the sacred fire, and all the other offerings to be thrown on the flames?'

'How should I know where they are?' snaps Sarala Mausi. 'I told you to bring whatever you needed with you.' But the pandit is not to be so easily intimidated: this is his moment of power and he knows it; he is indispensable. 'What did you expect?' he yells back. 'I told you the provisions would cost 1000 rupees, but you gave me only 250, which barely covers my own time. I can do nothing until you give me the full amount. Otherwise send for the things yourself.' Left to herself, my aunt would not succumb to such blackmail; but with so many guests waiting to pay their last respects, I persuade her that this is not the moment for conspicuous thrift. I quickly hand the man 1000 rupees and ask him to take my car and driver at once to the local shops to get what he needs.

Meera can't contain her amusement at the aunts' discomfiture. 'What did I tell you?' she chortles. 'They said they didn't need me to organize things, and now look what a mess they've made. As though any pandit gets the provisions at his own expense!'

An hour later, the puja has at last begun. The priest's Sanskrit chants are sonorous and hypnotic, not unlike Gregorian plainsong. But any dignity the occasion might have held is dispelled for me, not just by the earlier financial haggling, but by the ritual itself. As the deceased's only child, I am required to sit cross-legged on the floor, an improvised handkerchief covering my head, facing the priest across the large brazier that holds the burning sandalwood. The heat and smoke from the flames are blowing directly into my face. Has the priest skilfully arranged it so? Worse, every couple of minutes, at a signal from him, I am expected to dip a large tablespoon into a pot of ghee and various other comestibles and feed these to the sacred fire, which spits and leaps in response. It feels far more like some tortuous and embarrassing culinary penance than a commemorative ritual. As the minutes pass, the sweat rolls down my face, and the spoon grows so hot that it singes my fingers when I hold it. From time to time, the chanting finds an unexpected polyphony, as Sarala Mausi's contralto soars above the pandit's voice. She chats animatedly to those around her, complaining bitterly about everything from Delhi air pollution to the venality of the times in which priests are so greedy and unreliable.

A few days later, I make the final journey with Mother's ashes, accompanied by two loyal cousins. We drive out through the grand, red sandstone Mughal walls of the old city, past suburban housing estates and then commercial farms, into the adjacent state of Uttar Pradesh. We are heading for a small village on the banks of the Ganges, where we hope to escape the attentions of the hordes of predatory brahmins who throng all the main temple towns on the river, extorting blood-money from families who want to immerse the ashes of their loved ones without inauspicious curses. The plan is that we will make for a small tourist rest-house on the riverbank and then hire a boat, ostensibly for sightseeing. Once out of sight of greedy, priestly mendicants, we can scatter the ashes unmolested.

Unfortunately, the plan misfires. As soon as the car pulls up outside the rest-house, three rival pandits, with an equally unerring nose for profit, are upon us. We pretend not to notice them; but just as our boat is about to leave shore, one of them, no doubt in silent collusion with the boatman, jumps aboard. He has long, shoulder-length hair, a wild beard and eyes, and a small brass pitcher with which he scoops up some water from the river. While he chants Sanskrit prayers, I hesitantly open the cardboard box with the ashes, and find an inner container in dark red plastic. I open the lid, which has been taped shut, and prepare myself for the final act.

Who, if anyone, will perform these last rites for me, I wonder, and, will I care? For a moment, I feel awed by how transient, ephemeral and insignificant our lives seem against the backdrop of this vast river, which has flowed for thousands of years. Mother grew up on its banks, in a large riverside mansion in the city of Kanpur, a couple of hundred miles downstream. Now a dusty and decaying provincial town, it was a thriving, new industrial centre during the Raj. It was there that my grandfather launched his business empire in the 1920s, buying up a British-owned textile mill that had employed him as an engineer.

I remember too that, as the 'Cawnpore' of imperial history, it was the scene of one of the worst massacres of the Indian Mutiny. The rebel leader Nana Sahib was credited with piling hundreds of captive British women and children on to river barges and then drowning them with artillery fire. Historians still disagree about what really happened. Be that as it may, as children my mother and her siblings often watched the grisly funerary remains and floral offerings of hundreds of other cremations floating down the sacred river. As a precocious six-year-old, she once surprised her brother with the prescient observation: 'Just imagine, some day that will be one of us floating past.'

An incipient lump in my throat subsides as the pandit, suddenly aware that he is about to become superfluous, shouts at me to stop. 'Before scattering the ashes,' he bellows, 'you must let me bless you with sacred *ganga-jal*.' I hold out my hands over the side of the boat, as he pours icy cold water from his pitcher over them. 'Not yet!' he yells, as I reach once again for the plastic urn. 'First you must pay me 1000 rupees or your mother's soul will have no peace.' For a moment, I am overcome by rage. 'You filthy, crooked man,' I shout, waving my fist at him. 'You dare to call yourself a priest! If I hear another word out of you, it will be you we immerse in the river, not my mother's ashes.'

The pandit eventually yields to my cousin's compromise offer of Rs 500, and I am at last allowed to scatter the ashes. I am about to throw in the plastic urn as well when he snatches it from my hands. 'No, no, this will be very useful to me,' he says. 'Waste not, want not! I will keep it in sacred memory of your mother.'

Any funerary sadness dissipated by these shabby proceedings, the three of us drive back to Delhi in heated argument about the venal excesses of Hindu priesthood, compared with the more respectful and respectable observances of Christian and Muslim clerics. It is not long before our own appetites take over, as we pull over into a field in the shade of some trees. It is time for my cousin's picnic hamper to yield its delights. Not having had any breakfast, I am ravenous; and the 'roly-polies', curried chicken and lamb wrapped in paper-thin *rumali rotis*, are especially tempting.

Now that the ceremonies are over, my main task is to go through a large attaché-case packed with old papers, which Mother stored in one of her closets. Though its contents are dusty, they are permeated by the perfumed fragrance of her clothes. I spend my evenings sifting letters from old shopping receipts and an entirely unexpected horde of food recipes, some cut out from various magazines and others jotted down by hand, presumably from friends. These come as a surprise: unlike me, Mother appeared remarkably uninterested in food for most of her life. A vegetarian by choice, she was also a conspicuously small eater, especially as her diet became increasingly circumscribed by a variety of ailments. 'My dear, if you don't mind my asking, which part of you is sound?' quipped an uncle in Surrey, who had invited us to lunch and felt mildly let down by her lack of appetite.

Despite her public frugality about food, the recipes she collected ranged from rich European cakes and pies to mouth-watering Mughlai meat dishes, none of which I ever knew her to commission from her own cook. Had she kept them merely for the vicarious pleasure of browsing through them; or did she hope that she would be able to use them when she could once again entertain on the scale to which she was accustomed before her traumatic divorce?

The letters present me with a more troubling conundrum. Reading them feels like an invasion of her privacy; yet not to do so seems cowardly and negligent. Since they have been crammed together in no particular order, they leap back and forth across sixty years of her life. There are love letters she wrote to my father before their marriage (though mysteriously none from him in reply). When did he return them to her, before or after their messy and acrimonious divorce? There are also hundreds of letters I wrote to her: she must have kept them all. Many are in a childish scrawl, pining for her return during the long months I spent with my grandparents while my parents were away, and cunningly exaggerating the privations I had to suffer in her absence. Reading them is a reminder of much that I preferred to forget about my childhood and adolescence, most of all how adept both Mother and I were at manipulating each other's emotions.

Among the papers I also find some sporadic attempts at autobiography. Mother had a gift for writing and especially for telling a good story. It made her a successful children's author in her youth and she illustrated her own books with lively sketches. Later in life I nagged her to write about her own life for adults, hoping that autobiography might become an outlet for her frustrated nervous energy. She lacked the stamina for a substantial book, but left behind some fragments that are elegant, poignant and remarkably self-critical.

For the rest of my stay, these dusty old letters and papers become both an addiction and an occupation. At times I feel as though they are vital clues to my own story, even though I know the ending. At other moments, they almost literally bring Mother alive, resurrecting her in a sudden but familiar turn of phrase. For most of my life, I have cherished and nurtured my own solitude, always fearful it can be abruptly shattered by the intrusions of others. Mother, in particular, came to represent an overwhelming threat of invasion, in a near-permanent state of preparation for her ever-longer trips to London. Her presence became both a focus for my wider resentment of life's disappointments and an alibi for my own inertia.

Now that there is no one to blame but myself, and no one left to stand between me and the fading hopes of middle age, solitude has ceased to be comfortable. The past, trapped in a dusty attaché-case with the scent of roses, is now my refuge: a time when the world was young and anything seemed possible and people could make a difference. It is also an opportunity to reassess my complex triangular relationship with my parents and to offer them in death the understanding, acceptance and respect we found so difficult to achieve in life.

TWO

LOST BATTLES

In 1971 my mother and her favourite sister Sarala had quarrelled violently. It had begun with a political row about Mother electioneering for Prime Minister Indira Gandhi while Father was leading the Opposition against her. Aunt Sarala and her husband, Gogu, had been deeply and, in retrospect, rightly sceptical about Indira's left-wing populism and strongly critical of what they perceived—somewhat harshly—as an unprincipled bid by Mother to steal Father's political thunder. The quarrel had escalated rapidly into a major personal estrangement: for the next fifteen years, the two sisters did not speak to each other, even at family weddings and funerals. And then, in the 1980s, like a spent hurricane, their mutual rage subsided. Mother, encouraged by me, apologized. Aunt Sarala, more grudgingly, accepted, and friendly relations were restored.

In 1989 relations between them were good enough for Sarala Mausi to broker a divorce between my parents. It was the fourth attempt, and Mother only went through with it because she didn't want to alienate her sister yet again. The results were catastrophic: she had a mental and physical breakdown and had to be rushed to hospital with dehydration and kidney failure. For a couple of weeks she hovered between life and death. Sarala Mausi, to her credit, descended from the cool heights of Simla to sweltering Delhi to be at her bedside. Mother recovered; but the emotional scars took much longer to heal.

A year later, Mother accepted Sarala Mausi's invitation to her beautiful summer home in Simla. As the viceregal summer capital, it had been the scene of many happy teenage memories for both sisters, of a gilded age when their father had been in the viceroy's cabinet. Hoping it would cement their reconciliation, Mother went back enthusiastically after an absence of forty years. The reality was very different, and she recorded it in an elegiac fragment of introspection, written after her return to Delhi. I found it nine years later, after her death, in the magical attaché-case.

> The return to my home territory, the contrast between what I was in my youth and what I am today. A gripping feeling of nostalgia, followed by wave after wave of depression and helplessness. Nothing could be retrieved from the wreck of a life completely shattered by adversity and humiliation. Being with a sister who had once been the closest to me drove home the fear that was lurking in my mind: that I could never be in an equal relationship with her as in our youth. A feeling of inadequacy and loss of confidence – afraid of saying and doing the wrong thing.
>
> The only good that has emerged from this is that I know one can never go back to the past; that living in the past is turning away from the truth. Life moves forward and not backwards. The change is on a deeper scale – people change with their circumstances, and one has to come to an understanding with the present.

In another unusually self-critical fragment written around the same time, Mother blames her disasters on her own hubris, intoxicated with the self-importance of media celebrity, when she made front-page headlines for defying her husband and joining Indira Gandhi.

> I was so flushed with my own new identity and the importance and impact of what I had done, that it warped my outlook. Nobody questioned this move. They were too afraid that I would talk to Mrs. Gandhi and action would be taken against them. My brother-in-law did go around questioning what I had done, but if he had only done it in a more kindly way: come and talked to me gently, and let me feel he was a caring person. Nothing like that happened. He went around parties criticising me, and this only put my back up. I

became even more determined in my actions. A word of kindness and understanding would have helped, but there was no one to give this, and so I sank deeper into my follies.

Though critical of her brother-in-law, she accepts responsibility for her own part in the sibling rivalry that damaged her relationships with her sisters.

I must not blame my relations. We were never a family of doers and carers, much to our parents' distress and despair. They saw in each one of us an uncontrollable passion for self-destruction and a very selfish competitiveness. Some of my sisters were close to each other, but it was a closeness brought about by 'downing' the other ones. You made much of one sister, so that you could deflate another one.

I cannot understand how that attitude came about. Was it because my parents had favourites? For instance, I knew that if I played up to my mother I could deprive a sister of some favour. This disgusting trait was only found in our immediate family. Our cousins, who never had such a successful father, hung together and helped each other. This competitiveness was also true of my brothers: there was always one against the other. This jealousy was to grow worse as the years went by, and it has certainly led to the destruction of the family: the loss of the enormous wealth my father had built up out of hard work. I remember him saying: 'If you are wise, each one of you will have wealth for generations.' But this is something we lacked completely: wisdom of the heart, even wisdom of the world.

Mill after mill folded up, but nobody gave it a second's thought. My poor mother, after father's death, saw the shape of things to come. She tried to save something from the wreckage. She had lost faith in her sons, but she now wanted to save something for her daughters. She wrang her hands in despair when she saw even her daughters were pitted one against the other with petty jealousies and competitiveness. If we had not been so talented and attractive a family, we would have been a better family. But unfortunately each member was outstanding in qualities and always wanted to show off at the expense of the others. A wise friend once said in despair: 'What can you do with such lovely people, cast in such a grand mould, when all they want to do is dance on the edge of a precipice.'

The rise and fall of the Srivastava family, spanning half a century, was itself a historical saga of tragic proportions. Mother loved telling the story, and her close friend, the publisher Hamish Hamilton encouraged her to write it. She wrote simply and well: back in the 1940s and '50s, as a young wife and mother, she had written three very successful children's books: *The Story of Jawaharlal*, *The Story of Gandhi* and *The Story of the Buddha*; and she illustrated the first two herself with charming drawings. I remember her saying with pride: 'If you can write for children, you can write for anyone.' Yet, the potential family blockbuster always eluded her. The nearest she came to it were some tantalizing opening pages about her childhood, suggestive of the colour, simplicity and pathos she could have brought to the rest of the story.

There were seven of us children. I was Number 6, the second youngest. I was born on a hot and sultry morning in August. The date was the 9th, and the time not remembered but 'somewhere around 2.30 a.m.', so I was told by my mother when I pressed her to remember. The year must have been 'around the '20s'. It was difficult to remember such details in a home where four families lived together and were forever breeding babies.

We were a joint family, with my father the eldest and therefore the *karta* or doer. According to Hindu custom, his responsibility was to take on all the duties of his own father after his death, and that meant looking after his younger brothers and sister. I have no memories of my grandfather, as I was not born until after he died. He was said to have been a colourful figure: a man of considerable means, but a great spendthrift who lived in a lordly fashion and spent his fortune on good living and high thinking.

He was a man of letters of the Kayasth caste, scribes by origin who rose to powerful administrative positions under the Mughal emperors. Raja Janaki Prasad, my grandfather, was a middle-ranking landowner in the United Provinces, formerly the kingdom of Oudh. He was the British-appointed Tahsildar or tax-collector of his district, Basti. He was determined that his sons, and particularly the eldest, should be highly educated in all spheres.

My father went to school on an elephant in full regalia. It was a district school run by a Munshi who spoke fluent Persian, then the court language, but also had a smattering of English. My father proved to be an outstanding pupil, whose quest for learning went far beyond the poor Munshi's capacity. So it was decided he must go to the city, where he could get a more formal education at an English-medium school where subjects like mathematics and the sciences were taught.

The nearest school was in Kanpur or Cawnpore, as the British called it. They had set up textile industries there because of its advantageous position on the river Ganges. It was also served by a good railway connection and by the Grand Trunk Road, first built by the Mughals.

Young Jwala Prasad showed remarkable genius in both science and the humanities. He left school with flying colours and went on to take a Bachelor's degree in science at Kanpur's Christ Church College. Seeing his brilliance, his father decided that he should be sent abroad for training in cotton textiles. But before he left, at the age of 16, he was expected to marry.

My mother, Kailash, came from a family of culture and refinement of the same caste. She had been educated in the vernacular and spoke not a word of English. Unlike my father, she came from a rather Spartan family who believed that principles and nobility of character, sound moral values and high thinking were the worthwhile virtues to cultivate. She was just fourteen years old when she married. Jwala Prasad accepted her without any hesitation. He perceived in her those intrinsic virtues which he deeply admired. She was beautiful and sensitive in her perceptions. She would be a great companion to him, an asset in every way. Within a few months, the young couple sailed for England.

Describe the voyage and their experience of settling down in Manchester . . .

Here Mother's narrative is interrupted, and I have no way of filling in the gap. I know that a long sea journey to England in the early years of the twentieth century was a daunting experience for the most seasoned traveller, and for a teenaged Indian couple, who had never ventured beyond a provincial town, it must have been rather terrifying.

I've heard from a cousin that my grandmother Kailash's family were shocked by the idea of her crossing the seas, since orthodox Hindus still considered that a form of pollution that involved the loss of caste status. They threatened to disown her if my grandfather took her along, to which his characteristic reply was: 'Let them. I'm her family now. She no longer needs another.'

Another aunt says that it was my grandmother who insisted on going with her reluctant husband, who didn't want to be encumbered by a child-bride who spoke no English. According to this version, my grandmother was spirited enough to appeal to her father-in-law, saying: 'Even Lord Rama allowed Sita to accompany him into exile. How can you deny me that right?'

In any case, she went with him, and they found lodgings in Manchester, then still the textile capital of the world, with an extraordinary and unconventional couple: Shapurji Saklatvala, an aristocratic Parsi from Bombay, and his English wife, the outspoken and large-hearted daughter of a Yorkshire miner. The Saklatvalas later moved to London, where Comrade Sak, as he came to be known, was a leading figure in the British Communist Party and, in the 1920s, its first and only ever elected MP (for Battersea).

Half a century later, in the 1960s, his son, Beram Saklatvala, was the London manager of the giant Indian business house of Tata. He was a good friend of my parents, and we saw him often. On my first visit to London as an adult, in 1963, I remember him taking Mother and me to tea with his own mother, then widowed and in her eighties. She was a great character, full of anecdotes about my mother's parents, none of which I can now remember. I do recall Beram, with his mischievous sense of humour, teasing her with the suggestion that she had been such a wily Yorkshire lass, and my grandmother such an innocent, that when they both gave birth within a few weeks of each other she must have stolen him from my grandmother and substituted a daughter. Mother's eldest sister Queenie, he insisted, was really a Saklatvala and he a Srivastava. 'Can't you see the resemblance?' he asked with his arm round my delighted mother.

I also remember a couple of my grandmother's stories about her early years in England: about how she had to wear large Victorian skirts and learn to ride a bicycle. By the time I knew her, her English was good, though strongly accented. That had caused some amusement in Manchester. 'I used to ask them to pass the soap when we were dining, and demanded soup when I wanted to have a bath!' Here Mother resumes the story of her parents.

> The dullness and strange culture of the West would have demoralised any Indian girl. For Kailash, it was a great upheaval, coming straight from such an orthodox family, brought up with great strictness and simple living. The only men she had known before her marriage were her father and brothers. But being a highly intelligent and versatile young woman, she was quick to learn and to adapt herself to married life in a foreign country.
>
> Within two years of marriage, she became pregnant and gave birth to a baby boy, who died after a few months. The death of their first-born was a sad experience for the young couple, and more so for Kailash who had had to make such big adjustments in her life when she herself was only a child. But she was courageous and kept her spirits up by learning Western ways and encouraging her husband in his higher studies.
>
> Jwala Prasad proved to be a brilliant student. He took his degree at Manchester in Commerce and Science, along with several diplomas in textiles and other sciences. The ease with which he accumulated these academic prizes only proved his brilliance. Meanwhile, Kailash became pregnant again, and a bonny girl was born to them. They named her Lakshmi, after the goddess of wealth. It was not a name that was easy to remember for their English friends in Manchester,

who called her Queenie. The name stuck to her throughout her life, and now she is dead we still remember her as Queenie. Soon after her birth, Jwala Prasad heard that his father was ailing, and he decided to go back to India to look after him.

Mother's notes skip over the next decade in her parents' lives. They were a period of personal hardship and remarkable commercial success against all odds. My grandfather, armed with his newly acquired Western qualifications, had no difficulty finding work as a textile engineer, first with the Gujarati Sarabhai business empire in Ahmedabad, and later in Kanpur, where he had been educated, at the British-owned New Victoria Textile Mill. In a few years, he was doing well enough to buy out the British mill owner; and 'Victoria' became the launching pad for a chain of textile and sugar mills which made him the fifth-largest industrialist in India.

But life on the domestic front hadn't been easy to start with. His father died soon after his return from England, and Jwala Prasad had to pay off his large gambling debts and take on the responsibility of educating his two younger brothers and a sister. Meanwhile, his own family grew rapidly. My grandmother bore him another four daughters and two sons in a space of fifteen years. Mother was the penultimate, born in 1920, by which time the family were comfortably ensconced in a large mansion called 'Kailash Kutir' on the banks of the Ganges. Her earliest memory, which she recorded, was of the birth of her younger sister. Especially with hindsight, it was an event that would significantly alter the shape of her life.

> For four years I was the youngest in the family, and my memory dates back to that time. It was good to be the youngest and to be petted and spoiled by everyone. And then, on a cold night in February, as I sat on my little wooden potty, my Madrasi ayah told me to hurry up and do my business. *'Jaldi karo, Baby!* You now have two new sisters.'
>
> It did not register at first. 'Tell me another story, Ayah, and then I do my chichi, another story!' And then it dawned on me. I

stood up and let my knickers fall to the ground. '*Do* (two) babies, oh?' I asked with great alarm. '*Haan, do,*' she said, holding up two fingers. I caught her two fingers and shook them with all the strength I could muster. '*Nahin, nahin,*' I shouted. I was a spoilt four-and-a-half-year-old. I liked being called 'Baby' and petted by everybody.

I held on to Ayah's two fingers, and I shook my head of curls. '*Nahin!*' I shouted. 'Shoo, baby, you will go to bed and tomorrow morning you can see your sisters.' I was lifted up and put into a little wooden cot covered by a mosquito-net. The ayah patted me into slumber. '*Nini, baby, nini,*' she sang in a soft voice. I resisted her, but within a few minutes my eyes closed and I fell asleep.

My next memories are of two wooden cradles side by side, each with shining white mosquito-nets. It was all very quiet, and there were no ayahs or the younger maids around. This was quite unusual. There was always someone in the nursery, so that when I woke up they would rush and inform my Ayah. Feeling very neglected, I decided to climb out of my cot on my own, and I hoped I would fall and hurt myself, so that I would have my mother rush to me. This morning, however, nobody bothered about me, and I got out of my cot without any mishap and then went straight to the two cradles. I was just able to look into those cradles if I stood on my toes.

What I saw staggered me. In one cradle lay a little china-doll-like figure. She was pale as a lily. Her eyes were closed, and long black lashes rested on her porcelain cheek. Her little white hands were clenched, but when I tried to touch them she opened her fingers and clung on to mine. I was so entranced by the beauty of this lovely little thing that I could not move. I kept saying, 'Lily flower.' I do not know how long I must have stood completely bewitched, but I was brought back to earth with a bang. My Ayah came into the room and shouted, 'Don't go near her! Don't touch her! She is sick,' and pulled me away.

'Come and see your other little sister,' she said, and dragged me to the other cradle. There lay a fat and ugly little baby. Kicking her chubby little legs and clutching at her sheets. 'She is not my sister!' I yelled in anger. 'She is a big, black balloon. My sister is Lily-Flower.' Before I could have any more tantrums, I was taken out of the room. 'You have to be very quiet,' said Ayah. 'Your mother is not well, and Lily-Flower is even more ill. You must play in the garden and be very quiet.'

I was very quiet. I kept thinking of my sister Lily-Flower who would be with me wherever I went. I would show her the little fairy parks I had made of rose-petals in the orange grove and the lakes I had dug out and filled with fresh water so that the fairies could boat at night while I slept. I must be a good girl and listen to Ayah. And if I was especially good I would be allowed to go to Lily-Flower in the morning and hold her delicate white hand. The very thought made me gurgle with delight.

Unfortunately there was no such morning, because Lily-Flower died that night. I never saw her again. They wrapped up her tender, frail body in white cloth and took it away. Her cradle was folded up and put in a corner. The second cradle still stood there, and from it I could hear boisterous baby gurgles. Black Balloon was very much alive, but my little sister Lily-Flower had left me.

The healthy black balloon grew up to be my aunt Malati, who kept her rude health in a family plagued by heart and kidney ailments, and then suddenly and swiftly collapsed into a terminal decline when she turned eighty. Unlike her sisters, she never experienced the travails of creeping old age.

When I was a lonely child, growing up in Bombay in the 1950s, she brought sunshine and laughter into my life. She took me out for treats at the popular Swiss café Bombelli's, with its beautiful array of chocolates and cakes in the window. Often we went back to her bright, airy flat in a tall building called Belmont, at the summit of Malabar Hill, with wonderful views over the sea. She entertained me by singing popular tunes and strumming on her piano. And sometimes she turned on her radiogram, kicked off her high-heeled shoes and danced the Charleston, her sari falling off while I chortled with glee. She was pretty, with sparkling white teeth and beautiful, long, silky hair, which kept escaping its pins and cascading down her shoulders. She lacked Mother's poise and elegance, but she made up for it with energy and bounce.

Unfortunately, Malati had little in common with Mother. She was unashamedly extrovert, without any of Mother's shyness or reserve. Unlike her sisters, she had no pretensions to aesthetic or intellectual pursuits. Her idea of a good time was a few pegs of whisky, hearty jokes and a room full of people. Underneath her bubbly chatter there was also a shrewd instinct for money, inherited, she proudly proclaimed, from her father.

Mother and she fell out in the 1950s. There were frequent rows and each accused the other of maligning her behind her back. After my grandfather's death, his two youngest daughters competed for my grandmother's affections and inheritance. Malati, because she was the youngest, unmarried and the more wily, usually won. Mother attributed the quarrels to Malati's jealousy of her more talented older sister, but now I realize that Mother too had resented Malati almost literally from the cradle. Strange that such an idyllic childhood could have produced such deep sibling rivalry. In the few more pages Mother wrote, before her failing health brought the narrative to a close, there is little sign of the deep-seated tensions that must have lurked beneath the surface. Instead, she harks back to an enchanted childhood with a view that grew increasingly rose-tinted with the advancing years. It was a vista of glittering family and social events, over which her parents presided, interspersed with idyllic summers in the still unspoilt hill stations of the Raj.

> The family had moved up to Naini Tal, the summer capital of the United Provinces under the Raj. It was a charming little hill-station in the Himalayas. There was a large lake, where one could go yachting, and the mountains rose sharply from it into slopes of pines and *deodars*. The air was cool and fragrant, and the wooden cottages and chalets built on its slopes smelled of roses and pine-needles. Near the lake were the 'flats', the only bit of flat ground which could be used for ceremonial parades when the grandeur of the Raj was displayed in full pageantry on occasions like the King's birthday.

Naini Tal was well known in northern India for its excellent convent schools, where the English families could send their children for an education very similar to what they would have learned had they been in England. There was a fairly large Anglo-Indian community who also aspired to give their children a better life, but they were looked down on by the English children and by the very few privileged Indians whose parents held high posts in the government.

We belonged to such a family. My father was the Minister for Education in the U.P. government. Like all privileged children, we were sent to these English schools. In the hill-stations, schools opened in March and ended in December, when they would close for the winter months when the Himalayas were snowbound. The Anglo-Indian children came to these schools as boarders and lived in from March to December. But we, the more privileged, would live in our parents' homes and attend school as day-scholars.

We lived at home surrounded by servants and all our comforts, like the English girls, and the routine of our lives was very much the same. Our home in Naini Tal for sixteen years was Priory Lodge, a large mansion with dozens of rooms, built of timber, with lovely parquet flooring and enormous, rambling gardens filled with roses, with orange groves and stables where we kept our horses. As children, we rode to school on horseback every morning and came back every afternoon on foot, so that we had sturdy hill legs.

Although school opened on March the 15th, my father, being so privileged, would insist we did not have to go up to Naini Tal till April the 1st, when the weather was milder. Our leaving for the hills was quite an event. Our less privileged cousins, who had to stay behind in the plains and face an Indian summer, would get together to arrange farewell parties for us weeks before we actually left; and there would be a lot of hugging and crying as the day of our departure drew near.

We were a family of seven children – two brothers and five sisters. As was normal in Indian homes, the boys came first, and the girls had to fend for themselves. But in many ways we were unusual.

My father adored his daughters and never lost a chance to spoil them, and he always put the boys in their place. His lovely daughters were his pride and joy, and he lost no chance to show us off. Since he was no oil-painting himself, his English colleagues would rag him and ask how he had produced such a good-looking family.

Looking back on it, I think we must have been quite attractive. My mother was a beauty; everywhere she went, she was admired, especially by the British officials, who found her refreshingly unsophisticated and unaware of her own beauty. She was always surrounded by Englishmen, and my father would stand aside, watching her being fussed over. We her daughters had nowhere near her charm.

We were brought up like rich girls would be. We had a large retinue of maidservants and ayahs, and there were lots of chaprasis for the boys. The whole lot were supervised by an English or French governess. My parents had decided that for five years we would have an English governess, who would teach us exactly how an English girl was brought up in England. The following five years we would have a French governess, so that we spoke fluent French. But it never worked. At the end of her five years, our French governess left in despair, speaking fluent English, while none of us had learnt a word of French.

We would arrive in Naini Tal each year with our governess, our ayahs and an enormous number of attendants: a housekeeper, ———, cooks, pantry-boys, sweepers, *malis* [gardeners], horses, dogs, syces [ostlers], and trunks and trunks of school uniforms, carpets, curtains, crockery, cutlery, furniture, special beds and mattresses. Most of all this would be sent up in advance, so that we children did not walk into an empty house.

Leaving Kanpur and our cousins would be a big wrench. There were always terrible scenes of weeping and hanging on to each other at the railway station as the guard blew his whistle. It was all a bit exhausting, and it was a relief to get back to being normal. For about a month and a half, we the kids had this lovely hill-station to ourselves. Then came the summer exodus of the government, moving its headquarters to the hills to escape the summer heat in the plains. Overnight the little town of Naini Tal became the hub of the universe. There was feverish activity. Houses were opened, roads repaired, trees and avenues trimmed. Government House staff arrived, with young Englishmen in their resplendent uniforms. The little theatre was repainted, and actors came to stage Oscar Wilde. The shops in the Mall filled with the latest silks, foodstuffs, cakes and chocolates. The Yacht Club reopened sending white sails floating over the lake. It was fairyland, and oh such fun to be young, rich and in the thick of it.

At Priory Lodge, the upstairs belonged to the children and the downstairs to the grown ups. We had our own playroom and our dining-room, and our friends visited us when they wanted, without bumping into my father's colleagues. But in our own sort of way we were always included in our parents' lives. Lady Hailey, the Governor's wife, would bring her five poodles, and we were asked to come and play with them and roll with them on the drawing-room carpet. Or Lord Hailey would casually stroll up to the children's playroom and play Carom with us.

'Charades . . . Chalet plays . . . Purdah parties . . . Parades . . . Collecting funds for the Congress . . . Rickshaws and dandies . . . My sisters' courtships . . . Treasure-hunts . . . Communal riots . . . Dacoits . . . Government moves down for monsoon . . . My sisters' suitors . . . Simla . . . The weddings . . . Daddy . . .'

A tantalizing list of the chapters Mother meant to write but never did. She did leave two more vignettes about life at her parental home in Naini Tal, both written for some reason in the third person.

There was a hushed silence in the banqueting hall as the little girl rubbing her heavy-with-sleep-and-tears eyes looked at her father. The silence was broken by Lady Hailey leaping up from her seat and rushing to the child. 'Oh, you poor darling! Uncle MacEwan will be punished for hiding your books.' Lady Hailey put her arms round the child. 'Get up, MacEwan, you naughty man, and give the child her books.' MacEwan [presumably one of the Governor's aides-de-camp] got up hurriedly from his chair and, protesting loudly, came towards Lady H. 'I assure you, M'lady, I have not hidden her books. The servants must have misplaced them.'

'Nonsense,' said Lady H. 'Come on, all of you, let us look for the missing books. Follow me and form a chain behind me, and we shall go from room to room looking for them.'

At these words, all the guests rose, formed a chain and slowly wound their way through the house. Sir J.P.'s protests were ignored and the servants looked aghast as the dinner was abandoned and the long chain of guests wound their way out of the dining-room into the adjoining rooms. Sir J.P. and Lady Kailash smiled and joined them, for it became quite a game, with everyone enjoying themselves. At last, on the bay window seat, hidden by cushions, the missing books were found and returned to a beaming little girl. 'Thank you, thank you!' she said. She was kissed by Lady H. and then allowed to go back to bed.

It was a sunny morning in September. Sunlight flooded the spacious and elegant dining-room through the large French-windows. Dark blue velvet curtains, drawn apart, hung on the doors and windows. A deep red Persian carpet with a design of intertwining flowers and creepers in rich colours stretched from one end of the room to the other. A highly polished dining-table, large enough to seat 20 people, stood in the middle of the room. A huge silver bowl filled with roses stood on it. On the sideboards of deep brown teak, deeply carved, were silver dishes and salvers.

The room was filled with the chatter and laughter of children who sat near the French-windows at a smaller round table eating their breakfast. Presiding over them was a fat Englishwoman, who kept drawing their attention to their table-manners and pleading with them not to make too much noise. But they paid no attention to her admonitions.

'Oh, do look at your hair!' said Sarala. 'You haven't combed it.' She was a young girl of great beauty. Shakuntala [Mother] raised her hand to push back her curls, which hung in a tousled cluster on her neck.

Mrs. Elliot turned to her. 'Go to your room, dear, and tidy your hair. You will not get good marks for being neatly dressed with those curls flying all over the place.' Shakuntala got up obediently and ran out of the room and up the stairs. It was not really to brush her hair that she had so willingly obeyed Mrs Elliot. It was to see if her mother had woken up. Lady Kailash suffered from chronic insomnia and never slept before the early hours of the morning when she managed to snatch a few hours.

Shakuntala walked softly along the open verandah which led to her mother's room. She put her ear to the door, but heard no stirrings. Disappointed, she turned back as she could hear her sisters Sarala and Malati leaving for school. She caught up with them just as they reached the gate. Malati, the youngest of the three, was sitting in a *dandi*, which was being carried by four men. Being habitually lazy, she complained that her legs ached because her sisters walked too fast. Sarala walked in front of the *dandi*, setting a good pace with her long legs, and Shakuntala ran and caught her up.

It was a glorious morning in Naini Tal. Steep wooded hills surrounded the lake, which was fringed with weeping willows. At a height of over 6000 feet, Naini Tal had a magnificent view of the snow-capped upper ranges of the Himalayas. If one climbed its higher points, the highest being Cheena Peak, one was rewarded for this strenuous effort by a panoramic view of the snows on one side and the plains of the Gangetic basin on the other. It was an awe-inspiring sight.

Once a tiny village inhabited by hill-tribes, Naini Tal had been discovered by the British and developed to meet their needs. It contained everything that a small town in England would have had. The foothills leading to it had a fine rail service on the meter gauge. The railway ended when the climb uphill became too steep. Then one was transferred into a car or a bus, which negotiated the hairpin bends in first gear. But on entering the valley, the cars were not permitted any further. Only the British Governor of the province was allowed to be driven up by car to his residence at Government House, and a motorable road was built to enable him to do so. Having reached there, the Governor's car was garaged, and he used a rickshaw drawn by five men wherever he went. If he had a more athletic bent, he would ride a horse with his Indian footmen dressed in gold and scarlet with shining white turbans, and his British ADCs in their regimental uniforms. It was a colourful and impressive sight to see the Governor's party descending to the flats.

The lake, with the temple of Naina Devi, the town's presiding deity, at one corner, was skirted by the Mall Road, which encircled it, offering a shady walk under its weeping willows. A picturesque boat-house stood at another corner, and yachts with full-blown, white sails gracefully floated on the lake. The girls had a half-hour walk to their school. Their path wound up and down along the wooded hillside which, being fairly high up, gave a charming view of the lake when the trees were not too dense. The school was run by nuns, mostly for Anglo-Indian girls. Sarala, Shakuntala and Malati came from a far more privileged background and were also more intelligent than the average girls in their class. They had travelled widely in India and abroad. At home, they met outstanding Britishers and Indians from all walks of life. Their parents encouraged them to take an interest in politics and current affairs and to participate in adult discussions of a wide range of subjects.

Their father wanted his children to be knowledgeable, artistic and accomplished in all respects. Sir J.P. was a firm believer in the rights of women, and his daughters received exactly the same education as his sons. Unlike a typical Indian father, it could be said that he was more attached to his daughters than to his sons.

Mother was her own mother's favourite among the daughters, a status she cherished and fought hard to maintain until well after my grandmother's death. She was always flattered when people said how closely she resembled her mother; and, more important, she prided herself on having inherited my grandmother's sensitivity and obsessive fastidiousness, especially in matters of personal and domestic hygiene. Lady Kailash was undoubtedly fond and proud of Mother, but her greatest love among her children, true to traditional Indian form, was her eldest son, Sonny, with his irresistible charm and dazzling, matinee-idol good looks. Perhaps coming second to him accounts for some of my mother's emotional insecurity, in contrast with her sisters who learned early on to cope with emotional neglect and discrimination.

THREE

A DAUGHTER OF EMPIRE

As a child growing up in Bombay in the 1950s, in an era before television, my greatest delight, second only to reading, was being told bedtime stories. Often I had to make do with those of my Goan Catholic ayah or our moustachioed Muslim butler, but Mother's were my favourite. No doubt she embellished and exaggerated, and she romanticized her childhood and youth in inverse proportion to the frustrations and disappointments of her middle and later years. But looking back with a more sceptical historian's eye, I can see some important truths in her narratives.

The Srivastavas, the sub-caste name that Mother's family adopted as their anglicized surname, were certainly a very unusual family in northern India in the first half of the twentieth century. Their trajectory from declining and impoverished landed gentry to wealthy, haute bourgeois mill owners was part of a wider social transformation which Western education and rapid industrial growth were bringing about among India's upper classes during the Raj. But as Mother's narrative emphasizes, her family were virtually unique in the status given to their women members. That must have had a good deal to do with my grandparents' early years in Manchester, living with a very progressive couple like the Saklatvalas.

When they returned to Kanpur shortly before World War I, my grandmother had to adapt all over again to life in a dusty, provincial Indian town within a conventional Hindu joint family. But she appears to have made few concessions. At a time when most Indian women, Hindu and Muslim, were still in purdah, she was one of the few exceptions. She caused quite a stir by driving her own phaeton through the bazaars of Kanpur, playing tennis, acting as hostess for her aspiring and brilliant husband and mixing freely with his British colleagues and their wives at a time when racial barriers were still the norm.

My grandfather also encouraged her to join him in the embryonic parliamentary institutions that were evolving after the war. In the early 1930s, while the Congress led by Gandhi was boycotting the legislatures, Sir J.P. emerged as a prominent imperial loyalist, strongly committed to the British model of reform based on a gradual devolution of powers to bodies elected on a limited property and/or educational franchise. While he became Minister for Education in Lord Hailey's administration in the United Provinces, my grandmother was also elected to the provincial legislature as an independent.

Unlike her husband, she was sympathetic to Gandhi's nationalism and insisted that he stay at the family home when he visited Kanpur, while my grandfather absented himself to avoid embarrassment. She was also a vocal critic of officialdom in the legislature. She did not take kindly to being patronized by her husband when, on one memorable occasion, he declared in the chamber that he would explain a point of order to the Honourable Lady over lunch.

Unfortunately for my grandmother, her political career ended when the Congress decided to come in from the cold and contested elections to the provincial legislatures in 1937. She found herself facing a direct electoral challenge from Vijayalakshmi Pandit, sister of the Congress president, Jawaharlal Nehru. Mrs Pandit's supporters lampooned the Srivastavas as British toadies, and worse still, smeared Lady Kailash as a woman of loose morals, putting up posters with a photograph of her dancing with Lord Hailey at a Government House ball. Mrs Pandit won the election.

An unexpected footnote to the story emerged while I was researching at the Nehru Archives forty years later for my D. Phil. thesis. I came across a letter from Nehru to Lady Kailash Srivastava, apologizing profusely on his sister's behalf for the defamatory posters and assuring my grandmother that Mrs Pandit had no hand in them. Be that as it may, the apology was accepted, Mrs Pandit and Lady Kailash became friends, and I remember her visiting my grandmother in hospital during her final illness.

Mother's brief memoirs highlight the affluence, privilege and security of her childhood. But there was a darker side. My grandfather was notoriously unfaithful to his wife, and they quarrelled a good deal, sometimes about his mistresses, but also about her far greater religiosity and respect for Hindu ritual. Sir J.P. was a generous bon viveur who loved spending his money on the same lavish scale as he acquired it. He kept the best table in north India, and he loved his cigars, his Scotch and the attentions of beautiful courtesans, some of whom were the leading classical singers of their day.

I remember Mother describing a rather comical incident that occurred when she was a girl. Her mother, her eldest sister Queenie and her aunt (my grandfather's sister) drove together from Kanpur to Lucknow, where my grandfather had his official residence as a U.P. minister. They discovered him in flagrante delicto with his latest mistress, whereupon my grandmother produced a revolver from her handbag and made him throw out the poor woman at gunpoint. Whether true or apocryphal, it must have been disturbing for an adolescent girl.

Half a century later, when I was researching a book on the Raj, I interviewed a charming old lady called Dorothy Ganpathy. She had been Paul Scott's landlady in Bombay while he was writing his Raj trilogy and was believed to be the inspiration for one of its more memorable characters, Lady Chatterjee. 'Your grandfather, Sir J.P., was a dreadful man,' she announced over dinner. 'We all felt very sorry for Lady Kailash.' She went on to recall that my grandmother had come to see her [Dorothy's] father, who had been a leading lawyer in Delhi, to seek his advice about getting a divorce. He had advised her strongly to give up the idea, because, under Hindu law, she wouldn't get a penny and everyone would blame her.

She took the advice. For the next two decades till my grandfather's death, they lived on amicable terms, though increasingly apart. When he moved to Delhi to join the viceregal cabinet, she spent more of her time in Kanpur or abroad or visiting her daughters. For all his infidelities, he adored her. And she must have been deeply attached, too, because she never recovered from his death in 1956 at the age of sixty-three.

Much later, at a dinner party I went to with Mother, the ultra-socialist daughter of an old family friend held forth, to Mother's chagrin, about

Sir J.P. having had a parallel Muslim family with one of his courtesans, who had been ungenerously disowned by the Srivastavas and left in penury after his death. Only a decade ago, a woman with the unlikely name of Lotus Srivastava suddenly popped up in Kanpur, claiming to be Sir J.P.'s illegitimate daughter and filing lawsuits for a share of the family land.

It's clear from Mother's childhood memories that her parents, with their glittering public round of official functions, balls and tiger-shoots, were more often absent than present. The children were well cared for by their tutors and governesses, but they did have to struggle to get what little time their parents had left for them. Perhaps that explains why they were so competitive.

Their lives were protected but not always safe. One of the best bedtime stories Mother told me was about being separated from her parents, who were in Lucknow at the time, during a particularly violent communal riot, when a Muslim mob laid siege to their Kanpur house for a week. The men of the family, her uncles and cousins, kept all-night vigils with their rifles loaded, and everyone had to sleep in their clothes, ready to escape in the boats moored on the riverbank if the house was stormed by the mob. Eventually, my grandfather arrived with British troops and the siege was lifted.

Sir J.P. had good cause to prefer his daughters to his sons. His elder son, Sonny, his mother's darling, dutifully went to Manchester to study textiles like his father, but his main interest was in women. Soon after returning to India as one of the most eligible bachelors of the north, he fell in love with a thoroughly unsuitable, older, married woman, his mother's friend, the beautiful Maharani of Rajpipla. He was eventually extricated from her clutches and forced into an arranged marriage with the daughter of one of his father's business associates; but he never developed into the successor Sir J.P. longed for. The younger brother, Hari, was also not much of a businessman. He went to Cambridge instead of Manchester, and his main interests were singing, Romantic poetry and antique Chinese porcelain.

The daughters were made of rather stronger stuff. Queenie was her father's favourite, possibly because she was their first surviving child, born when they were still a struggling young couple in Manchester. Though she grew up to be the most level-headed of the five sisters, the pressures on her as a child must have been enormous, because her father expected her to be India's Renaissance woman. She was tutored in every art, science and skill, ranging from classical Indian music to flying an aeroplane. I recently saw a press report of her glittering wedding in 1936, attended by Lord and Lady Hailey. The biggest surprise was an aerobatics display by her colleagues from the Kanpur Flying Club, who sprinkled confetti on the amazed guests from a great height.

Sir J.P. was a great believer in modernity. He was one of the first Indians in the U.P. to acquire a motor car; and I remember Mother describing the excitement of the inaugural ride, when the whole family piled into it, with her brothers perched on the running boards. It's remarkable that the kind of Westernization my grandfather embraced didn't cut the family off from their Indian roots. The new home he built in Kanpur in the late 1930s epitomized his eclectic approach. The carved and pillared sandstone exterior was designed to evoke the façade of a medieval Hindu temple, but the interior was furnished in the latest art deco style with wonderfully geometrical furniture, lots of chrome and glass and wooden panelling and flooring, and the most up-to-date plumbing and electrical fittings.

In keeping with this eclecticism, my mother grew up as an excellent horsewoman, adept at painting English watercolours and dancing the foxtrot, but also schooled in Sanskrit, Urdu and Indian classical music and, most daring of all, in Indian classical dance, then still shunned by the 'respectable' for its associations with *devadasi*s or temple prostitutes. All five sisters had a university education. Queenie, the eldest, graduated in Kanpur, but by the time it was the second sister Sheela's turn, Sir J.P. decided she must go to Cambridge, and she went to Girton to do her Tripos.

Aunt Sheela was one of the first Indian women to be admitted, and the prospect of being separated from her family must have been daunting. She was to travel alone by ocean liner and her parents took her to Bombay where she would embark. At the departure dock,

Sir J.P. and Lady Srivastava met a rather austere, shabbily dressed Parsi family named Masani. Sir Rustom Masani, a lean, handsome man with a goatee, was then Vice Chancellor of Bombay University. He was seeing off his wife, Manijeh, and his daughter Mehra, who was going up to the London School of Economics. Sheela Srivastava and Mehra Masani were the same age, and Lady Srivastava begged Lady Masani to take her daughter under her wing during the voyage.

It was the first encounter between two families whose conflicts and tensions were to bedevil my parents' marriage and my own childhood. And it didn't get off to a good start. Many years later, I asked my aunt Mehra, whom I had grown to love dearly, how they got on during the voyage. 'Not very well,' she replied with her characteristic candour. 'We had very different values and interests. I found Sheela rather flighty. She was much more interested in dressing up and having a good time. She sat at the captain's table, and we didn't really see a lot of her.'

FOUR

AGAINST THE TIDE

In the late 1970s my father Minoo Masani published two volumes of political memoirs entitled *Bliss Was It in That Dawn* and *Against the Tide*. What follows is based on the sections about his childhood and adolescence, amplified by the stories I was told by my paternal grandparents, and two taped interviews I recorded, one with Father and the other—in some ways more revealing—with his sister Mehra.

Aunty Mehra was eight years younger than Father. Her brothers and parents were all terribly proud of her. She was one of the first career women in India and paid the price by remaining single. She had several close relationships, but they were all with men who were either married or too weak and dependent to make suitable partners. She was very handsome, in a masculine sort of way, tall and broadly built, with a square jaw, firm chin and mouth and beautiful, large brown eyes. Much later, people said I resembled her. I was always flattered; she, less so. But we grew to be very close friends and confidants. We instinctively understood each other. Prematurely crippled by arthritis, she retired to Deolali, once popular with the British Indian army for its good climate and health sanatoria. On my last visit to her there in 1989, I recorded some of her memories. She died a year later, and I still miss her sparkling laughter, her sharp intellect, her rich, contralto voice and, above all, her constant affection, so much less demanding or cloying than I found my mother's.

Mehra shared Father's talent for efficient organization, but she was far less confrontational and far more indulgent about other people's failings. And she had a sensitive and perceptive eye for personal details that Father chose to ignore. Her account of their shared childhood was much more revealing about what my grandparents and their various relatives were really like.

Father was born in Bombay in November 1905 in a middle-class home. His parents were Parsis, belonging to the smallest of India's minorities, Zoroastrian refugees from Iran who came to India some 1,200 years ago after Muslims conquered the Persian empire. The Masani children, three brothers and one sister, grew up in the fishing village of Versova, now a crowded, high-rise suburb of Bombay. In the early years of the twentieth century, it was well known for a creek, which had claimed many victims who had been swept away by its powerful ebbing current while bathing. Grandfather's house was situated just opposite the mouth of the creek. His sons, who grew up swimming across it almost every day, did not share the general fear symbolized by the signboard on the shore, which read 'Bathing Here Is Dangerous'.

'I remember taking a secret pride in swimming across the creek as the tide ebbed,' Father later wrote in his memoirs,

> knowing full well that if I miscalculated the strength of the current, I would be sucked away from the shores into the high seas. And then? Drowning? Or being eaten by big fish, or perhaps coming back with the next tide several hours later!
>
> One got a kick out of just about making it. Many's the time, battling the current, I recall my heart would beat faster at the thought that I was losing the battle. But then would follow the triumph of survival, of throwing oneself on the sand, all spent, and gradually regaining one's breath. . . .
>
> Swimming against the tide became so much of a habit, almost a part of my nature, I wonder whether in later life, particularly in my political activities and attitudes, the patterns of my childhood habit asserted themselves. Is it only a coincidence that right from 1932 onwards I have always been in opposition? When India was under British rule, I was an ardent nationalist and had three spells in prison. When India became independent, and nationalism and chauvinism

became the fashion, I moved on to a "one world" attitude. When very few in India had heard of socialism, I was an ardent socialist; but by the time Prime Minister Nehru made socialism the dominant state policy, I had published my little book *Socialism Reconsidered* and have since been indulging in Gandhian and Liberal heresies. I have met criticism of the changes in my views by quoting Gandhiji's reply in similar situations: 'Consistency is the virtue of an ass.'

Is there perchance something Irish in me, the like of which had moved that shipwrecked Irishman to open his eyes and ask the natives gathered round him: 'What is the government in this place?' and say before anyone could answer, 'In any case, I'm agin it.' Or is mine a passion to be on the side of the underdog, a strong sense of freedom and justice for whoever is down and out?

Be that as it may, Father had no regrets. He thoroughly enjoyed being in opposition. Jawaharlal Nehru, who spoke approvingly of his role as a Congress MP during the British days from 1945 to 1947, found him a nuisance when Congress came to power and Father became an outspoken backbench MP. In 1957 Father reverted to the Opposition benches, remaining there till 1971.

When I was still a child and Nehru still Prime Minister, I asked Father whether he would not have preferred being in government and doing the things he wanted to get done. He answered with a question: 'Yes, but *would* I have been able to do what I wanted? Or would I have had to do the things which Nehru wanted?'

Jawaharlal Nehru himself shared that view. Once in the 1960s, when someone suggested in Parliament that he should form a national government with able men from all parties and included Father's name, the Prime Minister replied: 'Just imagine what would happen. My friend Masani would obstruct almost everything I wanted to do, and I would certainly stop him from doing many things he might wish to do. We would soon be throwing things across the table at one another.' To this Father responded with a laugh and a hearty 'Hear, Hear!'

When he looked back on his political career in his memoirs, Father had no regrets.

Actually, it is great fun being in what is somewhat inaccurately described as 'the wilderness' provided you make the most of it and are not handicapped by pomposity. Harold Macmillan, when Prime Minister, once observed somewhat pityingly about Hugh Gaitskell, whom I knew and liked, that the joy of being Leader of the Opposition was to be able to say what one wanted, to strike out boldly and let oneself go, but that poor Gaitskell behaved as if he were Prime Minister, with all the cares and responsibilities of that office! Fortunately, I did not suffer from this particular handicap. My passion in life has been to do and say what I want.

As a precocious adolescent, he was much influenced by the writings of Fabian socialists like H.G. Wells and George Bernard Shaw. And much later in life, when his views were anything but socialist, he still quoted approvingly from poems of protest, like this one by Arthur Hugh Clough:

Say not, the struggle naught availeth,
The labour and the wounds are vain,
The enemy faints not, nor faileth,
And as things have been they remain.
For while tired waves, vainly breaking,
Seem here no painful inch to gain,
Far back, through creeks and inlets making,
Comes silent, flooding in, the main.
And not by eastern windows only,
When daylight comes, comes in the light,
In front, the sun climbs slow, how slowly,
But westward, look the land is bright.

'Whether mine is a life of wasted opportunities I do not know,' Father wrote in the foreword to his memoirs, 'but it is a life I would live again, if I had the option. Though against the tide, I have lived well and fully. I have been many times around the globe. I have enjoyed the love of beautiful women. I have friends and comrades in all continents.'

My grandfather, Sir Rustom Masani, came from a lower-middle-class background. His father had been a schoolmaster and was called Pandit because he was supposed to be a wizard with numbers, a clever man and very scholarly, but somewhat stern and with a temper. His mother was almost illiterate: she knew how to write her name and read the headlines in the newspapers, but that was about all. Both his parents died young. Rustom Masani had little use for his siblings—they didn't quite belong to the same world of high intellectual achievement. He had been the genius of the family and continued to be treated as such. He was unique among them in his love of learning, and at a very young age he had started writing. When he joined Elphinstone College, he was already editing a little journal and had started a lifelong interest in social reform. He became secretary of a newly established Parsi girls' educational trust. Very few girls in the community were educated then, and some public-spirited Parsis had decided that something must be done about it. And that was how my grandparents first met: he was visiting a girls' school where my grandmother, Manijeh Wadia, had recently become a fledgling teacher.

Manijeh belonged to one of the foremost aristocratic families of the Parsi community. There were fire-temples built in their name and they had landed estates in the suburbs of Bombay, given to them by the East India Company in return for services they had rendered. Manijeh grew up in the house of her paternal grandmother or Bapaiji. The old lady, according to Aunty Mehra, 'was thoroughly illiterate and a very foolish woman'. The apple of her eye was her youngest son, Mancherji. His elder brother, Nusserwanji, Manijeh's father, was an extremely gentle and civilized sort of man who couldn't put up any fight against his mother; but his wife could be fierce where her children were concerned and she constantly complained that they were not getting enough to eat.

When the Wadia family all sat down to a meal together, their Parsi major-domo would come in with a huge silver salver laden with all sorts of delicacies like chicken liver and prawns; and the grand old materfamilias would be served first. She would pick all the nicest morsels and put them all on her favourite son Mancherji's plate. By the time the tray got to the little children sitting at the end of the table, there was practically nothing left to eat. This would incense Nusserwanji's wife, who would start piling everything on to her own plate and then getting up and going to the end of the table to distribute it to her own children. Bapaiji would shout and scream at her, and there were dreadful scenes.

They all lived in a large, three-storey house in the Fort area of Bombay. Bapaiji, with her favourite son, was on the top floor; and the other two sons, in order of seniority, on the floors below. The old matriarch would stand at the top of the third floor stairs and her daughter-in-law at the bottom of the first floor stairs while they shouted and quarrelled about why the children hadn't had any milk that morning. As a child, Manijeh was deeply embarrassed by these rows; but in later years when she told her own children about them, they thought they were hilarious.

Manijeh's father, Nusserwanji, died very young, and her mother promptly decided to put an end to this domestic hell. She took her children and went back to her own parents', who lived in much more affluent circumstances in a beautiful house called 'Park Field', which at one time had been the British Governor's residence. It was in the suburbs of Bombay near Parel. They had horses and carriages and lived a very elegant life with gardeners and lots of servants and plenty of nice things to eat.

It was a life of luxury and ease, and Manijeh got used to the idea that everyone was good-humoured and good-tempered. But then suddenly her maternal grandfather, who was 'really quite stupid' according to Aunt Mehra, lost all his money speculating on the stock market. So they came down in the world and had to move to a much smaller, though still beautiful, house on Cumballa Hill. 'Great-grandfather would sit in the garden on a little swing and swing himself for hours, because there was nothing else he could do,' Mehra recalled. 'He was not fit for work of any kind; and having lost all his money, he was thoroughly demoralized.'

There was a big family tussle when Manijeh married, because the man she chose was not up to Wadia standards in terms of wealth or status. Everybody said: 'Who is this Masani? We've never heard such a name in our lives!' And others would say: 'Oh well, he's an up-and-coming young man.' 'Well, we don't care about that. You've got to marry so and so'—some cousin they'd already picked. But Granny was unshakable: 'Under no circumstances will I marry anyone other than Rustom Masani.'

She had a great champion in one of her aunts, who was quite taken with this romance, and said that of course she should marry him, why on earth not? So, ultimately, the two of them wore down the rest of the family and my grandparents got married. Rustom was still earning very little in his job with the Bombay municipality; no more than two or three hundred rupees a month. So they went to live in a small house in a congested, lower-middle-class area near Grant Road. They couldn't afford a servant and Manijeh had to do all the housework: sweep, swab, cook, wash up, everything. Her family said: 'Serves her right!'

Gradually life became easier as Rustom climbed the career ladder; and by the time their children were born they were living in a very pleasant house in Colaba. 'The difference between the Wadia and Masani families was always quite clear to us as children,' Aunt Mehra recalled. 'One knew that, if one went to maternal Great-grandmother's house, there would be flowers and priests chanting prayers in the home; they were a highly religious family. There would be constant *muktad*s in memory of various dead relations, with several days of continuous prayers. On such occasions, there were lovely things to eat, shining silverware laid out for the ceremonies and sandalwood fires burning. It was a beautiful sight, and although as children we didn't understand the significance of it, it was something we looked forward to.'

Rustom's Masani relations, by contrast, all lived in rather dingy little flats in the Grant Road area, in localities where well-bred people weren't supposed to go. It was impossible for his children not to realize that there was a big gulf between the two families. But both were beginning to westernize in different ways. Manijeh's aunt, the one who had championed her love marriage, had learnt to play the piano; and Manijeh herself was taught the piano, learned English at school and read books in English.

Both my Parsi grandparents were iconoclastic in religious matters. At the age of seven, Aunt Mehra asked her father: 'Do you believe in God?' He was quiet for a moment and then demanded: 'Why are you asking this?' She replied: 'I just want to know.' 'I don't know if there is a God,' he replied quietly. 'There might be one and there might not.

But in any case, I don't think it matters at all. You just have to be good and honest and decent and live a good life, that's all. There's no need to believe in God.'

Granny was more observant: she used to say her prayers occasionally and go to the fire-temple. But my grandparents were in full agreement that there was no need to impose religiosity on their children and they all grew up as agnostics.

My father was evidently a noisy and articulate infant, since an entry in his mother's diary on 8 March 1906 mentions that 'we call him parrot', and by August 1906 it was mentioned that he 'talked a great deal'. A year later, my grandmother wrote: 'He shows decidedly a will and stubbornness of his own.'

By the time he was seven or eight, he appears to have developed a marked trait for questioning anything that was put to him, earning the family pet name 'Mr Sanevaste', which in Gujarati means 'Mr Why'. This was the first evidence of a sceptical attitude to authority and dogma that persisted. Many years later, when he joined the London School of Economics and learnt that its motto was *Rerum Cognoscere Causas* (To Know the Cause of Things), he felt he had come to the right place.

Theirs was a far from typical middle-class Parsi home. Grandfather was unusual to the point of eccentricity, and all his children suffered some discomfort from being individualists themselves, the odd man—and the odd woman—out. 'Ploughing a lonely furrow is not everyone's idea of fun,' Father once admitted, 'but, brought up as we were, we had little choice.'

In Grandfather's scale of values, the intellect was supreme, and the importance he attached to intellectual attainments was accompanied by a contemptuous disregard for wealth and material comfort. 'His pride and indifference to worldly success made him somewhat egoistic and even unsociable,' was Father's judicious verdict. He was being polite. When I knew my grandfather, he was already in his seventies and much mellowed by age. But he had a reputation for being a terrible martinet in his youth, given to fierce and uncontrollable rages, especially at mealtimes.

He shunned socializing, and guests were seldom if ever invited to meals; which was just as well, because he was a food faddist and, ironically in the light of later medical knowledge, convinced that the more salt you had the better. Family meals tended to be nerve-racking events, with my long-suffering grandmother being ordered to remove one dish after another as he angrily pushed away his plate with his knife and fork.

Granny, who had married Grandfather when she was only eighteen, did her best to adjust herself to him, though not always successfully. Her early photographs show a smiling and cheerful woman with large soulful eyes, a square jaw and high cheekbones, the regularity of her Roman features and aquiline Parsi nose marred by too-prominent teeth. Like some other racially 'pure' Parsis of high birth, she had grey-blue eyes and very fair skin.

She came from good ship-building stock. Her great-grandfather was Naoroji Wadia, founder of a ship-building dynasty whose vessels were so good that they were used by British admirals as their flagships. One of his ships, the *Asia*, led the British fleet at the Battle of Navarino in 1827, after which Admiral Sir Pulteney Malcolm wrote: 'Tell my old friend Naoroji what a glorious part the *Asia* sustained in the battle and how proud I am of his success as a builder.'

Unlike his aristocratic Wadia in-laws, Grandfather was very much a self-made man. By the time my father, his eldest child, was born, he was Assistant Secretary of the Bombay Municipal Corporation, and the family were comfortably off with a horse and carriage, a sign of affluence in those days.

Grandfather was to occupy many important positions. He was Bombay's first Indian Municipal Commissioner, and then, after taking early retirement at fifty, continued to reinvent himself, first as Manager of the Central Bank of India, then as Rector and Vice Chancellor of Bombay University and eventually Leader of the National War Front during World War II. In his spare time he wrote several scholarly historical books and translations of Persian classics that are still in print.

During Father's childhood, Grandfather was still working for the municipal corporation. After school, Father and his younger brother used to go to his office for tea, after which they enjoyed watching the proceedings of the corporation from the vantage point of a stained glass window which opened on to the Council Chamber.

Grandfather was inclined to be belligerent with the British municipal commissioners and Governors. There were some with whom he started on bad terms and later became friends. The one he spoke of most was Sir George Lloyd, a very strong personality as Governor of Bombay. It was in his time that Grandfather was appointed Municipal Commissioner, a post that brought him into direct contact with the Governor. Apparently, when he once told the corporation that the government had blundered, Sir George was furious and summoned Grandfather to see him. Lloyd, having received him politely, declared: 'The government never blunders.' Grandfather questioned this logic and must have been persuasive, because from then on the two men became good friends.

Grandfather was intellectually well ahead of his time. He read British liberal literature—John Stuart Mill, Mountstuart Elphinstone, Macaulay, John Bright—and was a convinced nineteenth-century liberal in his thinking. Towards his children he was a most non-interfering parent. 'We made our decisions from a very young age about what we would study, what we would read and who our friends should be,' my father later wrote. 'Small wonder that none of us acquired what Arthur Koestler calls "the Bapu [father] complex" so common in India. On the contrary, we resisted Father's authority and adopted views in opposition to his.'

My grandmother was a counterpoise to Grandfather's reserved and somewhat forbidding character. 'She was a soft and sentimental person who wept easily,' Father recalled.

'When Papa lost his temper, she would cry and shiver and get asthma attacks. We children were always on her side. When I was old enough, thirteen or fourteen, I used to say: "Mama, what's the use of crying? Why don't you leave him?" But she didn't want to leave him; she was a typical Indian wife who would rather suffer than think of separation. Looking back, I think we were unfair to Papa. Mama could be very tactless, and she was inefficient and sloppy by his standards. But when your mother cries, you naturally want to support her against a bullying father.'

The four Masani children inherited their parents' physical and mental attributes in varying degrees. Like Grandfather, my father was impatient and drawn to academic and intellectual pursuits and later to public life. Despite Granny's efforts, none of her children had a strong family feeling—each of them went their own way. My uncle Keki was a constant irritant to my father during their childhood. Being younger, he would complain to my grandparents about Father bullying him, and they always took his side. But worse than this, he was habitually late in the mornings, making his elder brother late for school, so that they were both punished. There were scenes every morning, with Father pleading that he be allowed to go to school alone.

Uncle Keki, though he remained chaotic in his habits, grew up to become Bombay's first qualified psychotherapist, having trained in London both as a medical psychiatrist and a psychoanalyst. The youngest brother, Pesi, emigrated to America, where he became a very eminent mathematician at Pittsburgh University. And Aunt Mehra became the moving spirit of India's first national broadcasting network, All India Radio.

One of my father's earliest memories was of witnessing an injustice. The family were staying in a cottage called 'The Nook' in Colaba. Across the road was a police station, with an open-grilled lockup. On one occasion, my six-year-old father looked out of his window to see a policeman beating up a prisoner with a truncheon, a common way of extracting a confession. He rushed to Grandfather in tears and told him what he had seen, and Grandfather rushed across the road and managed to put a stop to it.

The family spent their holidays at various hill stations. One of these was Kotagiri, a little hamlet in the Nilgiri Hills in the south, where Grandfather had bought a cottage. There was a thick forest behind it, with a little rivulet flowing through it; Father spent many happy hours there, 'sitting alone, reclining against a tree, watching the water flow by and dreaming all kinds of dreams'. These holidays came to an end when Grandfather, always the good Samaritan, was persuaded by some Christian missionaries to sell the cottage to them for a song so that they could establish a little school for the children of one of the aboriginal tribes of the Nilgiris.

Granny suffered from very bad asthma, which she had outgrown by the time I knew her. She used to spend long periods in Khandala and Deolali, where the climate was drier and the air purer than in Bombay. 'In Deolali,' Father reminisced, 'she was prescribed ass's milk for her asthma. We children used to chase the donkey around the garden of the Coronation Hotel, run by Parsis at that time.'

One of Aunty Mehra's first memories was of the large, rambling house in the suburb of Versova, to which the growing Masani family had moved from Colaba. When Grandfather bought it, it was just a small bungalow; then he started extending and improving it. 'Right through those early years, there was nothing but workmen and cement and dust and dirt around the place,' Mehra recalled. 'But of course, as children, we didn't mind.'

She was five when the family moved there. Grandfather had decided that Bombay city was too polluted. 'This was in 1918,' Mehra laughed. 'And what he would say now if he saw the city I really cannot imagine. He thought the air was not healthy enough for children, that we would get all sorts of respiratory diseases. So there we were, out in Versova.'

It was a little fishing village, and the fisher folk took their catch to sell in Bombay. About a mile away from the village was a little cluster of houses called Seven Bungalows, and the Masanis were one of the seven, mostly middle-class Parsi families. One of the houses was a retreat for the Jesuit priests who taught at St Xavier's College in Bombay. Grandfather used to meet them on the beach, and they used to greet him and talk a little.

'Of course, there was not a thing you could do there,' Aunt Mehra reminisced. 'There was the beach and the Arabian Sea in front of you, and you stayed home and read when you weren't on the beach. In retrospect, this was a very good thing, because we never got accustomed to the idea that you must go to the movies, or go to see friends, that there must be some entertainment every evening to keep you alive.'

While she was too young to have regrets about leaving behind the hurly-burly of city life, her brothers felt differently. My father was especially annoyed about the move, because he felt he was missing out on all the things that other boys his age did.

Grandfather was a keen swimmer, and every morning and evening he went in for a dip. The children used to join him, and even before they could swim they paddled happily while he swam. The beach became the centre of their existence.

Initially Father, like me, went to Bombay's Anglican Cathedral School, even then the city's most elite educational institution. Like me, he appears to have been unhappy there, but he had the good fortune to be moved elsewhere, which I didn't.

'I was a thoughtful, introspective and somewhat frail child,' he wrote in his memoirs, 'and it was quite an experience to be thrown amongst the tough English and Anglo-Indian boys of the Cathedral School. Our Headmaster was named, not inaccurately, Mr. Savage. His canings were well known and dreaded. I luckily escaped these, but not the savagery of the boys. I remember being repeatedly clobbered after being forced into boxing bouts with bigger and stronger boys. Sometimes when I knew they were up to some mischief, I would run up the stairs and sit outside the Principal's lodgings and come down only when the lunch-break was over. However, I got tough gradually, and by the time I got to the second standard, I was actually walloping boys in the first.'

Despite this enforced apprenticeship in bullying, he was already a political nonconformist.

'I recall that I was very much for the Kaiser and against the Allies during World War I. Was this a result of the many thrashings I received from the English boys at the Cathedral School and a rather precocious application of the adage: "The enemy of your enemy is your friend"?'

There was a choir class at school, and the choir-master thought Father had a good voice. 'Masani,' he said, 'I'd like you to join the choir.' Father protested: 'Sir, but I'm not a Christian.'

'Oh, that's terrible. You're not a Christian? Then I'm sorry you can't join the choir. I withdraw my offer.'

When Father consistently came home with top grades in all his subjects, my grandparents decided that the academic standards at the Cathedral School obviously weren't high enough. So he was withdrawn, given private tuition at home for about six months and then enrolled in a more intellectually challenging and convivial school. The New High School was run by two Parsi headmasters—Jalbhai Bharda and Kaikobad Marzban—both strong personalities, but in entirely different ways.

Father remembered Jalbhai Bharda as an intellectual and a philosopher, a student of astronomy and a lover of poetry. Kind and gentle, he was a lovable man, careless and untidy in appearance. His Parsi skull-cap was old and crumpled, because when he wanted to give one of the boys a clout on the head, he would first remove his cap, place it protectively on the boy's head, and then give it a gentle bang. Once he asked Father: 'Who is your favourite poet?' And when he replied 'Sir Walter Scott', instead of saying Keats or Shelley, he was so outraged that he gave him the proverbial cap on his head followed by a clout.

His partner, Kaikobad Marzban, was quite a contrast, being meticulous in his appearance, with a shining new cap on his head, shiny black shoes and 'a waxed moustache which he was always curling *a la* Kaiser Wilhelm'.

Father used to take violin lessons from 'a sweet and bird-like' Florentine named Count Odone Savini who had settled in India. Under his tutelage, he took and passed the stiff examination conducted by the Trinity College of Music, London, which used to send an examiner to India every year for this purpose. By the time I knew him, music sadly had been driven out of his life by politics, never to return. But I remember that he was cross when Mother thoughtlessly sold off his prized violin to the local rag-and-bone man. A more distinguished pupil of Count Savini's was Mehli Mehta, father-to-be of the conductor Zubin. Father proudly recalled playing second violin to his first in a string quartet that used to perform at Savini's home.

At school, the only real friend Father had was Yusuf Meherally. 'The friendship developed during our last year or two of school,' Father wrote, 'and became somewhat intense about the time we were in college. While I was very fond of Yusuf, I found it difficult to reciprocate with the same intensity that he displayed, and he often called me a cold person. It was a matter of different temperaments.'

Could it also have been that Yusuf Meherally was consciously or otherwise in love with him, at a time when homosexuality was strictly taboo, especially in the nationalist circles in which they moved? Meherally, who became an icon of the Indian left, died tragically young soon after Independence. My parents nursed him during his final illness, and Father was heartbroken when he died. Though never a demonstrative man, his face always softened and his eyes misted over when he spoke of Yusuf.

'Yusuf influenced my choice of a vocation,' he once told me. 'While my father had wanted me to become a doctor, Yusuf convinced me that I was better suited to be a lawyer. His argument was that, with law, I could serve the country better in public life. I wonder!'

Occasionally, Father and some of his more political school-friends went to public meetings addressed by political celebrities. One such was the great liberal orator, Srinivasa Shastri, a moderate who opposed Gandhi's non-cooperation movement against the Raj. 'On February 4 1921, along with Yusuf and other friends, I went to the Excelsior Theatre to hear him,' Father noted in his diary. 'This was his third attempt to get a hearing, but he failed. As if we could hear anything! These rowdy non-cooperators, who themselves want freedom, do not want others even to oppose their opinions. We were all quite disgusted with this spirit.'

His main extracurricular activity at school was debating: 'I am pleased that, even as an adolescent, I fervently supported all the right causes such as women's emancipation and equality of the sexes.'

An annual fixture for him and his friends used to be the Aga Khan Hockey Tournament at the Bombay Gymkhana. Almost invariably, the finals match was between the Indian students of the Grant Medical College and the Sherwood Foresters, a British army regiment. Normally, the Grant Medical College won, and for the nationalistic Indian boys the great event of the year was to see them defeat the Sherwood Foresters.

At that time there was a rule that you couldn't matriculate till the age of sixteen. Since Father was only fourteen and two years ahead of his class, he thought he could play the fool and have a good time playing cricket and hockey. But he hadn't reckoned with Grandfather's reforming zeal.

He was by then a member of the University Senate, and he decided that the sixteen-year age qualification was a silly rule and that he should get it removed. He got a friend to move a resolution in the Senate abolishing the rule, and it was carried. Grandfather came home and said: 'Now Minoo, you better get ready for the Matriculation exam. We got the rule changed today.' 'What have you done?' Father protested. 'I'm not ready to pass. I'll fail in Mathematics.' 'Very bad! All right, you'll take private tuition.'

So Father managed to scrape through in maths and took his matriculation two years early. In 1921 he joined Elphinstone College, which was then supposed to be the best in Bombay. Founded in the mid-nineteenth century by an enlightened British Governor who believed in promoting Western learning, the college educated three generations of Masanis, starting with Grandfather and ending with me.

By then Yusuf Meherally and Father had both become vocal independence-walas, supporting Gandhi and non-cooperation with the British. But they got on remarkably well with the college principal, a red-faced, hard-drinking Irishman called Hamill. He used to dislike the Hindu boys, because they were in awe of him. They'd go and stand at his door, and he'd shout 'What?' and they'd all run away. But Yusuf and Father didn't run away. They chatted with him and cheeked him. 'I like you boys,' he would tell them. 'You're devils. Come on, let's go for a sail in the harbour.' He would take two or three of them out in his sailing boat, and they got quite intimate with him even though the other Indian students thought he was a monster.

Father and Yusuf made a formidable duo, and together they gave the lecturers a bad time, especially a Muslim mathematics professor with a big forehead and no chin. Father still had no use for mathematics, so he went to the bazaar, bought an alarm clock, set it for halfway through the lecture and put it below the lectern. When it went off, the students all applauded and laughed. The poor maths professor was dreadfully embarrassed. He said: 'I don't think it's funny.' And the more he said it wasn't funny, the more they all laughed.

They also provoked their economics professor by talking Marxism in his class. They were already socialists and they exaggerated their Marxism to annoy him. Whatever liberal proposition he advanced, they would object, 'Nonsense. Karl Marx says the reverse.' Many years later Father met him somewhere and apologized to him. 'Professor Parandekar,' he said, 'we were terrible to you. I'm so sorry.' He replied: 'Mr Masani, you and Meherally were the brightest students I had in my whole career. True, you gave me a bad time, but I don't bear a grudge. And I'm glad you're cured of the Marxism now.'

Father's penchant for challenging authority appears to have rubbed off on his younger siblings. When Aunty Mehra was ten, Granny decided she was not keeping as well as she should, that she was too thin and pinched, and must therefore be sent to a better climate. So she was packed off to St Joseph's Convent, a boarding school in Panchgani, a hill station in the Western Ghats, about seven hours from Bombay. It was run by European nuns, mostly French, Spanish and German. 'I got expelled from that school!' Mehra proudly told me. 'Whenever I say this, everyone is amazed that I of all people should have been expelled from school. But it did happen.'

She had been in the infirmary with mumps and since the Michaelmas holidays were approaching, the nuns had told her she needn't come back to class for the remaining few days of term. She used to spend her time wandering around while everybody else was in class and composing funny poems to entertain her friends when they came out of class for lunch.

'One day a girl saw us reading a poem and giggling over it, so I put it in my desk and went off to lunch. She took it out and read it and took it to the Sister Superior. But I had forgotten all about it and a few days passed. Then came music and elocution exams at the end of the week and I was expected to do well. A gold medal had been offered for the girl who got the highest marks. A Trinity College man used to come up to Panchgani to conduct the exams. When they were over, the normal routine was for us all to be called into the big assembly hall, where the results would be announced. On this occasion nothing happened, and we all waited. And then I was summoned to the Sister Superior's office. There she sat, looking very glum, with two senior sisters sitting next to her, one of whom taught French and the other, elocution. And there in front of Sister Superior was the poem.

'She asked: "Did you write this?" I said: "Yes, Mother." Sister Marie-Francoise, the French one, said: "Just look at this girl! If you knew her father, a perfect gentleman, and her mother, a perfect lady. And look at this child!" By this time, I was somewhat puzzled; I had no idea what all this was about. They asked: "Are you sorry you wrote this?" I replied: "No, I don't think so. There's nothing to be sorry about."

'"Oh, so you think there's nothing to be sorry about? You don't think that there's anything wrong with comparing the white nuns and the black nuns?"

'At that age, I was not in the least aware of colour or racial prejudice. But in a child's mind, I suppose these things do register unconsciously. And I'd noticed that, when they went to chapel, all the White nuns walked in front and all the Black nuns walked behind them. We also saw that in the refectory, where they had their meals, they always sat apart. With hindsight, there may have been good reasons for this, because the European nuns were all highly educated and they probably spoke French at table, and the poor little Indian Christian nuns were girls who were almost illiterate.

'All the same, the inequality had registered in my mind and I'd mentioned it in the poem, saying, "Poor Sister Mildred has to wear her eyes out darning socks all day, while Sister Stanislaw struts about reciting poetry", that kind of thing.

'They said: "Now you go straight up to bed and don't talk to any other girls." They wrote to my mother saying: "Please take away your child. She's a bad influence on the school." They sent her a copy of the poem. A few days later, I was summoned and told that my parents wanted me to return to Bombay. My packing had all been done and I was to leave the next morning by bus for Poona, where someone would put me on the train to Bombay.'

This summary expulsion must have been frightening for a child, but the family took it in their stride. When she arrived at Victoria Terminus in Bombay, her father and brothers had come to fetch her. 'My brothers were highly amused by all this and Father was not particularly perturbed either. But he said: "Your mother is very cross." When I got home, Mama was cold and distant and she said: "I could never have imagined that a child of mine could be so ungrateful. Think of all that these nuns have done for you. Look at yourself in the mirror and think of what you looked like when you went to Panchgani." And so it went on and I got quite upset, because I really didn't understand what it was all about.'

My grandmother wrote a letter of apology to Sister Gertrude. 'After all, she's only nine years old,' she wrote, 'and you shouldn't take it all so seriously. We're going to England in a few months for several years, so if you would take her back, we'd be very grateful, because it would spare us looking for a new school for her at this late stage.' Back came the reply: 'Of course, we'll be happy to have her back.' So back Mehra went.

Despite this precocious instance of a social conscience, the Masani children were not above practising their own, more subtle forms of racial discrimination. The family kept chickens, mostly for eggs but occasionally for the pot. The children had their favourites and gave them glamorous English names like Elizabeth and Victoria, while the less favoured hens got Parsi names like Aloo and Jeroo. When the moment came for one to be slaughtered, the children would plead with the cook to take Aloo or Jeroo and spare poor Vickie and Lizzie.

The year after Grandfather became Municipal Commissioner, the Bombay Corporation introduced elected councillors. Grandfather decided he would have none of it. He valued his independence and wasn't going to be pestered by corrupt, elected members who wanted municipal licences and permits for their friends and relations. So he took early retirement at the age of fifty.

The Central Bank of India then asked him to become its managing director. 'I know nothing at all about banking,' he said. 'I've spent all my life in municipal administration. But if you'll let me go to England for at least six months and work in a major bank there, I'd consider it and take a diploma in banking.' They were a little surprised by what seemed like an odd demand, but they were keen to have him, so they agreed. And that was how the whole family went to live in England.

They took a ship for London in April 1925. Father stayed behind in Bombay, waiting for his graduation results and followed the others a few months later, having decided to do a law degree at the London School of Economics and qualify as a barrister at Lincoln's Inn.

'In retrospect, it's amazing how little we were thrown off balance by the trip,' Aunt Mehra recalled. 'I shared a cabin with my parents. My brother Keki was sharing another cabin with an enormously fat old man who had the upper berth. Keki used to tell us how the upper berth used to sag under his weight, and he was always terribly afraid that one day the old man would just collapse on him; but he didn't. It was a ship called *The Olympia*, which was all one class, and Father took it for that reason, because he couldn't afford First Class for all of us.'

When they arrived in London, the family went to a boarding house in Cromwell Road, then as now a land of bedsits for new foreign arrivals. Mehra's first memory of London was of Kensington Gardens. A couple of months later her parents rented a place in Sutton, a beautiful detached house called 'Essendene', with four bedrooms and an attic and a very nice garden. Father and his brother Keki were up in one attic room and the family maid had the other. Their neighbours were two sweet old English ladies on one side and on the other, a family with grown-up children.

'We felt as if we'd lived there all our lives,' Aunt Mehra told me with some pride. 'It was a tribute particularly to my mother's adaptability. She made herself completely at home in no time and went about shopping and buying the groceries. She continued wearing a sari till one winter when she felt so miserable with all the slush on the pavements that she acquired a skirt, coat and hat. She didn't mind a bit going to market for the meat and so forth, which she would never have dreamt of doing in Bombay. She was forty, so not that young.'

The family had inherited Alice, the maid who had been with the owners of the house. 'She was a great help to us all and stayed for about a year and then left us to get married. Her successor was Agnes. She was always astonished at the vast quantities of toast we ate at breakfast. We'd say: "Agnes, six more toasts please." "My, what a lot of toast!" She cooked for us: English food, the usual lamb chops and boiled vegetables. My mother, who was quite a good cook herself, used to make the puddings.

Agnes loved Indian food, so whenever Mother asked: "What shall we cook today?" she'd say, "Let's have a nice curry." And Mama would say: "All right, but we had it only yesterday, so let's wait a day or two."'

Mehra was sent to a private school in Sutton. 'From the very first day, I never felt that I was in a strange place with strange children, although I was the only brown face there. Right from the principal downwards, everybody just took it for granted that there was this Indian girl in school, and there wasn't the slightest ripple of hostility. Curiosity, of course, there was about how we lived in India. One of the girls asked me if we lived in trees: the usual kind of joke you saw in *Punch* in those days. I fitted in extremely fast and did very well at school. I learned Latin and chemistry, which I never would have back in India. The standard was very high and we had excellent teachers.'

The only one ever to comment on her Indian origins was the chemistry teacher. 'She used to say: "Come along, come along. Hurry up! No page-boys here to attend on you!"—as if I'd come from some princely family. I used to laugh and say: "I don't have any page-boys."

'"Oh, yes, everyone in India has page-boys."'

Grandfather worked at the Midland Bank and also took an evening course in banking at the LSE, 'which he completed with flying colours, as one would have expected of him'. And then it was time for him to go back to India. 'You'd better stay on,' he told Granny, 'and let Mehra and the boys carry on with their studies.' So they stayed on without him for over a year. But then he fell quite ill and their Versova neighbours wrote and said it was time Granny came back, because he was quite alone. She got alarmed and decided to return and Mehra had to go back with her, uprooted from the school she had enjoyed so much. Father and Keki were deemed old enough to stay on in London on their own.

Grandfather was not a rich man, but he was determined that all his four children would have the best education he could afford. With considerable sacrifice of their own comfort, my grandparents managed to save just enough to give each of them an education abroad in the field of their own choice.

Father always loved travel, especially abroad. 'At sea and in the air,' he wrote, 'I am as comfortable as on land. On my very first voyage in 1925, at the height of the monsoon, I won bets with some fellow passengers that I would not get seasick.' The only disconcerting experience he had as a newcomer to England was that, at first, all English boys at the LSE looked alike to him, much as all Indians looked alike to the new British arrivals in Bombay.

He shared a very pleasant flat with Uncle Keki, then a medical student, in Middle Temple. There was a plaque on the building saying 'Oliver Goldsmith Lived Here'. They rented the flat from an exiled Russian princess who needed the money. They learned to clean their own shoes, make their own beds and wash their own dishes. This must have been something of a shock after India, where even a lower-middle-class home could afford a servant or two. 'There was no service, except for a cleaning lady,' Father noted. 'We learned for the first time to make our own eggs and tea.'

Much of their leisure time was spent at the Student Movement House in Russell Square, set up by the YMCA to look after foreign students: it was a home from home for all the German, French, Belgian and Indian students. They made some very good friends there among other foreign students, and it was where Uncle Keki met his first wife Birgitte, a Swedish student.

Father had won a small scholarship of £2, 3s and 9d. 'In those days, that was enough for a binge,' he proudly noted. 'You could take a girl out to a dinner-dance on a Saturday night for that amount, including a taxi to see her home. So I used to spend it on an evening out.'

He used the library in Lincoln's Inn, with its quiet and beautiful surroundings, to read law. He enjoyed telling a politically incorrect story about the rival library in Middle Temple, which was reputedly flooded by students from Africa, India, Ceylon and Burma. 'It was said that a bencher [senior barrister] was looking for an English friend and opened the library door to locate him. He found the entire room full of foreign students. At last he spotted a lone Englishman sitting in a corner. Advancing towards him, the bencher bowed low and said audibly: "Dr Livingston, I presume!"'

Father had a wonderful time during the four years he spent in London as a student. 'I was very popular, an excellent debater and a good sportsman,' he wrote, with no trace of false modesty. 'I was Captain of the University Badminton team and also played in the college tennis, cricket and hockey teams. My English contemporaries had no use for bookworms; they judged you by your all-round abilities. I became Chairman of the University Labour Party and of the University League of Nations Society and President of the India Society.'

On May Day 1926, he marched in procession to Hyde Park, holding aloft a red flag and chanting:

Rah Rah, Hoo Rah Rah!
Who the hell do you think we are?
Bolshies!

They also sang, without any inhibition, the *Song of the Red Army*, a very martial tune with the refrain: 'March, march, ye soldiers, and the world shall be free.'

On 6 September 1926 he attended the opening session of the League of Nations. Two days later, the Assembly of the League unanimously voted for the admission of Germany. On 10 September Father watched the German delegation take their seats, as Dr Stresemann, the Chancellor, and Aristide Briand, the French Prime Minister, embraced and made dramatic speeches. They jointly received the Nobel Peace Prize for achieving this historic reconciliation between France and Germany. Nobody had yet heard of Adolf Hitler.

A year later, Father stood for election as the Labour candidate for president of the university students' union. His main opponent was a Tory. He would have defeated him handsomely had it not been for an Indian fellow student called Krishna Menon. Later, Nehru's pro-Communist eminence grise, Krishna Menon was a moderate in those days and decided to stand against Father. The result was that the Indian and Labour vote was split, and Father lost to the Tory by a narrow margin. Perhaps that was the beginning of the deep hostility between the two men, which endured for the rest of their political careers.

Twenty-seventh February 1928 was the annual dinner of the LSE India Society of which Father was president. Being the political hothead he then was, he was not prepared to stand up for *God Save the King*. So he told the committee that he would not take the 'loyal toast' to the King-Emperor, and the committee voted by a majority to support his position. But Krishna Menon snitched about this to Sir William Beveridge, director of the LSE, who was to be the guest of honour. Sir William thereupon sent for Father and said that, in view of this intended *lèse majesté*, he would not be able to attend. 'If only I had not been told,' he said, 'it would have been perfectly all right.' Father went back to the committee and got the decision to boycott the toast revoked. Beveridge attended and, when the moment for the royal toast arrived, Father dutifully gulped down the obligatory glass of port.

FIVE

OFFICERS AND GENTLEMEN

All the Masani children had been radically politicized by their years in England. They had been there for the General Strike in 1926, during which Minoo, my father, 'could talk of nothing else', his sister Mehra remembered, 'and about how he was going to support the miners'. Granny became quite politicized too; Father made her read Shaw's *Intelligent Woman's Guide to Socialism*.

For Aunty Mehra, then fourteen, returning to Bombay and her old school, the Cathedral, came as something of a shock. The girls in her class were all considerably older than her and their attitude to everything was completely different: clothes, jewellery, boyfriends. Studies were not really of much consequence to them. And they thought her an extremely odd girl, because she came from a background where none of those feminine things mattered. 'English girls of my age, in those days at any rate, were just tomboys,' she remembered wistfully, 'not in the least interested in feminine graces.'

When Mehra started college in Bombay at Elphinstone in 1930, life improved because most of the students were quite nationalist. She became involved with running a little Swadeshi shop in college, which sold Indian-manufactured exercise books, pencils and chocolate. There was a patriotic fervour about the place. 'We picketed the college every week or so, in protest against the arrest of some nationalist or other. Principal Hamill would be furious, but what could he do? There we all were, standing at the college entrance asking people not to go in.'

Her anglophile father was not at all sympathetic: 'He thought all this was nonsense, that there was no possibility of India getting independence, and what would we be like if the British withdrew? He objected to my going to Congress meetings and joining processions, but he never actually stopped me.' As with the Srivastavas, the Masani children were in revolt against their father's pro-British views. Sir Rustom had recently been knighted for his services as Leader of the National War Front, which was mobilizing Indian support for the British war effort.

'Minoo, of course, was much more politically active than me,' Aunt Mehra recalled. 'I remember the day he first got arrested. He was editing the *Congress Bulletin*, a seditious, underground rag. I was one of those who distributed it secretly. I would collect it from a particular person and then stand at a predetermined spot. An actor friend of mine, who was in his element, would drive up in a Victoria carriage heavily disguised, sometimes as a Muslim with a *fez*, and sometimes in a dhoti pretending to be a farmer who had just come up to the city. I would hand over the bulletins to him, and he would pass them on to someone else in our distribution network.

'One day I got a phone call at college from Minoo, saying, "I'm in Arthur Road lockup." I asked why, and he said it was because of the *Bulletin*. "Will you go to the Taj [hotel] and get me some nice chicken sandwiches and some brioche?" I went and got them and took them to Arthur Road Jail by Victoria carriage. There were two Jewish confidence tricksters in the jail called Rosenfeld and Wemborg. Minoo used to share his provisions with them.'

My father's arrest annoyed Grandfather considerably, because it was in all the papers. Later, he was arrested again and sent to Nasik Road Prison in Poona. Aunt Mehra visited him once a month, sometimes with Granny, and they took books for him to read.

In 1942, while Father was in jail, Mehra was asked by the underground Bombay Congress leaders to lead a raid on the Wadala salt marshes and court arrest as part of Gandhi's campaign against the salt tax. Father's best friend, Yusuf Meherally, who had just been released from prison, scolded the Congress leader concerned, saying: 'You must be mad. She's only seventeen years old and you can't disturb her college education.

What will her family say if she's locked up? Minoo's in jail, so I feel I must put my foot down on his behalf.'

Mehra, meanwhile, knew nothing about Yusuf's intervention, so she made her preparations, packed a toothbrush and a change of clothes and confided in her younger brother Pesi so he could inform their parents if she didn't come home. When she arrived at the agreed meeting place, she was informed by her contact that the leadership had decided she wasn't to go after all. She went home crestfallen. 'Why have you come back?' young Pesi asked her, mortified because he felt that the more Masanis went to jail the more glory would reflect on him.

During those nationalist years, Mehra had very little contact with the British in Bombay, with one exception. A girl from her old Sutton school married a British Indian civil servant who became Collector of Bandra, the Bombay suburb. When she came to live in Bombay, they contacted Mehra; and she was invited a few times to their home, a lovely big house on Malabar Hill, the old type of bungalow with dozens of servants and a big garden. There she met their other English friends. 'I can't say I much enjoyed those occasions,' she later confessed. 'They were all much older than me, and it was obvious she was just trying to keep up an old association.'

By this time, Aunt Mehra was longing to go back to England and the London life she had grown to love. She applied to St Hugh's at Oxford and to the LSE; but the question was who was going to pay. Grandfather said he'd see what he could do about it, but it was hard to think how he would be able to raise enough money. One day Mehra was busy setting out Indian-made Godrej soaps on a table at a Swadeshi sale when Jal Naoroji—grandson of Dadabhai Naoroji, the 'Grand old Man of India', a Parsi who had been one of the founders of the Indian National Congress and the first Indian to be elected to the British House of Commons—came up to her and asked: 'Would you like to go to England, Mehra?' She said she'd love to, and he told her that a Parsi charitable trust he was involved with was about to offer scholarships for two girls to study in England. She was invited to an interview and offered one of the grants. She got £300 a year and, thrifty as she was, 'found that it was quite enough, and even allowed me to travel on the Continent'.

She travelled to England with Granny on a luxurious Lloyd Trestino liner. They had two adjoining First Class cabins, which they could afford because it was the monsoon and off-season. One of their fellow passengers was Sheela Srivastava, my mother's elder sister, who was on her way to Cambridge. They had to disembark at Genoa and Sheela travelled with them from there to London by train. Mehra had decided on the LSE over Oxford because of its political attraction and the advantages of being in London. 'Those were the great years at the LSE with Harold Laski and Arnold Toynbee and Lionel Robbins,' she told me. 'Karl Mannheim arrived there from Germany, along with other Jewish refugees from the Nazis. The first month, we couldn't make out what he was trying to say, because he knew no English. But he was a remarkable man: by the second month he was quite fluent and completely comprehensible.'

She lived at Crosby Hall in Chelsea, 'a very comfortable and pleasant place'. It was once the sixteenth-century home of Thomas More, and the dining hall with its minstrels' gallery had been part of the original building. 'Ever since then, I've always felt more at home in London than anywhere else,' Aunt Mehra confided from her final exile in remote Deolali.

She made several close friendships at the LSE that lasted most of her life. The closest was with Michael Vermeeren, who was from an aristocratic German family. I later found his letters to her and an album of photographs of the two of them in swimsuits holidaying at the Swiss lakes. She looks far more feminine and vulnerable than I ever knew her. They were clearly very much in love; and then suddenly the outbreak of war shattered their lives. Michael was called up by the German army and Mehra returned to India. Like so many others divided by the war, they lost contact with each other for many years.

Amid the upheavals of post-war Germany, Michael married another woman and settled in Spain. Then suddenly, in the late 1940s, he saw a press write-up and photograph of Mehra as a bright young star of Indian broadcasting. He wrote to her and they re-established contact. She became good friends with his wife and a godparent to his children, and they corresponded almost weekly till her death. He was devastated by it and wrote a heartbroken letter to my father. His wife had died a few months before, and he had been hoping to spend his twilight years with Aunt Mehra.

Talking to Mehra half a century later, one was left in little doubt that her LSE years had been the happiest of her life. 'I met people like Kingsley Martin and Noel Brailsford at meetings of the India League, where I used to hold forth. Krishna Menon always felt that a young woman in a sari would be a great draw, and I suppose he was right, so I used to be sent off to various provincial cities to speak for Indian independence.'

It was always taken for granted that she would take up a job after university. When she was ten, people would ask: 'So what are you going to be when you grow up?' 'I want to be a lawyer,' she would answer. And Grandfather would scoff: 'Pooh, what a stupid profession to choose. You should be a doctor.' And she would say: 'I'm not going to be a doctor. I don't want to study anatomy and zoology.' He carried on trying to persuade her to study medicine and much later she wished she'd taken his advice. 'I think I would have made a very good doctor, and I'd have been financially independent. You can go and set up your own medical practice wherever you want, without being beholden to anybody or having to put up with government officials.'

Her independence was always important to Aunt Mehra. When she came back to Bombay in 1938, the question was what she was to do. She thought of lecturing at a college and Grandfather was keen on that. But meanwhile she met Lionel Fielden, a former BBC executive who was in the process of setting up a countrywide broadcasting network for India, to be named All India Radio or AIR. He had already tried and failed to persuade my father to compromise his nationalist principles and join AIR, but Father suggested his sister would be more suitable, and Fielden persuaded her to join him. She had planned to go back to England in 1939, but it had become impossible because of the outbreak of war.

In 1940 AIR transferred her from Bombay to Delhi. 'I found it difficult to fit in there at first,' she recalled. 'People up north didn't really accept a young woman living on her own and working. All my colleagues were men, mostly Punjabis, and they found it very difficult to think of me as a person who should be treated exactly like everyone else. Even the Station Director was initially very hostile to my being posted there. But the Director-General insisted that they had to have me, and eventually they got used to my presence.'

It was a time of youthful optimism and dramatic changes were in the air. Fielden had been sent out by Lord Reith to help the Viceroy, Lord Linlithgow, set up a broadcasting system which would rally Indian public opinion behind the war effort. But this Reithian envoy, as Aunty Mehra later told me with delight, was adept at thwarting and subverting British officialdom. He was more or less openly homosexual, an unabashed intellectual (and therefore doubly suspect among officials) and generally iconoclastic in his opinions. Under him, AIR attracted some of the best minds in the country and, despite official censorship, became a beacon of free expression and radical opinion.

It was an intellectual climate in which Mehra could thrive and her personality and friendships blossomed in Delhi, where she was to spend most of her life. Unfortunately, AIR, despite her best efforts, deteriorated steadily after Independence, increasingly muzzled by political interference and denuded of talent by ministerial nepotism. As director of programmes, Mehra worked hard to maintain its early editorial independence and to secure its conversion into an autonomous corporation like the BBC. But the encroachments of what became effectively a one-party state were hard to resist, especially as her relationship to Father, after he became Leader of the embryonic Opposition, was used to discredit her in government circles.

Father's political career had already begun during his student years at the LSE, whence he returned to India steeped in Fabian intellectual values, passionately committed to fighting for socialism and against imperialism and a convert to radical social causes like female emancipation. But even at this stage, he was deeply suspicious of Soviet-style Communism, having witnessed alarming evidence of incipient autocracy and the cult of personality when he visited Moscow in Lenin's time in the 1920s. His worst fears were amply confirmed on a later visit in the 1930s during Stalin's purges.

Father's socialism and the political activism into which he threw himself made for a turbulent relationship with Grandfather. They had already clashed often enough over Father's championship of my long-suffering grandmother, and their heated political arguments now made matters worse. By the time I was born, they had come much closer, emotionally and politically; and Father could look back with great sympathy on Grandfather's role, even during their worst quarrels.

The more I think of it, my father was a great man. I'd like to think I take after him. When I came back from the LSE, Papa very generously put us up at Versova, and I used to practise at the Bar as a briefless barrister. I was passed over for the Law examinership at Bombay University, which would have paid me Rs. 2000 per exam. The third time my name came up, the Law Faculty recommended my name, along with some others, to the Syndicate. Unfortunately, Papa was in the chair. When he found my name on the list, he exclaimed: 'My son!' The Dean replied: 'Sir, it's nothing to do with that.'

'It has. Please strike off his name.'

'Sir Rustom,' the Dean pleaded, 'this is very unfair to us. Are you suggesting we're guilty of nepotism? And are you not being unfair to your son? He's been passed over for two years. This comes rather late to him, and it's well deserved.'

'No. While I chair this Syndicate, no son of mine will make one rupee out of this university.'

The Dean told me what had happened the next morning in the High Court. 'Your father was most unreasonable,' he said. 'For half an hour we argued on your behalf, but he wouldn't give in. There was a deadlock, and the meeting could not proceed. So in the end we had to bow to his decision.'

I went home to Versova seething. At dinner, I said: 'Papa, why did you come in my way? I would have earned some money that I badly need.' He kept quiet and carried on eating his food. I too clammed up. After dinner, he called me to his study. He had written out a cheque for Rs. 2000. 'Here's your money,' he said. 'Now stop complaining. This is a country full of nepotism. Everyone is helping his own sons and nephews. Somebody has got to set an example.

That's what I've done, and I'm sorry you're at the receiving end. Hence the Rs. 2000.'

I was so ashamed that I tore up the cheque and said: 'No, no, you're right.' Forty years later Rajaji [C. Rajagopalachari] told the story in his newspaper column. Indira Gandhi was then Prime Minister and her son Sanjay was her pet. 'Why doesn't Mrs. Gandhi follow Sir Rustom Masani's example?' Rajaji wrote. 'That's how she should treat Sanjay instead of pampering him.'

Father joined the bar of the Bombay High Court in 1929, soon after he returned from the LSE. He was delighted to be allowed to devil in the chambers of F. Coltman, the only leading English barrister then practising in Bombay.

'I could not have found a better place. Coltman had a flourishing practice. He was a rather dry and introspective person, and his strongest points were his precise drafting, his sticky advocacy in court, even on a hard wicket, and his unquestioned integrity. He was a hard taskmaster and expected us juniors to work really hard. I learned a great deal from him about the intricacies of legal language. After about three years, my political activities, of which I had no doubt he disapproved heartily, took me away from the Bar.'

Had he chosen, Father would no doubt have made a very successful barrister. He had all the qualifications: superb oratory as a public speaker, a razor-sharp mind, forensic debating skills and excellent organizing abilities. These were, of course, also powerful assets in his new political career. He threw himself into the Congress civil disobedience campaigns and had two terms in prison. The first was a two-month term of detention without trial in 1932. In January 1933 he was arrested again, pleaded guilty and received a sentence of one year's rigorous imprisonment, which he spent in Nasik Road Prison.

Father often used to say that the British Raj 'played cricket' in the way it dealt with nationalist agitators like himself. These Indian nationalists, after all, were the children of British education and liberal values, steeped in the literature of Western humanism and radicalism. Except in their treatment of avowed 'terrorists', the authorities used no torture or gratuitous violence and treated political prisoners with the respect they deserved, even during times of greatest crisis like the Quit India agitation during World War II. 'Had the British authorities not behaved like honourable officers and gentlemen,' Father always maintained, 'Gandhi's non-violent campaigns would never have been possible.'

'One of the finest things about prison life,' he later wrote, 'was the amount of reading one could do. I kept a notebook where I jotted down extracts from books and little quotations. I find that in one month alone I read an assortment of books which included the poetry of Landor, novels by Mauriac and Anatole France, economic geography and James Joyce's *Ulysses*. In a letter to Mama in September 1933, I mentioned that I had read about a hundred books during the first eight months of the year, but that I was now getting lazy and slacking a little.'

In 1934, after his release, he became one of the founders of the Congress Socialist Party, a left-wing bloc within the National Congress. This created tensions with Grandfather, with whom Father was still living at Versova.

Papa said he didn't mind socialism, but he did object to the concept of class war, which he considered pernicious. 'You are inciting class struggle,' he said. 'It's bad for the country, and I don't like it being done from my home.'

Although he hadn't asked me to leave the house, I thought he was right, and I decided that I must move into the city and find a job. I went to see a nationalist editor I knew who had just decided to launch a new paper called *The Daily Sun*. I explained that I needed to become independent of my father and asked him for a job. 'Wonderful!' he exclaimed. 'Would you like to be Assistant Editor?' I jumped at it. My job was to assist the editor, a venerable gentleman with a walrus moustache, and take full charge at night after he went home. My hours were from 9 at night till 5 in the morning, when the paper went to press. My salary was only Rs. 150, but I was delighted at the prospect of having the days free for my political activities.

When I told Papa that I'd got a job and was moving out, he said: 'What's all this?' I told him that I felt I had no right to sponge on him while I was busy advocating a class war he disapproved of. 'I never meant you to go,' he protested. 'I know you didn't,' I replied. 'But it was a well-deserved remark. I should have done this much earlier.' So Papa said: 'All right, provided you come and lunch with me every day at the Grand Hotel [of which he was a director]. You can't possibly feed yourself properly on Rs. 150 a month.'

And that's how Father survived as a political activist for the next five years. He had a good three-course lunch with Grandfather, and then in the evening he made do with half a bun and a cup of tea at the Cecil corner café on Hughes Road, opposite the small flat where he lived as a lodger with a political friend.

His flatmate, Lilubhai Merchant, was a young Gujarati who was in love with a Parsi girl called Coomi, but her widowed mother wouldn't hear of them marrying. 'I won't see your bloody face if you marry this Hindu,' she threatened her daughter. Coomi was intimidated by her mother's threats, but Father told Lilubhai to reassure her that it was all bluff and bluster. 'Parents say these things; they don't mean them. If she marries you, her mother will forgive her after one year. I guarantee it.'

In the end, Coomi and Lilubhai eloped with Father's encouragement, and her mother cut her off. 'The final outcome was rather funny,' Father told me with delight. 'A couple of years later, when I asked Lilubhai how things were going, he replied: "All right, but my mother-in-law has come to stay with us, and she won't budge. We don't know how to get rid of her. It would have been far better if she'd stuck to her original decision never again to see her daughter."'

Through the 1930s, Father was one of the leading firebrands of the Congress left. But his socialism didn't prevent him from having a great deal of respect for Mahatma Gandhi. He accompanied him on walking tours, tried unsuccessfully to recruit him to socialism and defended him against the virulent attacks of the Indian Communists. The Mahatma and he, though so different in most respects, shared a dry sense of humour and corresponded in terse, handwritten postcards.

Sir J.P. and Lady Kailash Srivastava (centre) in 1936 with their seven children. My mother, Shakuntala, is second from the left.

'Kailash', the Srivastava family home in Kanpur, looking neglected in the 1970s.

Lady Kailash Srivastava in the 1930s.

Sir J.P. Srivastava in full regalia as Viceroy's Executive Councillor and Knight Commander of Star of India, 1940s.

Manijeh Masani as a young woman.

Rustom Masani, circa 1900, as a young man.

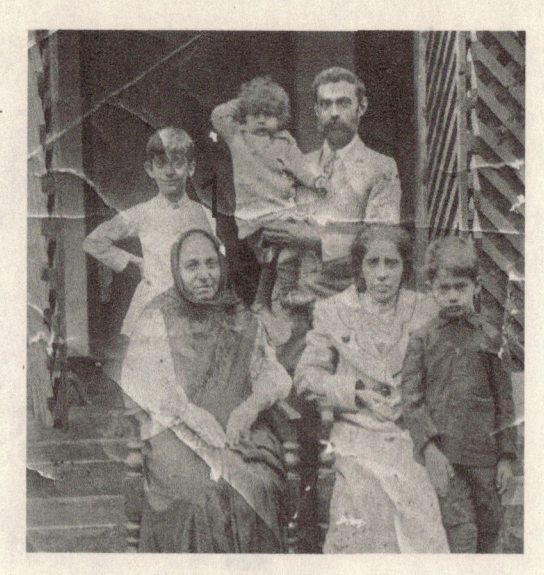

The Masanis, circa 1913. My father Minoo on the left and his sister Mehra in her father's arms.

Sir Rustom Masani (extreme left) in the 1930s as Vice Chancellor of Bombay University.

Minoo Masani, aged about five.

Father in the 1920s, a dapper young man.

Aunt Mehra in the 1930s, swimming in the Swiss lakes with her romantic friend, Michael Vermeeren.

Mehra Masani in the 1950s, a rising star of All India Radio, receiving Prime Minister Jawaharlal Nehru.

Father in his office as Mayor of Bombay, 1943.

As a Congress candidate backed by Pandit Nehru in 1945 at the hustings for the Indian Legislative Assembly.

Mother, Lucknow, 1943, shortly before she left home.

Giving a dance performance, Bombay, 1953.

In a Bharatnatyam pose.

During this period, Father was also close to Jawaharlal Nehru, whom he visited often at his family home, Anand Bhavan, in Allahabad. He was especially fond of Nehru's quiet and rather neglected wife Kamala. On one of his visits, he was at the Nehru breakfast table when Jawaharlal joked about a young Parsi nationalist called Feroze Gandhi who was infatuated with his wife. 'Minoo, can you imagine any man being in love with my wife?' he ungallantly remarked; to which Father replied with suitable chivalry: 'Of course I can! I could easily fall in love with her myself.' His gallantry won him a dazzling smile from Kamala Nehru. They remained good friends till her premature death in 1936, whereupon young Feroze Gandhi was to transfer his attentions to her daughter Indira, whom he eventually married.

In November 1939 Father sadly decided to cut himself off from the Socialist Party which he had helped conceive in Nasik Prison back in 1933. He was by then fiercely anti-Stalinist and frustrated by his own failure to prevent Communist infiltration of the Indian Socialist Party. He was also tired of eking out a miserable existence on the meagre bounty of a couple of wealthy friends. He wanted the dignity and economic independence of earning his own living. He announced his retirement from political life, started writing his first major book, *Our India*, and looked around for a job.

The book was a nationalist economic geography of India for older children. It was a resounding success and became a school textbook after Independence. A whole new generation of Indians who grew up on it still remember Minoo Masani best for being its author. In 1941 he joined India's leading business house, Tatas, and became their head of public relations and later *chef de cabinet* to the chairman, J.R.D. Tata. By then, his need for secure employment was also linked to developments in his personal life.

SIX

WEDDINGS AND DIVORCES

My father hated talking about his feelings and his previous marriages were never discussed when I was a child. The brief account he gave of his first marriage was extracted by my persistent questioning sixty years after it ended. It was at the LSE that he met Phyllis Atkinson, a fellow student from a middle-class Yorkshire family.

> Her parents were very upset about our relationship. I never met them. There was a Miss Gedge whom I knew in Bombay, a nice old lady and a good violinist. My parents spoke to her and she asked me to come and see her. She sized me up and said: 'So young man, you want to marry this girl.' I said, 'Yes, Ma'am.'
> 'But you know the parents object.'
> 'Yes, I know that.'
> 'Do you blame them?'
> I said: 'No, unfortunately it's a common prejudice among English parents these days.'
> This was in 1928. So she cross-examined me a little. And then she wrote a nice letter to Phyllis's parents saying: 'I know the parents of the boy. They're very nice people. He's a nice young man, and I think you should overcome your racial prejudice and not come in their way.' But her parents said, 'All right, you damned well get married on your own. We'll have nothing to do with it.'

They got married in London and then returned together to India in 1929 to live with my grandparents at Versova. The marriage lasted three years. While Father was in prison in 1932 during the Congress civil disobedience movement, Phyllis fell in love with another man.

'We separated and she went back to England and I took a divorce. She was meant to cable me from the boat if she changed her mind. When she got to London, she wrote saying that she had hovered around the ship's telex room, but couldn't make up her mind. "I was very torn," she wrote, "but in the end I decided it was better this way." She probably was right from her point of view. Coming back to Bombay, with this other man here, she must have felt that it would have been difficult to give him up.'

That was all Father would say on the subject. What I gleaned from other sources was that Phyllis Atkinson, despite her own youthful radicalism, or perhaps because of it, found it difficult to adjust to the role of the English wife of an Indian political firebrand. While Father threw himself into the politics of revolt and spent long months in prison, she was left isolated and bored with her austere in-laws in suburban Versova. So it wasn't altogether surprising that she started an affair with a wealthy, Parsi bon viveur. Her lover was already married to a beautiful woman of German and Parsi descent, Piroja or Pilli Fraser. Intentionally or otherwise, Father later had his revenge. He began a passionate affair with Pilli and eventually married her a decade later.

Despite having lost his first wife to another man, Father was irresistible to women for most of his long life. He was tall, with an agile, lean physique; he had strong features—a wide brow, a bow-shaped sensuous mouth, prominent teeth, an aquiline Parsi nose, a square jaw and a firm, dimpled chin; and his head, which became more visible as his hair thinned, was finely shaped. Mother later told me that a German anthropologist they met in Brazil, possibly a Nazi refugee, insisted on sketching him because he had the perfect Aryan face. The Parsis, of course, having originated in the Caucasus, had a stronger claim to Aryan purity than any German.

'Pilli was very beautiful, but very neurotic,' Father reluctantly replied when I quizzed him about his second wife. 'Dady Wadia, her first husband, was a typical, good-living Parsi. He was very unfaithful to her, a bit of a rake, and she couldn't bear it. She was a very sentimental person, and what she liked about me was my constancy. We were only married for a year.

'Her ex-husband blackmailed her over the children, and she couldn't make up her mind, which was forgivable from her point of view. He said she couldn't see her daughters if she didn't return. She wasn't capable of standing up to him. She was a very weak-minded woman I now realize. I sometimes meet her daughters, and one of them, Zarin, who has inherited her mother's looks, is quite fond of me. She felt I was good to her mother.'

That was all I could prise from him about his second marriage. But there were many other sources only too happy to fill in the gaps: his tempestuous relationship with Pilli had become one of the romantic legends of Bombay.

The story goes something like this. They had a long courtship, during which Father consoled Pilli for her husband's infidelities and became a close confidant to her and her two young daughters. In 1941 her husband agreed to sue her for divorce on grounds of her adultery with Father, who was cited as co-respondent.

This much is fact; and I found the evidence among his papers after his death in a divorce petition filed in the Parsi Matrimonial Court of Bombay in March 1941 in the case of *Wadia versus Wadia and Masani*. I also found a copy of the evidence the 'guilty' parties supplied in court: a receipt from the Daman Hotel (in Portuguese India), made out to Mr and Mrs Masani for one night's board and lodging at the rate of Rs 4 each. The bill included two bottles of lemonade, remarkably abstemious for a night of ostensibly steamy adultery.

More ominously, the plaintiff asked for custody of his children, and the court decreed that 'the question of custody of the two minor daughters of the marriage do stand over'. In practice, this meant that the girls stayed with their father, and Pilli was allowed to visit them at his home. She used to go there most evenings to give them their dinner and put them to bed. This was during World War II; there were blackouts in Bombay and rumours of imminent Japanese bombers. Pilli became distraught about leaving her daughters alone at night and started staying over at her ex-husband's.

Father eventually presented her with an ultimatum, and she decided to return to her first husband. One apocryphal story my mother enjoyed telling had Father waiting for Pilli in his car outside her ex-husband's home. She was to come down at 9.30 p.m. if she wanted to come home with him and save their marriage. Otherwise, he would assume she was staying for good. She came down, but five minutes late, by which time Father had driven off, never to return.

Pilli's own very colourful and, no doubt, equally fictionalized version, told at various Bombay dinner parties, was that Father had locked her in her bedroom at night to prevent her visiting her children. But she had climbed down from the window on her bed sheets, hailed a taxi in the midst of the blackout and escaped to her former home.

Whatever the manner of her departure, the three parties to this farcical marital triangle were back in the Parsi Matrimonial Court in August 1943, this time in the unopposed case of *Masani versus Masani and Wadia*. My father was the plaintiff suing his wife and her ex-husband for adultery. According to a lawyer friend of the family, the judge was understandably bemused. 'Mrs Masani, or should I call you Mrs Wadia,' he asked, 'are you quite sure you know whom you're divorcing and whom you're marrying?'

Pilli did remarry her first husband, and their second marriage was successful enough for them to produce a son. I remember being a little disappointed when I met Pilli fifteen years later to find that the Scarlet Woman of my imagination had become a plump and rather faded but kindly and warm lady, who used to chat with my mother while I swam with her son at the Willingdon Club pool.

Mother warmed to her and thoroughly enjoyed her stories at Father's expense. He was less pleased, and the friendship between his second and third wives was not allowed to develop. He avoided Pilli like the plague for the rest of her life, and it was my maternal grandmother who persuaded him to visit her briefly when she was dying prematurely of cancer in 1962.

Two thousand miles across the country, politics and marriage were also changing the lives of the Srivastava family in the textile town of Kanpur, then the Manchester of the East. In the mid-1930s, Sir J.P. had launched his political career by buying up the formerly British-owned daily, the *Pioneer*, and launching a Landowners' Party, along with various *taluqdar*s of the United Provinces. Defeated by the nationalist Congress in the 1937 provincial elections, he turned his attention to the capital, where the Viceroy's Cabinet still consisted of nominated and unelected executive councillors.

In 1940, following the outbreak of World War II, Sir J.P. was appointed Civil Defence Member of the Viceroy's Council, as much for his organizing abilities as for his staunch loyalty to King and Empire. In 1941, during the Congress-led Quit India movement, when Mahatma Gandhi went on a fast unto death, Sir J.P.'s advice to the Viceroy was: 'Let him. It's political blackmail and he doesn't really mean it. And if he does, it will be good riddance.' In 1943, at the height of the devastating Bengal famine, he was moved to the food portfolio, once again as a troubleshooter who would get food supplies moving. For six years, till the Congress ousted him in 1946, he was the political right-hand of two successive viceroys, Lords Linlithgow and Wavell, both of whom highly prized his friendship and advice.

Sir J.P., with his large Churchillian belly, a glass of whisky in one hand and a cigar in the other, was easy to caricature, and he became a favourite butt of nationalist cartoons and smear-stories in the tabloid press. He had come to represent the proverbial imperialist toady, growing fat on the blood and toil of the Indian masses. To his dismay, that was a view shared by some of his own children.

It all began with my mother's elder sister Sheela, who returned from Cambridge in 1939 as an armchair Communist who belonged to the Left Book Club and similar circles. She soon indoctrinated her younger sisters, Sarala and my mother, and the house became a hotbed of seditious chatter and intrigue. In her personal life, too, Sheela set an example which must have influenced Mother. She was in love with a glamorous Muslim intellectual, whom she had met at Cambridge. His name was Aga Hillali, and he later became independent Pakistan's Foreign Secretary. But back in the 1940s, he could not have been a less suitable match for Sir J.P.'s daughter.

The family was not overtly communal; indeed, the Kayasth caste, to which they belonged, had risen to prominence under the Mughal emperors and was closely integrated into north Indian Muslim culture. Nevertheless, they drew the line at inter-marriage, and it was still unthinkable for any Hindu girl of good family to marry a Muslim. And so, when Aga Hillali came to Kanpur to see Sir J.P. and ask for his daughter's hand, the answer was a firm no.

Mother once told me that she and her sisters hid outside the drawing room door and eavesdropped on this encounter. They were all agog when the rejected suitor leapt up on to one of the sofas and started jumping up and down while he denounced Sir J.P. as a reactionary communalist. He had to be forcibly removed, never to return. Faced with an ultimatum to give him up, Aunt Sheela complied and reluctantly married a promising Hindu ICS officer, Rajeshwar Dayal, who later became independent India's Foreign Secretary. Despite the rocky start, the Dayals and the Hillalis remained good friends for the rest of their lives.

In 1938 my mother passed her entrance exam for Cambridge, and Sarala and she were all set to follow Sheela there. The whole family travelled to England and Mother had her first glimpse of Cambridge. Later they toured the Continent in a huge nine-seater Daimler. And then disaster struck: outside a small Belgian village they were hit by a large lorry. There were only minor cuts and bruises, with one exception: my grandmother, who had a smashed hip and pelvis and severe internal injuries.

For months she hovered between life and death in a provincial Belgian hospital, with her anxious children and husband beside her. They lived with an aristocratic Belgian family who had kindly taken them in; and Mother and Sarala were courted by the teenaged sons of the house. Mother's Belgian beau, whom I later met as Baron Arnold ter Kint, remained a close and devoted friend till his death, a couple of years before hers.

My grandmother pulled through and lived another twenty-four years, but her health was always frail after that. Ever since I can remember, the family referred to 'The Accident' as the turning point in my grandmother's life. From a robust and adventurous young woman, she turned overnight into an elderly invalid.

Mother's Cambridge plans were finally dashed the following year, when war broke out. So she joined college in Lucknow, then the flourishing capital and cultural hub of British India's largest and most populous province. She lived in her father's palatial Lucknow home and took a first-class degree in history, politics and Sanskrit.

It was typical of the Indian cultural renaissance of this period that she also learned Kathak, the north Indian classical dance style, from its leading exponent, Acchan Maharaj of the Lucknow gharana, established under the patronage of the last independent king of Oudh, Wajid Ali Shah. Mother enjoyed telling me stories about the king's decadence, extravagance and love of the arts, all of which seemed inseparable. He scandalized both the British and his Muslim courtiers by dressing up as the Hindu god Krishna and dancing in public. A flabby and effeminate figure with large moustachios, he nevertheless danced with light abandon, one moment the mischievous Krishna, the next a flirtatious *gopi* (milkmaid). But the British were not charmed and, in 1856, on the eve of the Mutiny, they deposed him for misrule and annexed his kingdom, which became the heartland of British India as the United Provinces or U.P.

Mother later studied Bharat Natyam, the more ancient and Hindu classical dance of southern India, but Kathak, with its lilting melodies, graceful pirouettes and sinuous arm and hand movements, its blend of sensuality, storytelling and intricate, percussive footwork, was always her favourite style, and mine too. The dancer wears heavy brass anklets made up of hundreds of small bells, known as *ghungroo*s, and the most skilled refine their technique to the point of being able to vibrate a single bell.

Mother never reached that level of virtuosity, but she was a graceful and sensitive dancer with a flair for ravishing costumes. During her student years, she also studied painting at the Lucknow School of Art with Sudhir Khastagir, a well-known artist. Though she never developed an original or distinctive style, she sketched well and produced competent oil and watercolour landscapes and still lifes until well into her middle years.

Alone among her sisters Mother had decided that she wanted to work after university. For a while she helped out as a trainee journalist with Desmond Young, the British editor of her father's newspaper, the *Pioneer*. She also started studying for an M.A. in English literature. But she appears to have found her comfortable life in her father's shadow rather oppressive. She was by then passionately nationalist, and she also resented the over-persistent attentions of the wealthy young men who were courting her.

Apart from being the daughter of one of the wealthiest and most powerful men in the country, she had accomplishments of her own. Though not conventionally beautiful like her sister Sarala, she had what Indians call *chamak* or sparkle, especially for the opposite sex. 'Even when she was a teenager, men clustered around her like bees around a honey-pot,' her sister Sheela told me after her death; and Malati, her rival in life, mixed the metaphor and added: 'she had them eating out of her hand.'

She had an oval face with a long, graceful neck, small, elfin ears, a retroussé nose, large, liquid eyes and a mane of wavy, black hair. Her childhood pet name had been 'Shanky', because of her long legs, but by her late teens her figure was sylph-like, with a natural grace refined by her training in classical dance. Though she lacked the physical stamina of Sarala Mausi, also a classical dancer, she excelled in *abhinaya*, the subtle, facial expressions that are the soul of Indian dance. She was considered the most artistic of her brothers and sisters, with a keen aesthetic sense. At a time when Indian antiquities were still unfashionable, she was already an avid collector, picking up whatever fragments she could from the neglected archaeological sites her father passed by on his hunting expeditions or official tours.

Perhaps most fetching of all was her mischievous and irreverent sense of humour and her dislike of authority and pomposity, qualities that fuelled her rebellion against her father. She later wrote about her feelings in the third person.

> Shakuntala sat under the shade of the Neem tree with her hands cupping her chin and her elbows resting on her knees. She was worried and frustrated, and the tears trickled down her cheeks.

'What can I do? How can I fight against Father's power?' she muttered to herself. 'There must be some way for me to outwit him.' She looked at the pale blue sky above the leafy branches of the tree, as if expecting an answer to her question. A light breeze ruffled the leaves, and a couple of them drifted down, falling gently on her hair and her snow-white sari. She picked them up, one by one, and crushed them in her fingers with such fury expressing her utter helplessness. Shakuntala was twenty years old.

As the daughter of Sir J.P. Srivastava, the epitome of imperialist reaction, she was much in demand by her left-wing student colleagues, who wanted to put her at the front of their protest demonstrations. 'We were *lathi*-charged and arrested,' she later wrote. 'But because of my father's official position, I was forcibly put into the British Superintendent of Police's jeep and taken back to my father's house. I tried over and over again to court arrest along with my friends, but I was always taken back home.'

The final straw was the loss of her sister Sarala, to whom she had been intensely attached. In 1943 Sarala married a Punjabi ICS officer from one of the wealthiest families in Lahore. Despite wartime restrictions, the wedding in Kanpur was the grandest occasion Mother ever witnessed. Her father was at his political and commercial zenith, and no expense was spared. The Viceroy and dozens of Indian princes attended, arriving with the most lavish wedding gifts. The huge dining table, on which the gifts were displayed, groaned under their weight. On the lawns outside, some of India's leading artists performed for the guests. Begum Akhtar sang her romantic ghazals, Ram Gopal in his resplendent costumes performed the cosmic dance of Shiva, and Bismillah Khan played the *shehnai*, the traditional harbinger of happy unions and sad farewells.

Mother was heartbroken when her favourite sister left home. Sarala and she wept themselves to sleep every night for weeks before the day; and she was inconsolable when Sarala finally left for Lahore to live with her husband's family.

A few months later, Mother solved the dilemma of how to break free from her father. She slipped away from college with her bag already packed and boarded a train to Bombay. As soon as he got wind of this, her father wired the local police at various stops to intercept the train and force her to get off. But her compartment was full of British troops on their way home from the Burma front. She told them she was escaping from a tyrannical father, and they obligingly hid her in the toilet.

At Victoria Terminus in Bombay she was met by friends of her parents, with whom she lived for some months. Her father tried hard to persuade her to return. Sarala, the only one to whom she might have listened, was summoned from Lahore and sent to Bombay to fetch her back, but she returned empty-handed.

Bombay, then as now, was India's Big Apple, bustling with people, ideas and commerce. For a young woman from a sheltered home up north, it must have been a tremendous adventure, and my mother took to it like a duck to water. Her first priority was to find a job, and that's how she met Father.

The novelist Raja Rao was a close friend of her sister Sheela's. He took Mother to see Minoo Masani, then a senior executive at Tatas. It was love at first sight and they were both swept off their feet. He was much older than her, an experienced man of the world, and a glamorous nationalist figure who had just been elected the first Congress Mayor of Bombay. She was fresh, innocent and very pretty; the perfect antidote to his recent mésalliance with Pilli Wadia.

He got her a job on a nationalist daily called the *Free Press Journal*. She was responsible for the women's page of its Sunday edition and also had to work night shifts as a sub-editor. Father found her digs with the same couple, Lilubhai and Coomi Merchant, whom he had encouraged to elope a couple of years earlier. She lived with them for two years at their flat on Marine Drive—the sparkling, art deco seaside promenade described as the Queen's Necklace.

She later remembered walking to work at night through deserted streets during the wartime blackout. She was understandably nervous and did not know at the time that her father had quietly instructed the

Bombay police to watch over her. Unknown to her, her route took her past several plainclothes officers who made sure she was unmolested.

Through Father, she also met the underground leadership of the Quit India movement, romantic heroes and heroines like Aruna Asaf Ali, Jayaprakash Narayan and Yusuf Meherally. They encouraged her to return to her father's home for a while to try and spy on his official papers and ferret out secret information that the underground could use. She duly visited her father at his official residence in Delhi, but her career as a spy was short-lived. 'My father guessed my reason for coming home,' she later wrote. 'He arranged to leave false information on his desk, which I read and quietly passed on. After a while, to my great embarrassment, I realized the information was false.'

She returned to Bombay and her relationship with Father deepened. He was still living in financially straitened circumstances and drove an ancient Hillman Minx with a rusted roof. When it rained buckets during the Bombay monsoon, Mother and he had to wear solar topees to stay dry in the car. But they laughed off such minor hardships, and she seems to have been happier than I ever knew her.

India was by then moving inexorably towards independence, although the Viceroy, Lord Wavell, was making valiant efforts to broker a smooth transition that would avoid the partition demanded by the Muslim League. His approach was about to be overwhelmed by the impatience of Nehru and the Congress to seize power, matched by the desire of Britain's new Labour government to cut and run, the policy Lord Mountbatten was sent out to implement.

In November 1945 Father was elected to the Indian Legislative Assembly as a Congress representative from Bombay. Two years later, it became independent India's Constituent Assembly and he played an important part in its deliberations. Before Independence, he was the Congress Party's frontbench spokesman on food policy, a sensitive issue in the wake of the Bengal famine, which nationalists blamed on the Raj. Sir J.P. Srivastava was still Food Member in the Viceroy's government, and on several occasions he clashed swords with his future son-in-law on the floor of the Assembly; but these exchanges were always polite and good-humoured. Father later declared that India's last imperial legislature, though elected on a restricted franchise, was the most democratic and intellectually stimulating Parliament in which he ever served.

Mother was by now very much in love with him; and though proud of the public accolades he was getting, she fretted during his frequent trips to Delhi to attend the Assembly sessions.

29th January [1945]
8 a.m.

Darling,

You are gone and once again I am alone. As I watched the plane carrying you away from me, I felt that it was taking away a very important and vital part of me. But then, in another ten days, perhaps this very same plane will bring you back to me. And when I think of that, I feel happy again. Minoo, it was so wonderful having you here for these days, and thank you so much for coming. It meant a whole big heap to me.

I tried so hard to spot you inside the plane, but I just couldn't. Which side were you sitting on? Are you very, very busy in Delhi? I shall look forward to tomorrow's papers, just in case you have made another outburst.

Goodbye darling, I must have my bath and get ready for office. Look after yourself and think of me sometimes.

With all my love,
S

30th January
7.30 p.m.

Dearest Minoo,

I have just returned from a long walk by the sea. I thought of you all the time. I wonder if any of my thoughts ever reached you.

Darling, my heart is just bursting for love of you – such a complete, beautiful love, when one feels grateful just to be allowed to give without any yearning to receive. I seem to have got it badly, haven't I!

The flat is deserted. Sheela [her elder sister who was visiting] is out with Raja [Rao], and Malati has gone to Juhu [beach] with John. [Her youngest sister had joined her in Bombay and was in love with a handsome, young Scottish ICS officer called John Bowman.] I am alone, but I am neither lonely nor sad, because you are near me, and I feel such a nice, warm glow inside me as I think of you and all the wonderful times we have had together.

I got your telegram this morning. I am so glad you are well again. It really is rather distressing that every time you get away from me you feel better!

You will be glad to know that Acchan [her Lucknow dance teacher, who had arrived in Bombay] has agreed to teach me at Rs. 200 a month, and I shall be starting my lessons from tomorrow.

I have had no news from home [about their plans to marry], but as soon as I do I shall let you know. I saw in this evening's papers that Papa may be going to the U.K. and the U.S.A. I wonder if it is true.

Minoo darling, I want you to know that I am no longer afraid – afraid that you may hurt me. I had such awful fears at one time, but they seem to have all evaporated. You have been so kind, gentle and good with me, and it's with absolute confidence and faith that I say to you – 'into thine hands I commend my spirit'.

Good night beloved and God bless you for bringing me such happiness.

Yours ever,
Shakuntala

P.S. I am going to do a bit of reading for my M.A., and I think I shall start with Tennyson. If I come across any familiar passages, I shall know where I have heard them before!

~

Saturday 2nd February

Dearest,

Today being Saturday I had only half-day office. I am now going to settle down to my M.A. books. I am not going out anywhere, so that I can work right up to 8 o' clock, when Acchan comes for my dancing lesson.

I wrote to you earlier in the day, and here I am writing to you again. Have you received all my letters? Do let me know. You know I cannot help but feel a little fed up – I have written to you every day without fail, and I have only heard once from you. I do not want you to write unless you really feel like it, for I want from you only what your happiness can spare. That is not asking for too much, is it dearest?

I don't suppose you know as yet when you will be coming down, or if you can come down at all? I am not feeling quite up to the mark today – have got a slight touch of the 'flu. Tonight I am going to gladden your heart by taking a strong dose of Ninjol. You see, darling, how well I am looking after myself, and you really haven't to worry about me.

Yours with love,
S

~

Sunday February 3

Hello darling,

I am writing to you from bed. The 'flu got me down after all. It is nothing to worry about – just a bad cold and a little fever. You should see the fuss that is being made of me. Everyone is doing a flat spin round me. Malati called in Dr. Cooper. He has given me an injection and prescribed all sorts of mixtures, inhalers, nasal douches, etc., etc. Really I have never been so spoilt in all my life, so please don't worry about me, dearest. The doctor has asked me to stay in bed for a day or two, and I am going to do so – not because I need the rest, but because I know it will please you.

    I was to lunch with your mother today, but had to cut it. Sheela rang up and explained to her. I hope she will not misunderstand. I shall ring her up as soon as I am well.

    The other day when I went to see Yusuf [Meherally], he happened to mention how wrong it was of you not to have joined the Independence Day procession and to have gone [with me] to a cinema instead. Minoo dearest, I do not want you to neglect your career or your political activities because of me. It will make me very, very unhappy if you do. I don't know what came over me that day. I remember you did tell me that Yusuf had wanted you to join the procession, but in my selfishness I completely ignored your remark. Sweetheart, you must promise me that if any such occasion ever arises again, you will pull me up and tick me off. I do not mean to be selfish, but I think I am a little thoughtless at times.

    I have been having quite a bit of trouble about my dancing lessons. Our neighbours have been objecting to the noise, so I think I shall have to discontinue them.

    I have just had one letter from you. It would be nice if you would write more often.

Yours with all my love,
S.

Monday 4th February
7.30 p.m.

I received your second letter yesterday evening, dearest, a little after I had sent off my letter to you.

I was glad to hear that Mama had been nice to Mehra [my aunt] and you [in Delhi]. She rang up last night, and since the others were out she and I had a long chat together. Just before ringing off, she told me that she had met you, but had not been able to get to know or see very much of you, as she was afraid that it might embarrass you as a Congressman to mix with officials. I told her that she should certainly try and see more of you and that you too are keen to get to know them. Her tone sounded friendly, and I must say I was pleasantly surprised.

Personally, I think she is rather pleased by your speeches in the Assembly and by the fact that you are being made much of. Also Papa seems to have spoken very highly of you: she said something to that effect. I don't suppose she will be able to get in touch with you again this time, because she is flying to Bombay soon. She may, of course, change her programme, and in that case she will not come here till after Papa leaves for Europe.

Mama says that Papa may want to see all of us before he leaves, and in that case we shall have to fly up to Delhi. But like everything else, this too is most indefinite. If I have to go up to Delhi, I shall wire you, but I don't think this likely as Mama didn't sound too enthusiastic [presumably because she was far from keen to re-unite the lovers].

Good night darling and look after yourself and think of me sometimes.

With all my love
S.

Were there already signs in these early love letters of an emotional incompatibility that would become more pronounced with time? Father had become Mother's raison d'être, giving purpose and meaning to her life and a welcome substitute for the paternal authority she had resented in her own father. But it's also clear that she craved the same adulation from him and grew restless and even petulant when she had to share him with his career and other commitments.

Sir J.P.'s foreign trip, to which her letter refers, was not just a jaunt. He had by now accepted that the Raj was drawing to a close and with it the era of free market capitalism in which industrialists like himself had prospered. His textile and sugar mills had thrived on the low-tax regime in British India and the tax havens offered by several princely states. World War II, with its restriction of foreign imports and its spiralling demand for war supplies, had been an economic bonanza for India's young and dynamic private sector. All that was about to change with the arrival in power of the Congress Party, already committed to Nehruvian socialism, nationalization, redistributive taxation and centralized, Soviet-style planning.

Sir J.P., wisely in the circumstances, had decided that it was time to sell up his business empire and transfer his money abroad while that was still possible. That was the reason for his trip abroad and for the family meeting he called on the eve of his departure. Apparently, his plan was to buy a large estate in the south of France, with individual homes for each of his children. 'You can all live in comfort for the rest of your lives on what I invest,' he promised them. There was a cry of protest from both his sons, for once united in their insistence that he would be depriving them of their rightful inheritance as his business heirs. Their indulgent mother, Lady Kailash, weighed in on their side, and Sir J.P., against his better judgement of his sons' limitations and India's future economic climate, gave in and dropped the idea.

Mother's parents were very opposed to her marriage. From their viewpoint, my father, despite his oratory in the Assembly, could not have been a more unsuitable match for their daughter: an indigent nationalist, fifteen years her senior, already twice divorced and, unlike their other sons-in-law, not even a Hindu. Sensing her determination to go ahead with or without their consent, they shrewdly played for time.

It was agreed that she should return home to Kanpur for a few months to take her M.A. exams (for which she had been preparing in Bombay), and also to prepare her wedding trousseau. Back at her parental home, with Father still in Delhi, Mother could not contain her impatience.

~

Friday 15th March, Kanpur

Darling,

I got your second letter this evening. Your letters only take one day to get here. Do you post them at the station? I wonder why mine take longer to get to you, for I have been writing every day, and yet you say you haven't heard from me at all.

Today has been a very rushed day. I had a talk with Mama this morning. She has more or less given her consent to our getting married in April and is getting down to making my clothes etc. I spent the entire afternoon looking at jewellery and ordering things. Darling, I feel so excited and happy that I can scarcely write. I wonder if anyone has the right to be so happy.

Mama talked to Papa [in Delhi] on the telephone this morning and is ringing him up again tomorrow to tell him that I am determined to get married in April. She tried very hard to persuade me to wait for a few months, but gave it up when she saw how determined I was. Tomorrow, after she has talked to Papa and got his final consent, she will send for a *pandit* to find out a good date. [Such matters were still astrologically determined.]

I haven't had much time to study today with all this going on. I find it difficult to concentrate. You must excuse this very hurried letter. I thought I would dash off a few lines to tell you the good news.

What a pity the Assembly session is being prolonged. I shall be going to Bombay after my examination to do some of my [wedding] shopping there, but I shall try and come to Delhi for a few days before that.

Good night, dearest Minoo. I love you very, very much.

S.

March 19th, Kanpur

Dearest Minoo,

I have not written to you for two days. I'm sorry darling.

It was wonderful hearing your voice on the phone yesterday. Thank you so much for ringing up.

Mama is being so difficult again, and I cannot get her and Papa to fix a date. Papa now says that he must get a formal proposal from you before he can decide definitely. On the telephone, I asked you to write to him, thinking that you would prefer that to going over to Hardinge Avenue [Sir J.P.'s official residence] and talking to him. But if you prefer the latter, I don't in the least mind.

I told you that I would come to Delhi and that you could meet Papa then. But today Mama is being very difficult about my going to Delhi. She herself is leaving for Delhi in a day or two, but is dead opposed to my going there. I think she is afraid that if I do go, I will bring matters to a head and force her and Papa to decide something. She is playing for time. One day she tells me that she will agree to a date in May but not to April, and the next day she says that she won't hear of anything before July or October.

I think, darling, that this is our only chance to make them come to some sort of decision. I'm so tired of all this vacillation. I am hoping Mama will be reasonable about my going to Delhi and not make a scene. She was so for it two days back, and I can't understand why she is so against it now.

You can expect me on Saturday darling, but if there is a change in my programme I shall ring you up. I have not been able to put in very much work for my M.A. these days. All this has been worrying me quite a bit. The trouble is that I can't understand Mama at all. She takes me out shopping every day and is buying clothes and jewellery for me and yet won't fix a date. It doesn't make sense to me.

I am sorry darling to worry you with all my woes and troubles, but I know how very sympathetic you are.

Goodbye sweetheart.

Love
S.

~

My grandmother was obviously wily enough to have calculated that time and the pleasures of buying her trousseau might cool Mother's ardour; but the tactic didn't work. She was determined to marry in April and no later, and she had her way. They were married in Ceylon (now Sri Lanka) on 29 April 1946 under special licence. In India, at that time, a civil marriage was only possible if both parties renounced their religious faith, and this Mother was reluctant to do.

Sir J.P. refused his consent till the bitter end, but Lady Kailash was ambivalent. She arrived in Bombay with Mother's bridal jewellery and clothes, but in deference to her husband's feelings she did not attend the wedding. Mother's sisters Sheela and Malati represented her divided family at the civil ceremony in Colombo.

Father never forgave his in-laws for their opposition to the match. Forty years later he told me: 'They wanted me to go through with a Hindu ceremony like Feroze Gandhi [a Parsi who had recently married Indira Nehru]. I said: "To hell with Feroze Gandhi!"'

When I asked how he remembered his parents-in-law, his verdict was measured. 'Sir J.P. was a very likable buccaneer, a robber baron who made his money by rather rough methods; but he was full of fun. He was not a good husband; he was not a good father to his boys, but to the girls he was. He looked down upon his sons with great contempt as being useless, which they were. He had all the good and bad points of a self-made man: he was rather intolerant of pampered brats.

'Lady Srivastava was an accomplished and charming woman, but malign, with a chip on her shoulder; she didn't love humanity at all. She had a rough time with her husband, who was notoriously unfaithful to her. She was a "good" woman, in that sense, but full of malignancy to everyone else.'

It's significant that he resented the wiles of his mother-in-law more than the open opposition of her husband. Perhaps he also realized that she had a far stronger hold on her daughter's affections and would continue to play a major role in her life. There was no need for astrologers to predict that it was an inauspicious start to a marriage that would last forty-three years and take seventeen to dissolve.

SEVEN

AN ONLY CHILD

I was born in November 1947, a year and a half after my parents married and three months after India became independent. I was delivered by Bombay's leading obstetrician, Dr Shirodkar, who was already something of a legend. As a child, I ran into him occasionally with my mother; and although he was old enough to be her father, she had the same semi-flirtatious bond with him that she seemed to form with all her doctors, and there would be many in the years to come.

The birth was at St Elizabeth's, an exclusive maternity hospital on leafy Malabar Hill. It appears to have been the first of many confrontations between my mother and her mother-in-law. Cuckoo Granny—I called her that because she called me her 'little cuckoo'—had given birth to her own children before the First World War, and she had rather stern, Victorian attitudes to labour pains. Chloroform, she believed, could harm the baby; and it was Mother's duty to endure the pain without an anaesthetic.

When I was old enough to understand, I often heard Mother telling the story of how mine had been a 'dry birth' and therefore agonizingly painful. She had begged for chloroform and kind Dr Shirodkar would have been happy to oblige, but her sadistic mother-in-law had resisted strongly and she was made to suffer.

Perhaps that's why I was an only child, though Mother maintained that it was Father who had refused to let her have any more, because of his firm conviction that India needed strict controls on its population explosion and that people like him had to set an example. In our home, the personal was never far from the political.

I was a love-child; and by all accounts, including my mother's, I was showered with love from all sides as an infant. I was especially precious to the Masanis, as their first and only grandchild. As I grew up, that would be an onerous burden to carry.

Considering how hostile my relations with Father were to become, it feels strange to be reminded how close we were in my early years, and yet that was undoubtedly so. Some of my earliest memories are of cuddling up with him in bed on a Sunday afternoon, when he allowed himself a nap, and of tickling and teasing him to keep him awake, while he indulged me fondly and enjoyed the horseplay.

In those early years, my pet name was DD, which stood for Daddy's Darling, and he cared about me every bit as much as Mother did, if not more so. In a letter to Father on one of his trips abroad, she wrote: 'We are both well and both very lonesome for you. D.D. has been fine, and his stomach is behaving very well. I have stopped the drugs now and will be sending him to school tomorrow.'

Two days later, she wrote again in response to a letter from him. 'Zareer is in school just now, but when he gets back I shall read out to him the paragraph about the martinis [Father's favourite cocktail]. I'm sure he will be very amused. He is very well, so don't worry about him, darling. He sleeps with me in the air-conditioned room and enjoys that very much. Yesterday was first day of school. He was a little tearful in the morning, but cheered up very much when he got to school and found that Jangoo [a backward friend] has been promoted too. I got him a front desk, and he is quite happy now.'

But evidently all was not well with their marriage. 'When you get back from Europe,' Mother wrote in the same letter, 'I would like to talk to you about our relationship. I think you know how much I also care for you, and it is such a pity that we have been quarrelling so much in the last year. I wish we could arrive at a better understanding, and I would certainly like to make an effort in that direction. Anyway, let us talk it over when you get back.'

When did my parents start to fall out of love, and was I one of the causes? I have few memories of the most formative years in our triangular relationship, between the ages of five and ten. By the end of my first decade, the pattern had been well established. I feared and resented my father's bullying and hated him for taking my mother away from me for the long parliamentary sessions in Delhi. Father, for his part, saw me as a spoiled and indulged Mummy's boy, a 'cissie' as he put it, and insisted on trying to discipline me. Mother and I reacted like thwarted lovers, pining for each other and plotting against our mutual oppressor. Fairness or rationality didn't come into it.

Mother's family, with their pleasure-loving ways, tended to regard Father as a 'killjoy'; and it became one of the first labels I associated with him. Mother's sisters often told me the story of how Father used to insist she left me locked up alone in a New York apartment, so that she could accompany him on his public engagements. If, as they maintained, I was just a baby, that seems hard to understand, let alone reconcile with his own anxiety about me during those tender years.

Mother's diplomat brother-in-law, Rajeshwar Dayal, later claimed he was the first to incite me to childhood rebellion. 'You were the most obedient child I'd ever come across,' he told me, 'and I thought it wasn't natural. So I told you what your father really wanted was for you to do the opposite of what he said and that we should give him a pleasant surprise when he came back home.' Whether or not I swallowed the logic, I was delighted to practise defying the Killjoy whenever I could get away with it, and that became the pattern of our relationship.

We lived at 7 Altamount Road, on the crest of Cumballa Hill, one of the twin peaks of Bombay's most desirable residential area. In the 1950s, before high-rise tower-blocks took over, most of the houses still had large, rambling gardens, some thickly wooded with coconut palms and ancient banyan trees. I spent many happy hours cycling in our compound and walking the broad, tree-lined streets with my Goan ayah, generically named Mary, though her real name was far grander: Olivia Quadros.

It was Mary who bathed and dressed me and gave me my meals, though Mother sometimes joined in. Mary had a limited repertoire of two or three Portuguese ballads which she sang to me as lullabies. Sometimes, on Sundays, I went with her to Mass at the Catholic church, St Stephen's, down the hill. Its beautiful marbled interior and baroque, stucco façade has long since been replaced by an ugly concrete pile. Mary's husband was named, appropriately, Joseph; but he was a drunk and a ne'er-do-well, who called occasionally to ask her for financial handouts. They had a son called Benny, a dashing figure who worked as a car mechanic, and a slightly backward daughter called Joycie, who was my playmate during her school vacations when she came to visit. It was typical of the lives of domestic servants in those times that Mary had far closer contact with me than with her own children, who were farmed out to relations in Goa.

I loved her dearly and never quite forgave my mother for laying her off when I turned thirteen and was deemed too old to have an ayah, my parents for once in agreement. Two years later I tracked her down through our chauffeur and was distraught to discover that she was in hospital with cancer. I made Mother help her financially, and she returned to Goa to convalesce with her relations. We never heard from her again. Her dismissal still seems callous to me, but it was typical of the way our class discarded servants when they had served their purpose.

Our home was the upper floor of an old, spacious two-storey mansion, built in the nineteenth century in Bombay's distinctive Indo-Gothic style. We were tenants of an aristocratic half-French Muslim called Barodawalla du Randé, who lived in a separate villa in the same compound. Our house had beautiful mosaic floors, which were scrubbed with soap and water every week, high ceilings, a multitude of windows with elaborate wooden shutters and long verandas with elaborately carved, latticed, wooden railings looking out to the Arabian Sea, which lapped at the foot of Cumballa Hill. A solitary child given to introspection, I loved squatting by the veranda railings, watching the procession of street traders—rag-and-bone men, snake-charmers, vegetable sellers and many more—who wandered past, all with their distinctive street-cries. When I was feeling mischievous, I tipped jugs of water over surprised passers-by and hid behind the shutters when they looked up startled.

Father had lived there during his second marriage to Pilli and later as a bachelor. When Mother moved in, she claimed the flat was filthy and infested by bugs and cockroaches and spiders. She soon had it cleaned up and redecorated with her own very distinctive and unerring sense of style. Much before the ethnic Indian look became fashionable, she used simple but colourful handwoven cottons and silks, rush-mat floor coverings and blinds, and the antique Indian sculptures and paintings she had already started collecting. On the roof-terrace above, she created a beautiful tropical garden of potted plants and cane furniture, lit up with fairy lights for the dinner parties she enjoyed hosting.

Those dinner parties were planned and prepared for days ahead, and I looked forward to them with excitement and anticipation. The flat would be spring-cleaned, the silver polished, fresh flowers, candles and oil lamps strategically arranged and the dining table meticulously laid with silver and damask, with Mother applying the final decorative touches. On the night, I thoroughly enjoyed peeping from behind my bedroom curtain as the guests arrived, and a chosen few were sometimes brought backstage to say good night to me. And the next day, there would be the delight of eating the leftovers, especially the wonderful puddings—Byculla Soufflé, Cabinet Pudding, Mocha Cream and ginger snaps—at which our British-trained Muslim cook excelled.

There were, of course, several servants. Apart from Mary, the most memorable were Bhula, a small and wiry Gujarati who remained with us till his death in the 1980s, and Nanhey Khan, a tall, very grand and moustachioed Muslim butler, with whom Mother returned in triumph after a visit home to Kanpur. One of his duties was to read me Urdu stories, which he did with relish and great panache. I loved his stories, but also enjoyed teasing him. At dinner parties, as he strutted out to serve at table, I would clip a clothes-peg on the back of his formal black cap or pin a tail to the rear of his *achkan*. He grumbled, but always forgave me readily.

One prank, of which I feel more ashamed, was to misrepresent the contents of the monthly letters he received from his former British employer, Sir Tennant Sloane, a distinguished ICS officer who had retired back in England. My job was to translate them from English as Nanhey Khan listened with rapt attention and tears in his eyes. When I started letting my imagination run riot, he eventually smelled a rat and got the corrected version from my mother. But with characteristic tolerance and humour, he allowed me to carry on unsuspecting with my creative translations.

Towards the other servants he behaved like a fierce Malvolio, jealous of any who challenged his supremacy as major-domo. He particularly disliked Mary for her insubordination and laid little traps to discredit her with Mother. I saw it as my mission to defend her and did so fiercely.

During those early years at Altamount Road, our home seemed to brim with laughter, music and art. Mother carried on with her dancing lessons, learning new styles like Bharat Natyam, Kathakali and Manipuri. I would watch in fascination as a succession of different dance gurus arrived on different days of the week to practise with her in our large drawing room. The training became more intense in the run-up to the occasional charity performances she gave. I particularly enjoyed watching her dress up in the exquisite and distinctive costumes she designed for each different style. Her performances usually began with a couple of items of Bharat Natyam, the most ancient, classical and physically demanding of Indian dance forms; then, after a costume-change and interval, there would be the more sensuous and sinuous Mughal dance style, Kathak; and finally, after another costume-change into long skirts draped over bamboo crinolines, there would be an item or two of Manipuri, the north-eastern dance form with its slow and graceful twirling movements, or else some Kathakali from Kerala.

Despite her talent, Mother suffered from dreadful stage fright on the eve of her performances. Perhaps because of her competitive childhood, she dreaded failure, and her nerves were always on edge before any public event. The result was that her fears became self-fulfilling; and she tended to dance far better when she was free of those pressures to succeed. I remember one dance performance being cancelled on the day because she had taken an overdose of sleeping pills the night before in her desperation to get a decent night's sleep.

She was equally nervous before golf tournaments, although she won a succession of silver coffee-spoons in various competitions at the Willingdon Club. She had taken up golf in the early 1950s, as much as a social activity as for the game itself. The Willingdon had been set up in the 1920s by the liberal Viceroy after whom it was named; it was the first Bombay club to admit Indian members and became the hub of the city's westernized elite, a status it still retains. Its gracious white stucco buildings nestle within an eighteen-hole golf course, now one of the few green spaces left in Bombay's concrete jungle. Its carefully manicured greens and fairways were a delight to gaze upon from the veranda of the rustic golf-hut, where Mother and her friends sat and sipped cold gimlets, beer and whisky-sodas after their game.

The club was our home from home. Mother and I went there almost every afternoon, she to golf, while I swam in the pool and tucked into the delicious snack menu: chips, club sandwiches, waffles and chocolate cake. Mother dressed as carefully for golf as she did for a dinner party. Her white blouses were crisply laundered and she wore stylish American pedal pushers from Saks Fifth Avenue, which showed off her long, smooth and slender legs. She eschewed the ugly hob-nailed boots worn by some serious players and wore white leather shoes, freshly polished each day with Meltonian cream, which displayed her slender, neatly turned ankles to great advantage.

She played well with an excellent swing and a keen eye, and she cared passionately about winning. But even more important than the game were the personal relationships it fostered and soured. She usually played in a foursome; and I remember a succession of friendships, especially with her female partners or rivals, which turned into serious hostility over what Mother considered their unsporting, petty and jealous behaviour.

Her painting, which she still did regularly, was less stressful. Her large dressing room was also her studio, and I was intoxicated by its heady, competing scents of perfume, paint and turpentine. She painted still lifes, animals, birds and landscapes from sketches she drew during our summer holidays in the hills, mostly at Mahabaleshwar in the Western Ghats. I loved watching her paint and joined in enthusiastically with suggestions, peering over her shoulder as she deftly mixed her colours and magically transformed a figure here, a shadow there. Unfortunately, she didn't take the results seriously enough and tended to paint over a canvas once she'd finished it or got bored with it, so not many survived.

Just as Mother's dressing room opened up to me a world of exotic excitement, so too did our occasional trips to her family up north. Her relations with her parents had been strained by her marriage and later by Father's puritanical approach to any hint of financial irregularity. Sir J.P. had put substantial share holdings in all his daughters' names to avoid tax, and they were meant to pass back the untaxed income to him. Father insisted that he would not be party to such 'black marketeering' and made Mother sign back her shares to her angry father.

As a child, I was untroubled by such moral scruples. The Srivastavas to me represented all that was colourful, exciting and fun-loving, not least because they all gave me generous gifts and spoiled and petted me shamelessly on the infrequent occasions that we met. I was particularly fond of Nanna, my maternal grandmother, with her rich saris and jewellery, made-up face and stylish cigarette-holder. A greater contrast to my Cuckoo Granny, in her austere white cotton, was hard to imagine.

'Why don't you dress up and wear make-up and jewellery like Nanna?' I would taunt her. 'Because jewellery symbolizes the chains by which men lead women around like animals,' was her dour reply, based no doubt on the socialist tracts my father had made her read during his student years. Much as I respect her principles now, they cut little ice with me when I was five.

I remember an idyllic summer holiday in 1953 with Mummy and Nanna in Naini Tal, the Himalayan hill station where Mother had grown up. We stayed at the Swiss Hotel, still owned by an elderly Swiss couple; and the Srivastavas were favoured guests, having taken over a whole wing of the building. There were cross-country rides with Mother, visiting the favourite spots of her childhood, rowing on the lake, and exciting forays to the local bazaars. Presiding over it all was Nanna, by then in frail health, but still an imposing and indulgent figure in her black velvet dressing gown.

I enjoyed, for a change, being part of an extended family, with all my cousins to play with. Our leader was Meera, the eldest, who instigated all sorts of mischief. Those were still the days of 'thunder-boxes', large wooden thrones with enamel bowls, emptied several times a day by sweepers of the untouchable caste. The Swiss Hotel bathrooms all had back doors for this purpose. Egged on by Meera, we children would sneak in just after the sweepers had done their job and pee in the thunder-boxes of puzzled and unsuspecting residents.

A year later, I was back in the bosom of the Srivastava family, though the circumstances were less happy. Sir J.P. had died suddenly of heart and kidney failure at the age of only sixty-three. Lady Kailash was shattered and ill herself. The whole family gathered in Kanpur for the last rites. I was disconcerted and bewildered by the unusual spectacle of adults bursting into tears and weeping uncontrollably on each other's shoulders. But that didn't stop me from enjoying the unaccustomed company of my cousins, the lavish food and sweets with which we were plied and the large grounds of 'Kailash' with its own swimming pool and tennis courts.

I was a sickly child, mildly asthmatic and prone to flu and gastric infections. But illness had its compensations: I was put to bed, free to read my favourite books or daydream and be fussed over and ministered to by Mother. On that funereal trip to Kanpur, I had a long-drawn cough, but thoroughly enjoyed the added attentions of Nanna fussing over me and painting my throat to reduce the discomfort.

By then I was also a very well-travelled child. My first trip abroad had been at the age of six months, when I accompanied my parents on a one-year diplomatic posting in Rio de Janeiro. Father had dropped out of politics a year after Independence, having made an important contribution as a member of the Constituent Assembly. Disillusioned with the pro-Soviet and statist slant Prime Minister Nehru was giving the newly independent country, Father welcomed a sabbatical from Indian politics as the country's first Ambassador to South America, charged with setting up a network of embassies across that continent.

I was too young to have any personal memories of Brazil, but it formed a vital part of our collective unconscious, with my parents constantly reminiscing about the wonderful times they had there. They had both loved the relaxed, fun-loving atmosphere, the carnivals and the glittering parties and balls. Father had learned the samba and flirted with voluptuous Latin beauties, while Mother had charmed their chivalrous Brazilian hosts with her exotic Indian clothes and jewellery. Our Bombay home was full of the Latin American antiques and artefacts they had acquired there.

Later, when Father became Chairman of the UN Commission on Minorities, we made some long trips to New York, London and Switzerland. Mother wore an elegant and eye-catching, though politically incorrect, tiger-skin coat on these foreign visits; and I still remember how disconcerted I was when I saw my first real tiger at the New York zoo. It had been donated as a cub by Sir J.P., who had shot its mother on one of his frequent shoots. When I caught my first glimpse of the noble beast, I burst into tears and ran to Father screaming: 'The tiger is wearing Mummy's coat!' Father enjoyed teasing me about it. Whenever I came home as a child and asked him where Mother had gone, he would answer with mock gravity: 'A big tiger came and ate her up.'

In New York, we sub-let the apartment of a wealthy and very musical American lady, who had a treasured grand piano. When she came to tea one day, I caused my parents excruciating embarrassment by attacking the piano and hammering on its keys to show her how much I liked it; and she was too polite to protest. I also discovered the irresistible attractions of the black hole which was our incinerator chute. Its inexhaustible capacity to swallow up just about anything seemed magical, and I experimented with treasured pullovers and shoes that vanished while my parents were out. They suspected their Indian servant of stealing from them, until one day I was caught red-handed.

Switzerland brought the unaccustomed combination of chocolates and snow. I loved tobogganing at a resort we went to in the Swiss Alps, but was far more nervous about the ice-skating lessons Mother and I had from a handsome Swiss instructor. Most of all, I loved the mystery and grandeur of the aeroplanes in which we travelled. They appeared as vast as ocean liners to my child's eyes, especially the double-decker Stratocruisers with their upper berths of couchettes in which I would snuggle up with Mother.

Later, after I started school, Mother and I stayed behind when Father travelled abroad, which he did frequently to attend meetings of the Congress for Cultural Freedom, an anti-Communist grouping of intellectuals across the world that he had helped set up. Mother and I gave him shopping lists of the scarce, foreign luxuries which Nehru's protectionist policies had banned from the Indian market; and the day of his return was one of eager anticipation, which I looked forward to quite as much as my birthdays, with their promise of gifts to come. I still remember the smells of Europe which pervaded my parents' bedroom when Father's suitcases were opened: the scent of Swiss chocolates, French perfumes, the latest children's books from Hatchard's and handbags and woollens from Harrods.

After our return from Brazil, Father decided to return to work at Bombay's leading private business house, Tatas. He had worked there in the early 1940s as chief of publicity and now he became *chef de cabinet* to the chairman, J.R.D. Tata.

The Tatas lived in a beautiful, split-level bungalow perched on a dramatic cliff-top five minutes' walk from our home at Altamount Road. Jeh (half-French) and Thelly (his half-English wife) were childless, and for some years I became their semi-adoptive child, spending many happy Sunday mornings with Uncle Jeh in his workshop, while he mended cuckoo clocks and various other mechanical gadgets. His marriage was unhappy: he was notoriously unfaithful and his wife obsessively jealous. His French accent and Gallic charm made him irresistible to the ladies, and a succession of pretty women flitted in and out of his long life. One of them, I later discovered, was my mother. They golfed together and he took her for long evening drives. She later told me that their relationship had been serious enough for them to discuss marriage, but such plans had floundered on their reluctance to destroy Thelly's fragile sanity. They remained flirtatious friends till Jeh's death in the 1990s.

In 1957, when I was ten, an event occurred that was to change my childhood irrevocably. Father returned to active politics and won a by-election to Parliament from the then remote constituency of Ranchi in the tribal belt of Bihar. He had decided that the time was ripe to launch a national opposition party and offer an alternative to Nehru's socialistic one-party state. Along with C. Rajagopalachari, the brilliant and highly respected elder statesman who had been India's last Governor-General, Father was successful. In 1959 the Swatantra Party was launched on a platform of free-enterprise liberalism, and it soon became India's second-largest party, making Father the official Leader of the Opposition in Parliament until 1970. The party's dominant figures were businessmen and princes, but it also drew in a large number of bright young professionals and intellectuals who were fed up with Congress bureaucracy and statism and Nehru's pro-Soviet foreign policy. It would be another half-century before its ideals became the official policy of a Congress government led by Manmohan Singh.

In a family where the political always became personal, Father's immersion in national politics marked the end of my childhood. For one thing, it meant that he was away from home, travelling the country for much of the time; and that left me the man of the house and the focus of Mother's undivided attention for long periods. But it also meant that Mother, as a political wife and hostess, was expected to be with Father some of the time, especially during the parliamentary sessions in Delhi. And that meant leaving me behind in Bombay with my grandparents. Both circumstances encouraged me to develop highly precocious adult impulses and survival skills.

Mother was ambivalent about Father's political success. She certainly enjoyed the status and perks, which included a large, white stucco official residence in the heart of Lutyens's New Delhi. She enjoyed entertaining and attending the round of diplomatic dinners and cocktail parties in the capital. She was made much of, not just for her illustrious husband, but because foreign dignitaries were delighted to meet an Indian politician's wife who combined all the Western social graces with a strong passion for Indian art and culture. She often told me with pride how she was seated much higher at presidential banquets than her elder sisters, both married to senior civil servants.

On the other hand, she had no desire to accompany Father on his gruelling political travels, and she was bored and restless during his frequent absences. To fill the void, she relied increasingly on her circle of drones, a disparate and discordant band of male admirers.

First there was Dick Billimoria, an Eeyore-like recluse, lean and gaunt with hypochondriac starvation and quick to take offence. Mother teased him mercilessly, but he always came back for more. To be fair, he had a sense of humour. When Mother was being particularly capricious or changeable, he would smile quietly, shake his head and quote from the Sanskrit classic after which she had been named—'Shakuntala, and all at once is said!' At other times, when she was putting him off for someone else, he would recite wistfully: 'I shall always be true to thee, Cynara, in my fashion.'

Then came Noshir Limji, the very opposite in both appearance and temperament: good-looking, stocky, good-natured and, to quote Mother, 'rather bovine'. He ran Bombay's largest car dealership and declared that his main interests in life were 'fast cars and fast women'. Mother went out with him on long drives, but grumbled that he was always trying to 'paw' her.

Then there was Sir Hirji Jehangir, the reluctant heir to an immensely wealthy Parsi baronetcy. He was mildly schizophrenic and severely depressive, highly eccentric and absent-minded, with an upper-class British stutter. Though married to a martinet who tried hard to rein him in, he courted Mother assiduously. She gave him scant encouragement and was often irritable with him, but he remained one of her most loyal friends till she died.

And finally, there was Kishore Chand, for whom she happily dropped all the others. He was tall and very handsome, an Indian Clark Gable with a pencil-line, Hollywood moustache. A skilful, American-trained dentist, he had no intellectual pretensions, but was keen to rise in Bombay's snobbish social world. He came from a modest family of Punjabi refugees from Partition, and he was determined to find a crock of gold in Bombay. With his Punjabi-American background, he had little of the social finesse of Mother's circle, but he was eager to learn. For a decade, he gave her total devotion and obedience, at her beck and call when she needed him, quick to make himself scarce when she didn't. In short, he was the very opposite of Father, not least in his patient indulgence of me, and I loved him dearly.

Was it coincidence that Mother and I both started to fall out of love with Father around the same time? Her reason, she later told me, was that he had become a serial philanderer. My reason was that he was taking Mother away from me to Delhi and, perhaps more important, leaving me behind.

Parliament sat for about half the year, and while it did Father expected Mother to keep house for him in Delhi. She enjoyed it too, especially during the winter months when Delhi's crisp, sunny (alas, no longer!) and cold weather made a welcome change from tropical Bombay. But she fretted about being parted from me; and so the tussle began. I blamed Father for Mother's absence, and he resented me for making her anxious and fretful.

For me, Mother's departures were a double deprivation, because I was uprooted from my own home at Altamount Road, with its familiar routines and familial servants, and forced to live with my grandparents in Colaba, an area of Bombay which, though only six miles from Cumballa Hill, seemed foreign and remote to a shy and insecure ten-year-old. Grandfather was by then into his eighties and Granny in her seventies and although physically and mentally still remarkably fit, they were not ideal guardians or companions for a young child.

The first of these painful upheavals was in February 1958. I wrote to Mother every day in my untidy scrawl, and she kept every one of my letters. 'I miss you very, very much,' my litany of woe began. 'I did not sleep a wink last night, and feel as if I cannot eat a thing. Please come back as SOON [underlined thrice] as possible. Cuckoo Granny is very annoyed and says that I should not fret and cry because you have gone to Delhi . . . I am dying to see you, so please get away as soon as possible.'

After a few desultory inquiries about the Delhi house, I ended with the refrain: 'P.S. Come back as SOON [again underlined thrice] as possible.'

The next day I wrote that Granny was planning to take me to the Danny Kaye movie *Inspector General*. But although he was one of my favourites and I had loved him in *The Court Jester*, I was not easily diverted from my pining. 'I miss you very much and wish you would come back. Cuckoo Granny is very opposed to my missing you so much. Please come back as soon as possible.'

The cinema was undoubtedly my greatest joy during those childhood years. I particularly loved historical costume dramas with heroes like *The Scarlet Pimpernel*, *Ivanhoe* and the *Knights of the Round Table*. The 1950s were the heyday of Bombay's cinema houses, with their grand, art deco buildings and their evocative names: the Eros, Metro, Regal, New Empire and Excelsior. They were my escape and refuge, and they never failed to divert me from my fretting and pining.

Granny was determined not to let my pleas bring Mother rushing back to Bombay. Four days after her departure, she wrote reassuring her that: 'Zareer is as happy as a bird. I told him to write and tell you that he is not depressed. It seems he thinks it a good thing to be depressed!' But her efforts to counter this Srivastava penchant for melancholia were in vain. The very next day, I wrote: 'Cuckoo Granny is being very nice and has been trying to cheer me up . . . But I have not got used to your not being here. I am very miserable and cannot sleep at night.'

As the weeks passed, I grew more accustomed to my new routine, and there were compensations. Although I resented them for having supplanted my mother, my grandparents did their best to include me in their lives. Grandfather had by then retired from public office and spent his retirement writing historical books and presiding over two charities close to his heart, the Kama Oriental Institute and the Byramji Jeejeebhoy Home for Orphaned Children. Granny was also very actively involved with the orphanage and spent much of her spare time attending spiritual meetings at Theosophy Lodge, run by her charming and dynamic French sister-in-law, Sophia Wadia.

I loved the musty scent of old paper in Grandfather's room, which was crammed from floor to ceiling with books. He had mellowed with age and was far more tolerant with me than he had been with his own children. As a small child, I was allowed to sit on his knee and tug with curiosity at his goatee, the first I had ever encountered. Later, he encouraged me to browse in his library and was delighted by my love of history. He bought me an abridged edition of Gibbon's *Decline and Fall*, and I used to read aloud from it to the two of them after dinner. I can still remember Granny's pained and embarrassed expression when I got to a bit about a victorious Roman warlord castrating his more recalcitrant prisoners, while their wives pleaded with him not to take away those parts of their menfolk that they loved best.

Unlike my parents, Granny and Grandfather shunned all dinner engagements, and so we three spent our evenings together in cosy domesticity, devising our own entertainment in an era before television. When we were not reading to each other, we played cards: rummy and a simpleton's form of bridge. In March 1958 I wrote proudly to Mother: 'Cuckoo Granny has taught me to play chess and now I am quite good at it. I play with her every night and usually win. It is a difficult game and requires a lot of thinking. Do you know how to play? If you do, then we can play together when you come back from Delhi.' No such luck: Mother preferred Scrabble to chess.

Granny and I had our fallings out, too, usually when she tried to stop me doing what I wanted. A typical instance was when she refused me permission to go to a funfair with a schoolfriend because I had a bad cough. 'I was terribly disappointed,' I complained to Mother, 'as the fair only comes once in two or three years. Please write to her and try and persuade her to let me go.'

Disagreements like these would soon seem like minor pinpricks. My parents were about to clash swords about radical changes in my schooling and upbringing; and the conflict would draw me inexorably into their more fundamental marital tensions.

EIGHT

TOUGH LOVE

Scouring my father's private papers some years after his death, I found an intriguing bundle relating to his divorce from my mother. Although they were not actually divorced till 1989, the earliest papers date as far back as 1960. Among them is a handwritten aide-memoire cataloguing his frustrated attempts to intervene in my upbringing. With his orderly, barrister's mind, he had compiled a brief to strengthen his case against Mother.

1956 & 1957: Efforts to make Zareer take some interest in games, and Shakuntala to talk to him in Hindi, failed consistently, despite warnings repeatedly given.

Late in 1957: Shakuntala was given choice between sending Z to boarding-school or day-school in Delhi. She preferred Delhi. With her consent, Zareer was admitted to the Modern [High School, Delhi] from April 1958.

March 1958: Under pressure from Shakuntala, who now wanted Zareer sent to boarding-school from January 1959, Minoo yielded and withdrew Zareer's name from the Modern.

August/September 1958: Having visited Sonaver [sic] and Ajmer [two north Indian boarding schools], Shakuntala decided on Mayo College [Ajmer], and Zareer was admitted for January 1959.

Early December 1958: Shakuntala changed her mind and wanted to change back to the Modern, but Kapur [the principal] was non-committal.

Late December 1958: Shakuntala started pressing for Doon [another boarding school north of Delhi]. Minoo agreed, and saw Sir C.D. Deshmukh [Chairman of the school's Board of Trustees] about it.
Beginning of January 1959: Martin [Principal of the Doon] interviewed Zareer in Bombay. Minoo agreed to waiting till January 29th for Zareer to join.
Middle of January 1959: Under pressure of Shakuntala's ill health, Minoo yielded again and agreed to waiting till mid-year for Doon and wrote to Martin. The only condition was that Minoo should from then on take all decisions re Zareer. This was agreed to by Shakuntala and Zareer, but was uniformly and consistently ignored. When pointed out, they said it had not been promised seriously.
May 1959: Z admitted to Doon. War of nerves over this.
June 1959: Under pressure, Minoo agreed to withdraw Z, provided that both S and Z agreed that Minoo would take all decisions re Zareer. They agreed solemnly, but again cheated.

With hindsight, these jottings are a testament to Father's determination to impose some paternal discipline on me. If he and Mother had reached a consensus, it would have spared us all a great deal of grief. But the question of my upbringing was becoming inseparably entangled with their deeper marital tensions.

In the spring of 1958, when my admission to a boarding school was being considered, Kishore Uncle accompanied Mother and me when we went on holiday to Wellington, a beautiful, ex-colonial military cantonment in the Nilgiri Hills. Since Kishore Uncle's presence was meant to be a secret, the trip had all the excitement and intoxication of forbidden fruit. I remember that Mother and I would duck down and hide in our car seats if we happened to pass other visitors from Bombay on the roads. Nevertheless, there must have been some successful sightings of the three of us together, and I have little doubt that the gossip filtered back to Father in Bombay.

'Wellington is beautiful and we have a lovely suite in the Club,' Mother wrote to him. 'I am writing to you sitting in the garden, which is a mass of colour. I wish you could see it. The weather is perfect – cold at night and cool in the day. Mrs. Regal, the housekeeper, is taking good care of us, and Colonel Umrao Singh [the local army commander] is arranging for me to ride [cavalry horses]. Please don't worry about us. If you could only see this place and how comfortable we are!'

Kishore Uncle had come into my life at the very moment when it seemed as though Father was trying to send me away from home. Kishore felt no call to deny me anything, and his love seemed unconditional. He called me his 'Pet' and no doubt he meant it. I transferred my affections to him, and he became both a second father and my closest friend and confidant. Our pact was sealed when he bought me a beautiful golden cocker spaniel from a kennel near Wellington. Although my parents had kept dogs ever since I could remember, Russet, as I named him, was my first very own pet. I loved him dearly, and he was my loyal companion for a decade. Being parted from him became yet another reason for my resenting the stay with my grandparents, because their landlord prohibited dogs in their flat at Mereweather Road in Colaba.

'After leaving you at the airport,' I wrote to Mother in August 1958, 'I went back home and found Russet looking very forlorn. He sends his licks and dribbles.' Although I had to shift to my grandparents, I insisted on visiting him every day after school and taking him for a run at the race course, where dogs could be exercised when there were no races.

'Zareer is well,' Granny wrote to Mother a few days later. 'He does not give me trouble as I let him do what he wishes – going daily to see Russet and poring over novels! He prefers to play cards to chess – feeling lazy I suppose. During the holidays I shall arrange to send him to the pictures. He eats well, but says he always reads before sleeping. I do not allow it, so he keeps talking or playing cards. I love his company but wish he had more friends – more social.'

I had recently had to start wearing spectacles for short-sightedness; and my grandparents were convinced it was being made worse by too much reading, especially by artificial light. They had a rather Victorian distrust of fiction, with the sole exception of Dickens, and urged me to save my eyes for sterner stuff than 'storybooks'.

Life with them had its lighter side as well. 'Cuckoo Granny would like to know whether I am allowed to drink a little wine,' I asked Mother in one of my letters. 'There is a bottle here which Grandfather was advised to get by the doctor.' The bottle in question was Hall's Wine, which my otherwise abstemious grandfather insisted he took for his health—just one glass a day, measured out like medicine. I can't remember if I was allowed to join him, but I do remember him, glass in hand, quoting Persian couplets from Omar Khayyam:

'Drink wine. This is life eternal. This is all that youth will give you. It is the season for wine, roses and drunken friends. Be happy for this moment. This moment is your life.'

It was conspicuously not the philosophy by which he lived his otherwise stoic and Spartan life.

Like mother, I loved animals and spent many happy hours watching a family of kites nesting in a small park that my room at Mereweather Road overlooked. 'There is a big tree where the eagles have made their nest,' I wrote to Mother. 'A few days ago the mother eagle hatched her egg and a sweet little baby eagle came out. When I am in my bathtub I watch the mother nursing it and the father bringing food for it.' The next day, I added: 'Today the Eagles had two more babies!' Was there just a trace of envy about this picture of avian family bliss?

My daily visits to Russet at Altamount Road were, for a time, disrupted when my grandparents found themselves without a chauffeur. 'A new driver was found today,' I complained to Mother, 'but Cuckoo Granny does not like his driving, so we sacked him this evening after we got back. We hope to get a good driver soon.' But the next day I added in desperation: 'The Employment Bureau sent another driver, but as Grandfather thought he was not good we sacked him as well.'

In April 1959 Father at last had his way, and I left home for the first time to join the Doon School. The school had been modelled on Eton and the headmaster was an Englishman. It was located in spacious and attractive grounds in Dehra Dun in the Himalayan foothills. Because my Srivastava and Sahgal cousins were already there, Mother and I had finally settled on it as the least objectionable of the schools to which Father wanted to send me.

Mother took me there, and my last night of freedom was spent with her at the circuit house, where we stayed. I cried myself to sleep, but kept waking to hear her crying quietly in the next room, where she stayed up sewing name tags on to various bits of my new school uniform. 'On Sunday after you left I was very unhappy,' I wrote to her the next day. 'Mrs. S— [our house matron] took me up to her room, and Vijay and Arjun [my cousins] tried to cheer me up. Again at night I felt very unhappy. I miss you and Russet very much. I just don't understand why you have put me here. I absolutely hate it. The boys are so dirty. They skip their bath. Many things of mine have disappeared: my toothpaste and 2 hankies . . . I can't tell you how much I miss home and I am most unhappy here.'

But children are remarkably resilient; and only two days later I was writing with glee that the teachers, contrary to expectations, thought my Hindi good and that the school was 'knocking Mayo College [the team that was visiting] into a cocked hat in all the events'. I added that we had had a screening of the film *The Sea Devils*, which was 'very good', and were about to have a performance of a play called *The Invisible Duke*. Life was beginning to look up.

I had entered remarkably quickly into the school esprit de corps. Four days after I joined, I was writing triumphantly to Mother: 'The Mayo College boys departed for Ajmer feeling very sorry for themselves. We beat them at everything – athletics, hockey, cricket, squash and tennis.' 'The school is swarming with bees,' I added with mild exaggeration. 'There have been two cases of boys' faces being completely chewed up by them. The boys fainted on the spot and are now in hospital. So now I am very careful not to pass near any trees.'

Certain school habits still shocked me. 'The standard of cleanliness here upsets me considerably,' I primly confided. 'The boys only clean their teeth once [a day], and they only apply soap while bathing on alternate days; that is if they do bathe, as all the Sardars [Sikhs] hardly bathe. The swimming-pool is absolutely filthy. It is full of toads, and some boys are silly enough to take their bicycles into it.'

My letters were full of the whirl of school life, crammed with a busy schedule of classes, P.T., swimming, athletics and games. I still preferred to avoid the last, but enjoyed the rest. I also enjoyed being scholastically well ahead of my classmates, since my previous Bombay school, the Cathedral, had had higher academic standards.

For the first time in my life, I started making friends and was surprised to find how easy it was once I started.

'There are lots of raw lychees and mangoes in the school grounds,' I wrote to Mother a month after my arrival. 'They are not actually the school's but belong to a certain gentleman. Nevertheless we all raid the lychee and mango trees, but if we are seen by a prefect we get a yellow card, which prevents us from going to the tuck-shop. The ripe lychees and mangoes are guarded by a *chowkidar* for full 24 hours. But the boys still organise raids, which take place after midnight when the *chowkidar* is very drowsy. Last night two boys from our own dorm organised a raid at 4 a.m.. They managed to get a hatful of delicious, red, big lychees without the *chowkidar*'s knowledge. Vijay, Arjun and I all got one lychee each. This evening towards the end of the Diving Contest my friend Ravinderbir Singh of Jind [a Sikh princeling known as Robin] and I sneaked away and broke off three ripe mangoes each. I have quite a few friends here.'

I went on to list no less than eight boys, four of whom were from the princely families that still dominated the school intake. By now I felt secure enough to make light of the fact that my swimming trunks and towel had gone missing, presumed stolen by older boys. And I even felt safe enough to cut myself free of the apron-strings of our school matron, the Dame, to give her her proper title. She stored for us the extra goodies our parents sent: chocolate, cheese, mangoes and so on; and we were allowed to visit her private rooms for our treats, safe from the pilfering of school bullies. What came as a revelation was that these goodies were not safe from pilfering even when they were in the Dame's custody.

'I noticed that my mangoes were disappearing,' I confided to Mother, 'I then noticed that four packets of chocolate were missing too, and I think she gave them to her young nephews who spend the day with her.' What I hadn't bargained for was that the wily Dame was steaming open my letters to make sure she hadn't been rumbled. When she read what

I'd written about her, she went ballistic and claimed she had happened upon it by accident while sealing an envelope I had forgotten to glue.

I was unrepentant. 'She opened the letter intentionally and read it,' I wrote to Mother. 'She says that the envelope had opened and, while gluing it again, she had read one line, which she had thought very suspicious. She had then read the whole letter. But that is a lie, as when she showed it to me the envelope showed every sign of being forced open carefully. Even if it had come loose, she could not have read the line, because I had only written on one side of the sheet of paper, and the written side was folded inside and only the blank side was visible.' As the Dame learned to her cost, I had inherited my father's forensic and relentless logic.

My letters to Mother were full of anxious inquiries about Russet, to whom I sent unaltered love. I even fretted lest he grow too attached to Father in my absence. To Father himself, there were hardly any references, let alone effusions of love. Clearly, by now I regarded him as the enemy. He had succeeded in banishing me from home, but I was not beaten. Term was about to end, and the long summer holidays beckoned with Mother and Russet and Kishore Uncle awaiting me in Bombay.

But first I had to survive the last night of term, called 'Golden Night'. 'It is the custom here to frighten new boys on Golden Night,' I wrote to Mother and enclosed an anonymous written threat I had received. 'Thou hast been chosen as the next victim of the T.T. Secret Society [Terrible Three]. On the night of the third thou shalt be trapped and shalt be beaten up with both fist and boot. Thou shalt then be tied to a chair for the whole night, whilst we enjoy a pleasant sleep in comfortable beds. BEWARE. Terrible Tom, Leader of the T.T.'

This far-from-sinister note might well have been the handiwork of my cousins, but it did the trick. Aunt Mehra kindly agreed to drive up from Delhi to fetch me; and my housemaster gave permission for me to spend the dreaded Golden Night with her at the circuit house.

I sometimes wonder how different life might have been if I had stayed on at the Doon School. I would certainly have been less involved in my parents' marriage; and without me there to egg them on, they might well have reached a happier accommodation. Would I, too, have been a happier child? I had missed Mother and my dog at school, but there had been compensations. For the first time in my life I had made friends of my own and discovered that I could survive away from home.

I returned home to Bombay for my summer holidays like a conquering hero, flushed with success, basking in the renewed adoration of Mother, Mary, Russet and Kishore Uncle and, for a change, even the respect of Father. I boasted of my exploits at school, the pranks I had got up to and the adversities over which I had triumphed. Among the latter, I dwelt at some length on the dirty habits and bullying practised by the older boys and mentioned coyly their penchant for sexually molesting the younger and prettier boys and 'trying to make babies' with them.

It was an exaggeration typical of my fertile imagination, because homosexuality at the Doon was mostly limited to romantic crushes, and its sexual consummation rarely went beyond mutual masturbation. I had certainly not witnessed any buggery. Nevertheless, Mother, far from being impressed by my sang-froid, was appalled; until she realized that she now held a trump card over Father. She confronted him with my tales of sexual abuse, accused him of having sent me to a den of iniquity, wept bitter tears of anger and reproach, and compelled him to agree that I should not return to boarding school.

My own feelings were ambiguous. I was delighted that I had been vindicated and Father forced to capitulate. But I did miss the Doon and the company of my cousins and new friends. At the Cathedral in Bombay, I had always been a loner, with perhaps just one special friend at a time, prone to mockery and bullying because of my bookish ways and dislike of games. And so it continued after my return. The one compensation was the undoubtedly high standard of teaching, especially in subjects like English literature, French and history, at which I excelled.

Prima in Indis, Gateway of India, door of the East with its face to
the West,
Here in Bombay we are living and learning India our country to
give you our best . . .

So began our school song, set to the tune of the Harrow 'Boating Song'. Most of our teachers were Anglo-Indians, with a couple of 'real' Englishmen thrown in. The principal, Mr Gunnery, was unmistakably the real thing, a large man who blushed as red as a beetroot and stuttered like an artillery barrage. Like everyone else, I had been in awe of him at first. But then Mother tamed him into docile submission. He became a frequent visitor during our summer vacations in the hill station of Mahabaleshwar, and he was one of her golfing companions.

The teacher I most admired was Mr Glynne-Howell, a middle-aged Anglo-Indian with a neat, pencil-line moustache, dyed auburn hair, a beautiful tenor voice and enormous Falstaffian pot belly. He taught us Shakespeare, and my love of blank verse owed much to his eloquent declamations as he rolled down the aisle of our classroom, book in one hand, while the other, with a distinctive gold and cornelian ring, elegantly marked time to iambic pentameter. He had the most beautiful handwriting I have ever seen, and he illuminated our essays with pithy comments in multicoloured inks from a selection of carefully tended fountain pens he kept before him in a leather case. He particularly loved the role of Orsino in *Twelfth Night*, which he claimed he had performed in his slender youth; and it is a testament to his skills that we willingly suspended disbelief, forgot his belly and imagined him as the handsome lovelorn Duke of Illyria.

Much to the disapproval of Father and my grandparents, back at the Cathedral I rapidly returned to my familiar dislike of games and other team activities. 'Yesterday was the Scout meeting,' I wrote to Mother in Delhi in August 1959, 'but I did not attend as I was not well. Today was the Scouts' Efficiency Contest. I did not attend this also as I was not quite recovered and the contest consisted of marching in the hot sun at midday. I thought I had better not risk it. Please send an excuse for the Scoutmaster saying that I had a bad cold and a little fever.'

A day later I added: 'If you have not done so already, please do not bother to send me an excuse to account for my absence from the Scout meetings as Cuckoo Granny has agreed to do so after some persuasion! I do hope she does not make things hot for me by complaining to Daddy as she normally does!!'

By this time I saw Granny as Father's spy and felt they were plotting to thwart me at every turn. 'Today I am most unhappy,' I wrote to Mother a few days after the Scout event. 'This is the cause: Cuckoo Granny suspected that I had more than Rs. 10 [my weekly pocket money] in my wallet. One day she took her own Revelation [suitcase] key, opened my Revelation and saw the money I had in my wallet. I have just realised this must have happened. When Daddy [on a visit to Bombay] had lunch with her today she must have told him, and together they opened the Revelation again and took away the wallet!!! This evening, when I realised that it was missing, I fully suspected what had happened. Sure enough, my suspicions were confirmed when Daddy turned up with the wallet saying that I had misplaced it and he had found it! I knew that this was not true, as the last time I had opened my Revelation the wallet was still there. However neither of them have openly declared that they found Rs. 40 [my secret stash from Mother] in the suitcase. When Daddy returned the wallet to me, there were only Rs. 10 in it. He had pocketed the rest. I had another Rs. 10 in my drawer, which they did not search! That was lucky. I am feeling most upset about this, as I had planned to use all the money on a birthday present for you, and now all my plans are ruined. I really hate Daddy and Cuckoo Granny for this. Grandfather also knew about it. Why don't you write a stinker to Cuckoo Granny as I am most unhappy.'

My taste for rich food, which my mother indulged, had also become a bone of contention. 'Daddy has left a set of instructions with Cuckoo Granny,' I complained to Mother. '1) my eggs must be rotated [i.e., not always fried as I liked], 2) I can only have ham twice a week, 3) I can only have cream on alternate days, 4) every evening I do not take Rusty to the Race Course I must go for a walk with the *hamal* [manservant].'

These restrictions were not unreasonable, but they did seem petty and irksome, and I magnified them into a prison regime. I decided to get my own back at Granny by going for a different sort of walk from the ones she approved. I dressed up in her old dressing gown, with a pillow tied round my middle, draped a shawl over my head, and marched up and down the road below her balcony pretending to be a deranged Parsi woman, screaming obscenities at passers-by. For half an hour poor Granny looked on with embarrassment from her balcony, furtively beckoning me to come up, though reluctant to acknowledge me as her own.

The last laugh was on me. When I had had enough and wanted to come back up, the burly Pathan watchman at the entrance did not recognize me and refused to let me in. I eventually had to sneak past him and leg it up to my grandparents' flat with the watchman in hot pursuit brandishing his stick and threatening to beat me to a pulp. Luckily, Granny opened her front door just in time to vouch reluctantly for the fact that this strange creature really was her grandchild.

My relationship with my grandparents suffered considerably from conflicts of identity as I grew up. The Parsis had a strong sense of racial superiority over other darker-skinned Indians. My grandparents, though enlightened for their time, were not free from its prejudices. Mother maintained that Cuckoo Granny had shocked Nanna at the time of my parents' marriage by confiding that they would have preferred an English daughter-in-law with fairer skin. The story was probably apocryphal, but I do remember Granny scrubbing me in the bath and offering the consolation that it would lighten my skin, which was dark by Parsi standards.

On a more serious note, my grandparents were insistent that I must have a Navjot, the Parsi initiation ceremony, which had similar connotations to a Jewish bar mitzvah. I resisted it tooth and nail, insisting that I was a Hindu like Mother. Hindu mythology, with its large pantheon of gods and goddesses who fought, loved and made merry, much like their Greek counterparts, was far more attractive to a child's imagination than the monotheistic austerity of Zoroastrianism. Although Mother only did puja during the main Hindu festivals, she often entertained me with epic tales from the Ramayana and the Mahabharata. In my childhood fantasies, I had joined Rama and his monkey army in their forest exile, watched the trials of his wife Sita, forced to prove her innocence by walking through fire, trembled at the threats of Ravana and his evil cohorts and rejoiced at his defeat and destruction, celebrated each year at Dussehra, when giant effigies of the demon king were burned on the beaches and maidans.

Mother usually celebrated Diwali, the Hindu New Year, with a traditional gambling party. Our house was decorated with flickering oil lamps, and I revelled in the fireworks, which I was allowed to light myself as I grew older. I also loved the spring festival of Holi, when we sprayed each other with coloured water loaded into flit-guns. By contrast, my occasional visits with Granny to the Parsi fire-temple, usually on Navroz, the Parsi New Year, seemed onerous and irksome. The white robes of the priests looked drab and their chanting of the ancient Persian prayers sounded nasal and incomprehensible. The only excitement was the hiss and crackle of the sandalwood we threw into the sacred fire, burning in a large, central brazier, and the wonderfully fragrant smoke that rose from it.

My Parsi grandparents disliked superstition and were largely agnostic, but they valued the ethics of Zoroastrianism, and Grandfather had written a scholarly book about it called *The Religion of the Good Life*. They were bewildered and annoyed by my childish delight in pagan Hindu ritual and idolatry, and they blamed Mother's family for encouraging it. Nanna had given me a silver medallion of the elephant-god Ganesha, who fascinated me, and I sometimes wore it on a chain round my neck. When my Masani grandparents asked me not to wear it in their home, I promptly defied them by appearing with it one evening when they had Parsi visitors and twirling it nonchalantly before their disapproving eyes. When the visitors left, Grandfather angrily ordered me from the room, shouting, 'You dog!' 'Yes, I am a dog,' I retorted defiantly, 'but I'm a Hindu dog.'

Despite his atheism, Father was adamant that I must have a Navjot to satisfy his parents. I was reluctantly coaxed and intimidated into learning the obligatory prayers from the Zend-Avesta, the Zoroastrian prayer book, which had to be memorized parrot-fashion because they were in ancient Persian, which even the priests no longer understood. What I dreaded most was the traditional rite of sipping cow's urine during the ceremony. But I need not have worried; my grandparents were too enlightened for such undiluted mumbo-jumbo. On the day, a silver goblet with a colourless liquid was simply passed beneath my nose; and though I sniffed hard I could smell no cow-pee. I could also have been spared all those tiresome hours memorizing the prayers with a priestly tutor. When the moment of recitation came, my mind went blank and I simply mimed along with the chanting priests.

The rest of the day passed in a whirl of pleasure. I was delighted to be the centre of attention at the traditional evening banquet, dressed up in a traditional white *dugli* with gold buttons and an impressive black Parsi hat, which resembled a bowler. I was thrilled by all the gifts it was customary to receive, and especially delighted by the indulgent presence of my beloved Hindu Nanna, who had come to Bombay for the occasion.

Despite the occasional Hindu–Parsi tensions I have mentioned, my childhood was remarkably free of religious bigotry or sectarian conflict. Our home was overwhelmingly secular and eclectic. In those years when the British Raj was still a recent presence, both the Srivastavas and the Masanis celebrated Christmas with as much gusto as any Indian festival. I loved the decorated trees, the plum puddings and, most of all, the mystery of my Christmas stocking, miraculously brimming with all the goodies my parents had asked me to note down on my Christmas list so that they could pass it on to Santa Claus.

By the time I was nine, I began to get curious about how Santa managed the miracle; and so one Christmas at my Masani grandparents' country cottage in Igatpuri (a hill resort near Bombay) I decided to stay up and find out. Several times I sat up to look as poor Cuckoo Granny made unsuccessful forays into my bedroom, retiring frustrated as soon as I spotted her. Eventually I fell asleep and woke to find the usual miracle accomplished and my stocking full. But Granny, exhausted by her sleepless night, had had enough. When I pressed her for an answer about whether Father Christmas really existed, she snapped back: 'What do *you* think?' I had my answer, and when I returned to Bombay I triumphantly told Mother I had discovered the truth about Santa Claus and that Granny had all but admitted it. She was furious. When Father came home she burst into tears and said: 'Your old witch of a mother has ruined Christmas for him.' In our home, laughter and tears were never far apart.

I have never had regrets about growing up without any organized religion, the product of a hybrid and multicultural home long before that became fashionable. It made me feel special, but it also reinforced my isolation and singled me out as different, especially at school, where mixed marriages were still very rare among parents of my contemporaries. 'What do you know? You're just a half-breed! You're neither a real Hindu nor a Parsi,' was a frequent jibe from the school bullies; and at some level it must have rankled. For the rest of my life, it made me both envious of in-groups and proud to be an outsider.

In 1959 we had to abandon our hilltop home on Altamount Road and move down to a block of flats on the sea face at Breach Candy. Our old home had been sold to property developers by the late landlord's heirs, and it was to be demolished and replaced by one of the high-rise blocks that were springing up all over Bombay, swallowing up the few gardens and open spaces that remained. I had resisted the move with all my heart, begging my parents not to succumb to the inevitable. But once we were settled into our airy new flat with its beautiful sea views, I had few regrets.

The building dated back to the 1930s and had the light art deco styling of its time. Best of all, it overlooked the Breach Candy Swimming Baths, a vast open-air pool then still reserved for foreigners. I spent many titillating hours on our balcony, watching handsome young men, stripped to their trunks, swimming, sun bathing and playing volleyball. Father sometimes joined me to enjoy the view, and I couldn't help noticing that his gaze was directed at the women in their skimpy bikinis.

Unfortunately, the move coincided with a dramatic deterioration in my parents' marriage, in which I was rapidly becoming an active protagonist. After a particularly bad row in 1960, Father took the initiative in suggesting that they formally end the marriage and go their separate ways. He admitted that he was in love with someone else and wished to marry her. In the months that followed, Mother fought an intense rearguard action against the idea of divorce. She had an entirely irrational terror of it, partly as an emotional rejection and partly because she feared its impact on her social status. Divorces were still few and far between in our social circles, and divorced women were considered a failure, unless they remarried higher up the social ladder. Marriage to Kishore, which was all that was currently on offer, would not have been enough to rehabilitate Mother in the eyes of her own family and friends.

So she prevaricated and ducked and weaved, while Father tried to pin her down. Under pressure from Kishore and me, both of whom wanted nothing more than to have her to ourselves, free of Father, she warned that, if she gave her consent, he might trick her and try and deny her custody of me. The prospect of falling into Father's custody scared me far more than any prison sentence. At other times, she said a divorce would kill her poor mother, who was strongly opposed to it on moral grounds. When Nanna, on the contrary, proposed that we should leave Father and live with her, free of any financial or other worries, Mother claimed that the strain of divorce would destroy her own health. She had developed high blood pressure and was also prone to kidney infections.

About this time, Father scribbled an aide-memoire about the state of their marriage, which I later found among his papers. 'S's picture needs correcting,' it began, and went on to describe a marriage based on 'general dissatisfaction and unappreciation, tepid' with an emotional 'vacuum'. There followed a list of subheadings, beginning:

'1. Zareer – no common ground. His mind poisoned against me . . . Status quo bad for him.

'2. Money – S's spending always in excess.

'3. Friendships – S's Double Standard – Noshir in Mahabaleshwar, Kishore also in Mahabaleshwar and gave her dog, Hirji gave her air-conditioner. But called me lecherous . . . She said every bit of feeling for me gone, my presence a blight, only carrying on because of Z.'

So on every count, Father believed she was the guilty party. But he did not wish to press matters to a hotly contested and very public divorce. He tried to persuade Mother to agree to an amicable divorce by mutual consent, but she refused. Her position was that he must agree to be the guilty party in a suit for adultery; and this of course would have been politically very damaging at a time when he had just become parliamentary leader of the infant Swatantra Party. Mother had friends of her own in high places. The Prime Minister, Jawaharlal Nehru, had always been fond of her, ever since she had written her very successful children's book about him. I remember the warmth with which he embraced her when we ran into him unexpectedly one day at Delhi airport. Krishna Menon, his all-powerful Defence Minister and eminence grise, was also an old friend of Mother's and had retained a soft corner for her long after he and Father fell out.

And so, on both sides, discretion proved the better part of valour: Father agreed to a one-year trial reconciliation, and the divorce negotiations petered out. They both promised to eschew all others and be faithful to each other. But Mother continued to see Kishore, who came on holidays with us to Mahabaleshwar. And Father continued to see the woman he would have married if Mother had agreed to a divorce; she was by then working for him in one of the voluntary organizations he had launched. Occasionally, when my parents quarrelled, I heard them bring up each other's alleged infidelities, but more often their rows were about money, because Mother claimed it was impossible to manage on the tight domestic budget to which Father constrained her, while he complained that she was squandering his meagre savings. On his return to active politics, he had had to relinquish his well-paid job with Tatas and had set up a small management consultancy to bring in a modest income.

It was Nanna who came to the rescue with financial bailouts that enabled Mother to buy the luxuries Father denied her. Nanna had never liked Father and made no secret now of the fact that she considered him a callous husband and a brutal father. She fretted about Mother's poor health and Father's alleged neglect of her. I have two anxious letters she wrote to Mother in April 1962:

> At first I thought you had an operation and did not inform me. Now I see that you lay ill with high temperature for 8 days and didn't inform me. I am your mother and it is my right that you inform me.
>
> Your son is still a child, and you were lying there alone so ill. Your husband doesn't care about you. I saw that for myself when I was in Bombay last time. So why do you hide these things from me? While I still live, your well-being is my concern. I feel great sorrow

that you hid things from me. I was crying so much when we spoke on the phone that I could not find out properly about your condition.

Shanky darling, write and tell me whether you have a kidney stone. Don't lie to me. Does the doctor say you need an operation immediately or after waiting a while? Write everything. I will send you to Europe to have it done there.

A few days later, she wrote again:

I did not cry for anything except that you poor thing have had no one in the house to look after you when you have been so ill. Darling, why don't you keep a nurse? I will pay, but you must have a nurse as soon as you feel unwell. I must send you an ayah now. I must also send you to England for treatment, but with whom? I will remain half-mad here sending you alone there . . . I am not too well, otherwise I would have come just now. I have been running a slow fever after my flu.

I cry for your poor luck. Have faith in God. Your days will come too when you will be happy, and later Zareer will shine and show those who have been calling him all the worst they can think of.

Nanna came to Bombay a month later. Mother had recovered by then, and it was decided that she was well enough to go abroad on her own for a holiday and medical check-ups. Nanna paid for the trip, but was too ill herself with severe angina to go with her. I was left alone with Father, who had promised Mother to be on his best behaviour with both Nanna and me while she was away.

His letters to Mother suggest that his efforts at reconciliation were genuine, and her response somewhat grudging.

'I can't tell you how sad I've been feeling,' he wrote to her in London. 'I've been trying so hard to get closer to you but just don't get a chance to do so. There are two things I can sincerely say to you. First, that I do care for you and your happiness and wish for nothing more than to be with you and Zareer. Secondly, that I need you and feel lost without your nearness.

'Please, darling, can't we both let bygones be bygones and come together again? I wish you would give another thought to my suggestion that we have a little holiday together. You know, we haven't had a holiday together since that lovely month in the snow at Crans in 1952. Please let's give it a try.'

Meanwhile, the truce back home between Father and me proved short-lived.

'This evening we had a little row,' I wrote to Mother, 'although I tried my best to follow your advice [to humour Father]. He told me that I would have to go and lunch with the Old Witch [Cuckoo Granny] tomorrow. I quite truthfully replied that tomorrow would be inconvenient for me. He said that it was compulsory for me to go and see her at least once a week, whether it was convenient for me or not. He said until I had had lunch with her I could not have Chinese lunch [my favourite].

'I just can't take any more. Do you know every day I get up at 6.00 a.m. to study. Sunday is the only day I can relax and he is taking that away from me.

'You remember you told me that if I gave in on certain things he would give in on others. So after thinking it over, I went to tell him that I was willing to go and see Cuckoo Granny as often as he wanted me to. However, before I had a chance to say a word he started on a long tirade about my sleeping late on Sundays . . .

'After having pushed you off by promising to be very nice to me, he has determined to enjoy himself by bullying me about every single thing.'

A month later, matters were no better. 'I am really desperate – and here I am not exaggerating,' I wrote to Mother. 'Daddy is driving me to the point of distraction – literally. He does nothing but bully me all day – so much so that at night I don't sleep well. I can't concentrate on my studies, and every time I hear a little sound I jump with fear, thinking it is he. I do not know who to turn to and I don't know how long I can stand it. I have a splitting headache just now. I can't stand it for another day, another hour. But I suppose I'll have to stand it till you return.

'To tell you the truth, I shall be quite hurt if you are going to spend a week with him in Istanbul after he has thus maltreated me. However, you go ahead and do as you wish. I don't want to come in the way of your trip.'

Mother quite sensibly ignored my plea not to reward Father's bad behaviour with the holiday *a deux* that he wanted. On her way back from Europe, she met him in Turkey and they had a pleasant time together. A few months later, I suffered another blow to my hopes of preventing their reconciliation. Nanna, my main ally against Father, died in Bombay at the relatively young age of sixty-seven.

Especially during Mother's absence abroad, Nanna and I had grown ever closer. I visited her religiously every evening and spent hours by her sickbed, where she lay looking like a fragile china doll, always immaculate in her silk pyjamas, her beautiful silver hair neatly brushed, her face discreetly made up, with her pearl tops, the only jewellery she now wore. We exchanged confidences, laughed and joked about the eccentricities of my Masani grandparents and generally cheered each other up. Father, of course, thought this most unhealthy, especially since I was so reluctant to visit Cuckoo Granny, but he could not prevent it.

On 12 November 1962, Nanna died of pneumonia and heart failure in her bedroom at Belmont, my aunt Malati's flat. It was my birthday, and I had been looking forward to spending some of it with her. I was in the room watching as she struggled for breath, bravely reassuring everyone that there was no need to panic and that she would be all right. She saw me standing there and with the last ounce of her failing strength gestured to me to leave the room; five minutes later she died.

The cardiologist in attendance was a famous but bungling, tubby and middle-aged Parsi who preferred socializing with his patients to treating them. He had decided the crisis had passed and was enjoying tea with us in the drawing room when Mother came running down the corridor shouting: 'Doctor, please come! Her pulse has gone!' We looked on in anguish as he unbuttoned her pyjama-top, massaged her heart and gave her the kiss of life; it seemed like an obscene violation of someone who had been so fastidious in life. I remember Mother rocking back and forth uncontrollably in paroxysms of grief as her sister Sarala held her and tried to comfort her. I was fourteen; it was my first encounter with death, and I felt as though the world had ended.

Mother was devastated too; the knowledge that Nanna was there behind her had been a source of strength in her battles with Father. Now she was more inclined to make her peace with him and he reciprocated with an olive branch. While Mother flew to Kanpur on a plane that had been chartered to fly Nanna's body back for the funeral, Father stayed back with me in Bombay because my O Level exams were only a week away. But he gave Mother the emotional support she needed, anticipating that sibling rivalry might be about to break out among the volatile Srivastavas. The sisters had already been at loggerheads over Nanna's medical care in her last days, with Mother insisting her condition was critical and trying unsuccessfully to get the others to hospitalize her. Events had proved her right.

'I have been thinking of you all the time since you left,' Father wrote to Mother in Kanpur. 'Please look after yourself, darling, and don't fall ill while you are in Kanpur . . . Pixiekins, please try to avoid unpleasantness with anyone there. Whatever has happened has happened. You did your best, and now nothing can help.'

Their own reconciliation was still fragile. Shortly after her return from Kanpur, they had another major quarrel and were not on speaking terms for some days. Father wrote her this pained note of self-justification:

'While you were away in Kanpur, my mind and heart were with you and I had no other thought in my head. You yourself said how sweet I was being to you. It's hurt therefore when you called me a liar and accused me of all kinds of things without any rhyme or reason whatsoever. Please, darling, I beg of you to put suspicion out of your mind and not let it torment you and me like this. I love you. Please let me get close to you and don't push me away like this.'

Clearly, there were problems of trust from which their relationship had not recovered. About this time, Mother jotted down various predictions and advice about her marriage from an astrologer she had consulted. 'I shall try to leave Minoo. No friends will stand by me after that. They are all selfish. There is only one person I should stay with and that is Minoo, and he will keep me happy. There is pain for me through another woman, but she cannot harm me. I can destroy Minoo's *kirti* [career line] to a certain extent. There is no other marriage for Minoo. All advice given to me to leave him is wrong advice. Turn to prayers and meditation, and guidance will come to you from there. Do not be guided by any person.'

Throughout her life, Mother sought out new fortune tellers with all the eagerness and anticipation of someone desperate for reassurance. They varied in the future joys they promised her, but they were all unanimous on one point: she must not divorce Father. It was what she wanted to hear, and so she drew back from the precipice and their marriage returned to a kind of normality. Father by then was in his late fifties and Mother, over forty; though neither yet considered themselves middle-aged, their physical relationship had ended in the storms of 1960. From now on, they would at best be friends and partners rather than lovers.

NINE

A POLITICAL WIFE

The mid to late 1960s were a relatively calm and uneventful period in our family life. In 1963 I began university in Bombay, at Elphinstone College, where Father and Grandfather had preceded me. Miraculously, I made up for my isolation at school by making lots of new friends, and I soon had a busy social life. I was active in the debating and dramatics societies and edited the college magazine. My new life left me little time or inclination to be a protagonist in my parents' marriage. They, for their part, were getting on far better. Also, Father had by this time given up trying to discipline me, and for the first time expressed grudging approval of my academic and extracurricular successes.

My parents' emotional battles were soon supplanted for me by my own thwarted adolescent romanticism. In my first year at Elphinstone, I had fallen passionately in love with a sophisticated and glamorous final-year student. He was highly sought after by my female friends and held court among them with all the regal splendour of a peacock. I was amazed and delighted when he returned my adulation, and our secret love was consummated on my sixteenth birthday. The secrecy itself made for an amazing intensity. A knowing glance across a room full of friends, or a furtive brush of a hand, were all we needed to kindle our passions.

For a few weeks I walked on air, happier than I have ever been before or since; I was the chosen one. And then he dropped me, abruptly, without warning or explanation. Overnight my world collapsed. At first I thought I must unwittingly have done something to offend him; all I had to do was discover what it was, and I would be magically reinstated in his love. It took months for me to realize that he had simply tired of me and decided to move on to heterosexuality and an ambitious career.

At first, there was no one in whom I could confide and it was a heavy emotional burden to carry alone. I spent long evenings locked in my room in the dark, listening to romantic music, tears rolling down my cheeks. Occasionally, Father banged on the door to rouse me. He complained that all this lying in the dark listening to music was unhealthy and jokingly referred to me as Cleopatra. Mother more indulgently smiled and turned a blind eye.

Forty years on, it's hard to imagine how different my life might have been without the isolation imposed by what was still regarded as sexual 'inversion'. The sexual revolution was just beginning: even in Bombay, we read and performed the works of Tennessee Williams, Carson McCullers, Edward Albee, Terence Rattigan and J.D. Salinger. But homosexuality was never mentioned in our own circles.

And yet, for me there had never really been any doubt about my sexual orientation. My earliest romantic crushes had been on men and older boys, despite sporadic and excruciating efforts to dance with girls at our school socials. Was my sexuality the result of nature or nurture? I fitted the classic, Oedipal cliché of an overly close mother and a hostile or absent father; but it's hard to imagine I would have turned out differently with a closer father. Certainly, I had no childhood fear or distrust of women. All the most important people in my life had been female, and as an adult my closest friends were too.

It was to an understanding and perceptive female friend that I first confided my heartbreak and loss. She was comforting and supportive and offered to break the news gently to my mother. I went out and left them alone to talk; and when I returned, filled with apprehension about Mother's reaction, I was greeted by unconditional acceptance and reassurance. 'I don't see what the problem is!' Mother exclaimed. 'Why didn't you tell me earlier? There's nothing to be ashamed of.' She went on to mention several men in my parents' social circle who were bisexual or 'inclined the other way'; but she did suggest that it would be better not to let Father into the secret.

Was Mother's support entirely altruistic? Was she perhaps just a mite flattered that she would never have to face any female competition for my love? That realization may have dawned later, over the years; but I'm sure her immediate reaction was spontaneous and very generous. She had never been prudish in such matters and I think she was genuinely pleased that I had confided in her. She must have noticed my melancholic moping for some months, and now she was relieved to know the cause.

Confiding in Mother strengthened the bond between us and made me feel less hopeless. We both recognized that my sort of love had no future in India; and so it was on enlightened and permissive Albion that we set our hopes. It had always been assumed that I would go to Oxbridge after graduating in Bombay. That goal became the purpose and justification for my remaining years at Elphinstone, and Britain beckoned as enticingly to my emotional and sexual privations as it did to any economic migrant.

I had not been abroad since my early childhood, and when Mother took me with her to London and Paris in the mid-1960s, it was a grand tour full of cultural anticipation and excitement. Mother was an excellent guide. In Paris, she introduced me to the masterpieces of Impressionism then displayed at the Jeu de Paume, and we marvelled together at the muscular modernism of the sculptures at the Rodin Museum and the exotic, baroque splendours of Versailles.

London, by contrast, was like a homecoming, evoking the familiar sights and sounds with which I had grown up in the novels of Agatha Christie and Conan Doyle and the bedtime stories of my grandparents. Here we concentrated on the theatre and on visits to stately homes like Hatfield and Syon House, full of associations with the historical personalities who had fascinated me in my studies of English history. And in search of the authentic London, we also had tea and walnut cake at Lyons Corner House and enjoyed the wonders of the Tube with its multicoloured maze of lines and stations.

London was Mother's favourite city, and she loved the discreet charm of its upper classes. Her own attractions had won her an impressive circle of (predominantly male) friends and admirers who included the celebrated author Arthur Koestler, the publisher Hamish Hamilton, the conductor Lorin Maazel and the Earl of Harewood, musical patron and the Queen's first cousin. Mother, always elegantly attired, glided smoothly and effortlessly through these gilded circles, while I, still painfully shy and gauche, followed hesitantly in her wake.

And yet, when the long-awaited move to a British university came, my hopes of emotional fulfilment were drowned by my terror of life in a cold climate, separated for the first time from Mother and the rest of my familiar world. On closer inspection, the dreaming spires looked dark and forbidding and the medieval college interiors damp and icy at a time when central heating was still a rare luxury. Long accustomed to my own en suite bathroom at home, I was particularly appalled by the scarce and rather primitive shared toilet and bathing facilities.

Having failed to get into the colleges of my choice, I had been offered a place by the School of Oriental and African Studies in London and by St Edmund Hall at Oxford. 'Teddy' Hall was just beginning to shed its former prowess for rugger and rowing blues, in favour of a new and more academic intake, of which I was part. After much agonizing, I chose it over SOAS (considered far too 'native' by my parents); but I was still deeply suspicious of its sporty reputation and afraid of being a misfit, as I had been at school.

My fears proved self-fulfilling and I made hardly any friends during my undergraduate years at Oxford. Ignoring Father's sensible advice, I avoided the discomforts of living in college in favour of more comfortable but isolated digs outside. Worst of all, I failed to discover a welcoming gay scene in Oxford, if indeed one yet existed in the late '60s.

Mother had come with me to help me settle in at the beginning of term. Her presence was a mixed blessing. She came armed with introductions and gifts for various academic hoi-polloi, who she hoped would invite me over after she left: Sir William and Lady Hayter at New College, Lord and Lady Redcliffe-Maud at Univ (University College), Professor Plamenatz at All Souls, and Sir Isaiah Berlin and his graceful and very wealthy French wife, Aline. Mother charmed them all, and they reciprocated by inviting me to a series of sherry parties. I attended dutifully, though my shyness made these occasions excruciating for me.

When Mother finally flew back to India, it was with the promise that I would follow her there only three weeks later for my Christmas vacation. Even so, we wrote to each other at least twice a week, and this continued for the next three years.

'I am sorry you are not making more friends,' Mother wrote a couple of weeks after her departure. 'You will have to go all out, as the English are so reticent. The first term is always the hardest, and I'm certain you will be happier in a couple of months' time.'

She, too, felt our separation keenly, especially when I returned to Oxford after the Christmas break. 'You have been away for four hours only,' she wrote, 'and you cannot imagine how much I am missing you . . . I am writing to you from the office. I had to rush away outside, as I miss you terribly when I am in the flat. Russet and I went into your room and tried to comfort each other.'

Mother was by then working part-time as a sales executive with Bombay's largest travel business. It supplemented her income, always a sore point between her and Father. She used the extra funds to finance what she called her 'treasure-hunt', a passionate and almost obsessive search for antiquities. She had been collecting Indian art since the 1940s, long before it became fashionable. Now, with her keen eye for beauty, she tracked down a succession of striking paintings and sculptures, usually at bargain prices.

She read widely on the subject of Indian antiquities and established very convenient friendships with two leading experts, Dr Motichandra, Curator of the Prince of Wales Museum in Bombay, and Dr Sivaramamurti, his counterpart at the National Museum in Delhi. She would breeze in to see them with her latest potential acquisitions, and they, charmed by her enthusiasm, generously provided her with hours of free inspection and authentication. Collecting became the centre of her life, with the overarching justification that she would present her collection to me on my twenty-first birthday.

Although she missed me, Mother seems to have been much happier during these years than ever before or after. My absence had brought Father and her closer, and they had become good friends, tolerant of each other's foibles. Father was then at the peak of his political career as

Leader of the Opposition in Parliament; and Mother and he both enjoyed the whirl of diplomatic and other parties at which they were made much of in Delhi. They made a glamorous and invincible team: good-looking, intelligent and very charming.

'Yesterday we went to Mrs. Pandit's reception for Rajiv Gandhi and his [Italian] wife,' Mother wrote to me in a typical roundup of her weekly social calendar. 'I can't tell you how dim the girl is, and she comes from a working-class family. I really don't know what he saw in her. Madame Malraux, the wife of the French Minister for Culture, is here and is giving a piano recital. We shall be going to that this evening, and then to dinner afterwards at a party in her honour.'

A month later, she informed me: 'I met Maharishi Mahesh Yogi's impresario, and it appears that I made quite an impression on him, for every day I get a phone call from the ashram at Rishikesh saying that the Maharishi wants to see me and is keen I accompany him on his world tour. It is such a tempting offer that I must admit to you I am in two minds. To travel all round the world and stay at the best hotels, all free of charge! Daddy of course insists I turn down the offer and, in his words, "not become party to the biggest fraud in history". What are your views on the subject? Please let me know, as it will help me to make up my mind.'

I doubt if I was any more encouraging than Father, and the Maharishi was left to conquer the Beatles and the West without Mother's aid. Apart from her social skills, she had also become a loyal, though not uncritical, political wife. She used to campaign for Father during elections in his Gujarat constituency of Rajkot, although she tended to avoid his more gruelling political tours on grounds of health. As a Hindu, she was particularly useful to him in countering the propaganda of the Hindu nationalist Jan Sangh, who were his main challengers. When they tried to smear him as a beef-eating Parsi, Mother came to his rescue as the loyal Hindu wife who was photographed garlanding local cows and petting their calves.

Mother and I continued to correspond about developments in India and abroad. 'I hope Daddy is pulling his weight in Parliament,' I wrote to her rather patronizingly in March 1968. 'Does he know that the Indian Parliament has made a complete laughing stock of itself all over the world by standing in silence for the three Rhodesian "martyrs", who were guilty of the most ghastly and bloody crimes and would have been hanged long ago in any other country of the world. Not even a single African country thought of making such a "ridiculous and disgusting gesture". That's how the London *Times* described it.'

Although we were separated by time and distance, Mother and I remained each other's closest confidants. When I hinted to her that Britain had not proved to be the emotional promised land of my dreams, she was full of solicitude. 'I am worried and unhappy about your being upset about something,' she wrote instantly. 'Please darling, do write and tell me what it is. You know how much I love you and what companionship and understanding there is between us. I have shared all my most intimate thoughts and feelings with you and you have always understood me and helped and advised me. It is because of this that I have been able to tide over the darkest and saddest moments in my life so far. Let us keep our relationship on this solid basis, and no matter what is troubling you, you can be sure I will stretch out my hand to help you. You must not think of me as just a mother. I would like to be a friend as well, and please remember that I will never betray your confidence.'

Significantly, she went on to add that she was not alone in her concern for me. My absence had made Father's heart, too, grow fonder. 'Daddy read your letter to me and is also worried. He loves you very much. I realise now, when you are not here, that his affection for you is deep and genuine. However, if you do not feel like confiding in him, I shall not say a word to him and treat your letter as completely confidential.' Two months later, when Father was about to visit London, she reiterated: 'If there is anything on your mind, do confide in Daddy. I can't tell you how much he loves you.'

Unfortunately, old emotional habits died hard, and I did not act on her advice to take Father into my confidence. I felt sure he would condemn my sexuality as yet another result of my pampered childhood. But I probably underestimated him. How different my life and theirs might have been if I'd followed Mother's advice and trusted him.

Around this time, I had fallen in love for the second time. The object of my affections was rather different from my college hero in Bombay, but just as unattainable. He was intellectually brilliant and emotionally sensitive but, as I later discovered, clinically schizophrenic and, worst of all, in love himself with someone equally unattainable. For the next two years, I courted him assiduously, but it ended in tears and bitter disappointment. For much of this time, I toyed with ideas of suicide. I never attempted it, but hardly a day passed when I did not contemplate it and fantasize about ways and means, about how best to make a noble, painless and glorious end.

Two years passed, and my thwarted romantic obsession was superseded by the anxiety of impending final exams. I was convinced I was going to end up with an ignominious Third. Mother wrote me soothing letters, assuring me that, whatever the outcome, I need not worry. She was keen to have me back in India and sent glowing accounts of all the scintillating artists and intellectuals she knew in Delhi whom I would enjoy meeting. When I expressed a preference for Bombay, she replied generously: 'You can have the Breach Candy flat more or less to yourself as we are there so little, and I shall buy you a car. I can speak to Jeh [JRD] about a job in Tatas or to Khushwant [Singh] to get you a job in a newspaper. I think Khushwant is leaving the *Illustrated Weekly* [as editor] next year, and if you can take over from him that would be wonderful.'

She clearly had high ambitions for me, but added thoughtfully: 'I will not press you or push you into anything that you do not want to do. There is plenty of time to think things over and make up your mind later.'

Then came an unexpectedly harsh blow. In April 1970, Cuckoo Granny died at the age of eighty-five, after a painful operation for bowel cancer. Grandfather had preceded her five years earlier at the very ripe age of ninety-one, active, healthy and busy till the very last day, when a massive coronary took him within hours. Granny's decline was more gradual and prolonged, and it affected me more than I had expected, despite all my childhood spats with her.

By the time I left for Oxford, she had become a proud, soft and indulgent grandmother with little trace of the old disciplinarian. She wrote often, gently chiding me for not replying: 'When you do get time, scribble me a few words – it will make me happy.' 'Do not please *over*work. I hope you take enough nourishment and eat enough,' she fussed in her last letter to me. 'It would be good to see you plump. It will not be out of place with your height.' A far cry from the days when she had rationed my consumption of ham, cream and chocolate.

In the same letter, she confided that she had fallen and hurt her 'sitting parts', so had to use an air-ring to sit on. She was on a visit to Aunt Mehra in Delhi. A couple of weeks later, there was a far more serious development: she was diagnosed with an enormous tumour in the intestines. Mother wrote to keep me informed, while unfairly blaming Mehra for neglecting her mother and illogically attributing the cancer to the earlier fall. 'Poor Granny!' she wrote. 'When she fell, I told Mehra that she should be x-rayed, but of course Mehra dismissed the idea. I'm sure that if the x-ray had been taken at that time, the growth would not have developed. You will recall that the same thing happened to Grandfather. It is strange that both Papa and Mama fell in Mehra's house. Papa died of neglect, and Mama may also die due to this fall. It is almost sinister, but do not worry, darling.'

Though unable to resist such insinuations about Aunt Mehra's murderous neglect of her infirm parents, Mother does appear to have been genuinely distressed by the passing of her once hostile mother-in-law. 'Poor thing. She is in awful pain and is being very brave indeed,' she wrote a few days later. 'It is a pathetic sight to see her.' After a colectomy and colostomy, Granny rallied for a few days. 'She is still too weak to talk,' Mother wrote, 'but there is a tremendous difference for the better. Till yesterday, she was in a coma. This morning she recognised me. I read your letter to her, and she smiled and listened to it. Poor Mama, she looks so pathetic and helpless. But she is no longer in pain, and that is something to be thankful for. I have been going to the hospital every day for quite a few hours, and all our other activities have come to a standstill.'

It was a short reprieve, and a week later Granny faded away. 'She had a quiet and beautiful funeral,' Mother informed me, 'and has been buried here [in Delhi] in the Parsee Burial-ground under a mango tree in a lovely garden. I was allowed to attend the funeral.'

It was a reference to the traditional exclusion of non-Parsis from all Zoroastrian religious rites. It was a point on which Mother had always been sensitive, and her indignation had been compounded by what she perceived as her continuing treatment as an outsider by the Masani family. A typical example was a row between Father and her over a clause in Grandfather's will over a property he owned in the Bombay suburb of Santa Cruz.

The Executors, Father and Aunt Mehra, had the discretion to decide whether to give their proverbially indigent brother Keki a life interest in the rents from the building or to sell it and buy him an annuity. Aunt Mehra decided that the latter option would be simpler and more beneficial and Father consented. Mother, however, was furious. She believed that I, as one of the other heirs, had been done out of my rightful inheritance; and of course the subsequent boom in Bombay real estate was to prove her right.

'You know perfectly well,' she wrote angrily to Father, 'that this will hit Zareer's interests and that you as a father should have pressed for the first option. How unlike you are to Keki, who has his wife and child's interest at heart! I have realised for some time that you have no thought for me, but I did expect you to at least think of Zareer's future. I know that you are as usual going to say that I have no right to take any interest in Papa's Will when he and I were hardly on the best of terms. But it is your attitude which is completely unnatural. My opinion counts for so little in all matters.'

Perhaps the vehemence of her anger and frustration owed something to her general state of health. She was approaching fifty, menopausal and prone to high blood pressure and chronic kidney infections. She was also in the early stages of what would now be diagnosed as a clinical depression, with insomnia, panic attacks and major mood swings. A fashionable Hungarian émigré psychiatrist in London had been dosing her with Valium, but the medication, though addictive, was producing diminishing returns.

Apart from occasional family quarrels, there were deeper undercurrents of tension in the marriage, stirred up by the spectre of infidelities past and potential. Kishore Uncle had by then dropped out of Mother's circle of admirers, resigning himself to marriage with a less glamorous but more available Englishwoman. But there was still Sir Hirji, the eccentric baronet, whose attentions were particularly embarrassing because his formidable mother, the dowager Lady Jehangir, was the cousin and best friend of my own Cuckoo Granny.

For years, Granny had urged Father to put a stop to Mother's friendship with Hirji, on the grounds that it was distressing his wife and putting strains on Granny's own friendship with Lady Jehangir. But Hirji was not easily deterred. He wrote to Mother: 'I took the first opportunity of asking my mother of the rift she had with Lady Masani because of our friendship. My mother assures me that there has been no rift whatever in their long and close friendship of 35 years and that she will ask Lady Masani what she means by saying that their friendship was being spoilt by ours. So you can expect some more fireworks when Lady Masani returns from Delhi. If your health can take the strain of a domestic fireside chat between the two elder ladies and ourselves, I shall be delighted for you to join our select circle.'

Unfortunately, the matter was not confined to the family circle. There now began a barrage of anonymous letters, postcards and telegrams addressed to Father, accusing him of being both a pimp and a cuckold and of prostituting his wife to Sir Hirji and others in return for cash. This poison-mail lasted for about three years—from 1966 to 1969—and miraculously ceased whenever Mother stopped seeing Sir Hirji. Both Mother and Father were convinced that the author was his jilted wife, but she denied it strenuously. Hirji countered with the allegation that they were probably being sent by one of Father's jealous mistresses.

'Your house has been turned into a brothel,' said one typical example of the poison pen. 'Positive proof of it is that Sir Hirji Jehangir visited your wife yesterday at 2.30 p.m. in your own home seen by all. It is said that these visits are with your sanction, and much gain can be got thereby. Your wife is also cited as a go-between in the highly irregular affairs of her former lover Dr. Chand, who has jilted her for an English girl, and her present rich baronet, from whom she has extracted vast sums of money for Dr. Chand.' Despite their lack of logic or credibility, the hate-mail was undoubtedly a great embarrassment to Father, especially when it arrived in the form of open postcards addressed to his parliamentary office, warning: 'When you get up to speak on public accountability today, ponder on your own private accounts and the source whereby your family is maintained, a fine example of an M.P. who lets his wife loose for prostitution, thereby making a neat business.'

As Mother spent more time in Delhi and saw less of Hirji, the letters gradually petered out. But they were replaced by a new focus of suspicion and jealousy. Sometime in the mid-'60s Mother had begun a close friendship with a handsome American called Hoppy (I can't remember his Christian name because we never used it). He and his wife were old friends from the time my parents had spent in New York in the early 1950s. Now he was a senior manager with Coca Cola and visited India regularly to promote the corporation's growing and very lucrative local bottling franchises.

Mother became a consultant to the company and helped introduce Hoppy and his colleagues to influential Indians. Her work involved travelling with Hoppy when he was in India, and she also went with him to a couple of Coca Cola board meetings abroad. Hoppy appears to have fallen in love with her; but her own feelings were equivocal. She enjoyed the attention, but she drew back from the kind of serious involvement that would have wrecked his marriage and her own.

Sometime in 1969 she appears to have turned down his advances. I found Hoppy's injured response recently; and significantly, it was among a bundle of papers Father had filed away in connection with his later divorce from Mother. 'Love is something which I find impossible to turn on and off like a water-tap,' Hoppy reproached her in this plaintive letter which Father had apparently intercepted. 'If you can, you are indeed lucky – or cold – or were not in love to start with.'

This letter appears to have provoked some serious tensions between my parents. Father, with his strongly pro-American and private enterprise ideology, had no political objections to Mother's affiliation with Coca Cola, but he does appear to have been genuinely jealous. 'There has been considerable tension during Hoppy's visit,' Mother confided to me in

November 1969. 'Minoo was unfriendly and made his attitude clear. In view of this, Hoppy feels my taking up a job under him will expose me to considerable tension, which might even lead to a break-up between Minoo and me. He has therefore advised me to discontinue my job, so as not to bring matters to a head.'

'I simply cannot understand Minoo,' she complained, in a reference to the intercepted letter, 'My mail is pilfered, and he is always checking up on my whereabouts. I feel I am being watched all the time. Anyway, I shall try and have a frank talk with Minoo and see if I cannot persuade him that we co-exist on a sensible arrangement. I cannot lose my friends one by one, and now my job too is endangered by his aggressive antagonism.'

Hoppy had been holding out the possibility of a highly paid, full-time job for Mother in Coca Cola, and she seems to have been torn between conflicting emotions. 'The more I see of him, the less I like him,' she confided to me in December 1969. 'I am beginning to have serious doubts whether I want to work for him or not. Sarala and Gogu [her sister and brother-in-law], who know him well, find him coarse, unreliable and selfish. I am beginning to agree with them.'

Two weeks later, she was less critical of Hoppy, but also less attracted by the job. 'I have more or less decided not to continue with Coca-Cola. Hoppy is a very nice but very unreliable person. One can never predict what he is going to do next. Jeh [J.R.D. Tata], who also met him, felt that he was a typical American businessman and could be very ruthless. It is very difficult to work for Americans. Although they are generous, they observe no procedures, and I do find it rather tiresome. Also, there is such a lot of political goings on in the firm, and I find myself dragged into it all the time.'

The same letter was full of praise for her newest male friend, the Sikh author and journalist Khushwant Singh. 'Khushwant, who writes to me regularly [from Bombay], insists I do an article for *The Illustrated Weekly* on Indian classical dancing and is offering to pay me well. He is such an interesting and sensitive person, and I like him more and more.'

In the next few months, Hoppy and Coca Cola faded out of our lives, and relations between my parents improved. By now, personal tensions had in any case been submerged in the political tidal wave that was sweeping India. Prime Minister Indira Gandhi, tired of being fettered by the big beasts of her Congress Party, was making a bid for supreme power. The outcome was to have a far more profound effect on my parents' marriage and my own future than any of us could have imagined at the time.

For most of my life, I had tended to accept Father's strongly argued political views, but three years at Oxford had slowly but surely politicized and radicalized me. The Vietnam War and the protests against it had proved for me, as for so many others, the major catalyst. It is a measure of how political we were as a family that these arguments figured prominently in my correspondence with my parents.

In May 1970 I had sent Mother various press clippings from London criticizing the American bombing of Cambodia. 'I agree with you basically that American interference in South East Asia is wrong,' she replied, 'but I cannot help feeling that, as country after country falls to Chinese Communism, the danger to India gets more grave. We are going through a very difficult time. The Naxalites [Maoist guerrillas] are active in practically all the states, and they are spreading a reign of terror throughout the country. With this background, the Chinese danger becomes very real. England can afford to take a critical attitude, but I wonder if the English would feel the same way if the British Isles were situated in South East Asia. It is so easy to be critical of someone else's action when you know you are quite safe from Chinese aggression. Also England does like to snipe at the USA whenever it can. It is suffering from an inferiority complex and can never accept the fact that it is a second-class power. This does not mean I am justifying the brutality of the American police. I strongly condemn the firing at the campus, but at the same time the American intellectual is very confused, and I cannot agree with them on a number of issues.'

Mother concluded this cogent rebuttal of the anti-war case by assuring me that her views were her own. 'You must not think that Daddy has brainwashed me. I disagree violently with him on the Swatantra Party stand on the privileges and Privy Purse of the princes. If the Party is to gain ground, it has to have a more go-ahead attitude.'

A month later, Father came to London on a brief visit. We must have argued fiercely about politics, for I wrote complaining to Mother: 'He has a closed mind. I hate to say it, but I think he has the makings of a Fascist dictator. Whenever we argue, I feel like going off and joining the Indian Communist Party. Who knows, I might when I return! Daddy says he is planning to visit Saigon. But he's so bigoted that I doubt if he'll gain much. His belief in the "World Communist Conspiracy" is as pathetic and superstitious as the "Conspiracy of Satan", which the Spanish Inquisition used to trot out. After the Sino-Soviet polemic, it should be clear to anyone that there's no such thing as World Communism. There's Russian imperialism, Chinese imperialism and Vietnamese imperialism. There are already grave tensions between Peking and Moscow. While I appreciate the threat to India from the Naxalites, the threat is from China, not Hanoi, and the Vietnam War is no concern of ours.'

I ran on for two more pages about how the Americans were playing into the hands of the Communists, because their presence in Indo-China was driving more and more nationalists into the arms of the Viet Cong. 'It's only when people fight their own battles,' I lectured, 'that they learn to stand on their own feet. This is where Hanoi scores. I'm all for supplying arms to Cambodia and Laos, but not fighting their battles for them. The best solution would be if the U.S. pulled out of South Vietnam, where no one except the Saigon clique wants them, in return for a North Vietnamese withdrawal from Cambodia and Laos, who are the real sufferers.'

Having come rather late to political protest, I was rapidly becoming obsessed by it. Even a reading of E.M. Forster's novel, *A Passage to India*, provided grist to my anti-American mill. 'I found it most gripping and read it at one sitting,' I wrote to Mother. 'Apart from the sheer poetry and excitement, it was so thought-provoking. It is such a sensitive portrayal of the unbridgeable gulf between two alien civilisations and of the utter futility of the British Raj. How remarkable that Forster in 1924 should have had so penetrating an insight into the absurdity and uselessness of "westernisation", an insight which still eludes the Americans and other neo-colonialists. A very depressing book, I admit, but very true.'

These were also the days of Enoch Powell's campaign against immigration, and I was quick to spot a moral here for Father. 'Daddy will be glad to know that Powell has taken his cue,' I wrote sarcastically to Mother. 'When the Home Office exposed his figures on immigration as grossly exaggerated, he announced that the Home Office had been infiltrated by "Commies". Most people think he is teetering on the brink of insanity. At any rate, he has dragged the Tories down with him, and Labour seems set for a landslide majority. Even loyal Tories like Yvonne and Jamie [our good friends, the Hamish Hamiltons] are going to vote Labour or Liberal.' My own vote, I proudly announced, would go to the Liberals.

Political radicalism had, at long last, given me a sense of belonging at Oxford, where I now had some good friends. But these changes came just as it was time to go back home to India for good, armed with an upper Second instead of the Third I had feared. 'Oxford has been such a stimulating and mind-expanding place,' I wrote to Mother, 'that I shall be very sorry to leave.' I was keen to stay on and do a doctorate at St Antony's, but I failed to get a scholarship, and Father was adamant that he could not afford to fund a postgraduate course at Oxford.

Through my Oxford years, I had remained closely in touch with political developments in India, which had been moving towards a major unravelling of the established party system, as Mrs Gandhi sought to consolidate her hold on power and the Opposition planned a counter-offensive. Mother had kept me well informed. In December 1968 she wrote about 'sinister moves' by the Hindu nationalist Jan Sangh to take over Father's secular Swatantra Party under cover of a merger. She complained that 'the old fox' Rajaji, the founding father of Swatantra, was unofficially encouraging these moves, which would see Father replaced as Leader of the Opposition by A.B. Vajpayee, the Jan Sangh leader (who became Prime Minister in the late 1990s). 'If this comes off,' she concluded, 'I hope Daddy will resign.' He was on a trip to London at the time and she asked me to brief him on the plotting that was going on behind his back.

With or without Rajaji's support, Father successfully scotched the move. But then came the dramatic split in the ruling Congress Party, which presented the Opposition with a real chance of bringing down Mrs Gandhi's government. She had expelled her opponents within her own party, known pejoratively as 'the Syndicate', and was trying to project herself as the voice of youth, dynamism and radical change. The two wings of Congress fought bitterly for the mantle of legitimacy, which carried with it the party organization and funds and the inheritance of Gandhi and Nehru.

'The mob is out on the streets,' Mother wrote to me in the summer of 1969, 'and there is a lot of slogan-shouting, etc. What emerges from all this is difficult to predict, but it looks at the moment as if we are heading for chaos. Indira's position in Parliament is very precarious. People who had supported her on the first day are slowly edging away. The Communists have openly said that they will support her only on her socialistic measures. She is running into troubled waters and will probably have to face a mid-term poll if she is to have a clear majority in Parliament and not depend on Communist support. But nobody wants another general election, including a great many of her supporters. Such is the game of politics – no wonder only the ruthless survive!'

Mother was perceptive about the reality underlying the slogans. 'The foreign press,' she complained, 'has I see come down thumpingly on Indira's side. They have not the faintest idea of what is going on and as usual are backing the wrong side. The more objective Indian papers such as *The Indian Express* and *Statesman* have rightly described this deplorable situation as a faction fight and nothing to do whatsoever with any principles or ideology.'

One example of this populist opportunism was the way both sides had exploited the issue of abolishing the privileges of the Indian princes, guaranteed by treaty and the Indian Constitution. Mrs Gandhi had announced that she wanted to abolish them and amend the Constitution, only to backtrack when she needed princely support in Parliament. The issue was thereupon cynically taken up by the opposing Congress faction, who demanded immediate abolition of princely privileges, in an attempt to outbid Mrs Gandhi's radicalism.

A few months later Mother wrote describing how Indira had been consolidating her position by bribing opponents with the loaves and fishes of office. 'The patronage she has is enormous, and she can easily buy off many who are disgruntled. Daddy feels that she will last till 1972, unless of course there is a mid-term poll, and then one cannot tell how she will fare. It is clear, however, that the motley crowd she has collected are all at loggerheads already, and she is in perpetual danger of losing the majority in the House.'

The main beneficiaries of this political instability were the two Communist parties, on whom Mrs Gandhi depended for her government's survival. Father never tired of reminding her, on the floor of the House, that Communist support would be, judging by past precedents elsewhere in the world, like 'the rope that supports the hanged man'. He challenged her to follow the example of democratic Prime Ministers in France and Italy and declare that she would not allow Communist votes to be counted in determining whether she had a majority. 'Unfortunately,' he wrote to me, 'Mrs. Gandhi did not accept my challenge and agree to exclude Communist votes from computation.'

Instead, she had taken the battle into the opposition parties themselves, seeking to split them by buying over the waverers and by using her patronage at the Centre to topple unfriendly state governments. Father, with his long and unblemished record, now emerged as the champion of political rectitude, mercilessly and successfully rooting out and expelling opportunists from the ranks of his own party. But he had one major disadvantage. As a Parsi, he could never hope to be accepted as Prime-Minister-in-waiting by a predominantly Hindu country. And partly for that reason, he could not persuade his political allies to unite against Mrs Gandhi on a principled platform based on a common programme. To cap it all, he would soon have to face a damaging political rebellion inside his own home.

TEN

THE INDIRA WAVE

My return from Oxford coincided with the denouement of India's political power struggle. The disunity of Indira Gandhi's opponents and her own capacity for shrewd populism was turning the tide decisively in her favour, though quite how dramatically we could not have imagined. Nor could we have anticipated then that the wave that swept her to absolute power would also shatter our own family life beyond repair.

I had returned to Delhi a loose cannon. I was by now politically well to the left of Father. I was also resentful of his attempts to press me into taking up a job. To be fair, he left the choice to me. Business, teaching, journalism, the foreign service, were all possibilities that were mooted. But what I really wanted was to return to Oxford as soon as I had the necessary funding to pursue a doctorate at St Antony's. At least as important as any academic motivation was the elusive holy grail of 'the relationship' that seemed far more attainable in permissive Britain than in homophobic India.

Of course, Father knew nothing of my personal motives, since they were never discussed with him. He saw me as an idler who was trying to shirk my responsibilities and sponge on Mother's generosity. The spectre of her good-for-nothing brothers was an ever-present warning of the consequences. Mother, meanwhile, was torn between her own delight at having me back home and her desire to see me happy and fulfilled. Her response was to be more indulgent than ever and to humour my every whim.

In the months that followed my return, these emotional and political ingredients proved an explosive mixture. I identified increasingly with Indira, whom Father by now saw as a pro-Communist, would-be dictator. We argued heatedly, both at home and at dinner parties, and Mother usually took my side.

And then came Indira's coup de grâce, a snap mid-term election early in 1971, which put the Opposition on the defensive. In response to her election slogan, *Garibi Hatao*, all that her opponents could come up with was *Indira Hatao*. The opposition parties formed an electoral pact known as the Grand Alliance, but it lacked a common programme other than the purely negative aim of ousting 'That Woman'. Father worked hard to knock heads together to produce a principled Opposition manifesto, but failed to overcome the opportunism of colleagues who wanted to try and outbid Mrs Gandhi's populism. At one point, he even walked out of the inter-party talks, provoking much press speculation.

Mother was delighted. 'I can see the so-called "Grand Alliance" has become a complete farce,' she wrote to him from Delhi. 'I am so glad you are having nothing to do with it.' And then, in the same letter, she dropped a bombshell. 'Zareer has joined the Congress (R) [Indira's faction] and I wondered if you would mind my also doing so. I feel it is the only party that can give India a stable government. This will certainly not come in the way of my working for you in Rajkot [Father's constituency], as I also feel that leaders and worthwhile people from other democratic parties should be supported, as ultimately Indira will have to have a coalition government. Let us hope it will be a Cabinet of Talents, and I'm sure she would ask outstanding people to support her, provided they agree with her on certain basic principles. I certainly feel you, for instance, have more in common with her than with the Congress (O) [the opposing faction led by Morarji Desai].'

Mother may have been naïve to imagine that Mrs Gandhi really wanted to attract principled outsiders into her cabinet, or that Father might consider joining her; but she was not alone in thinking that the elections would produce a hung Parliament and a coalition government. That was the feeling among most of the national press and also at the hustings, where I was now active. I had been drawn into the Congress election campaign through Romesh and Raj Thapar and their coterie of left-wing, pro-Indira intellectuals, whom Father had long reviled as 'Commie fellow travellers'. I was helping to produce a mobile street play with music and dance, which travelled around Delhi on the back of a lorry, canvassing support for Indira and lampooning the Grand Alliance. I also addressed various Congress election meetings in the old city, where much political capital was made of my youthful rebellion against a misguided father.

Father's response to my political rebellion was tolerant, though he did remind me that, when he was my age, he had left his father's home to pursue socialist politics and that I might at least consider earning my own living. He was less tolerant about Mother's activities. She had retreated from the idea of joining the Congress, but spurred on by me she started canvassing in a personal capacity for Indira's candidate in Old Delhi. From Father's point of view, she could not have picked a worse candidate. Mrs Subhadra Joshi was closely linked with the pro-Moscow Communist Party, an ardent admirer of the Stalinist East German regime and the moving spirit behind the Indo-GDR Friendship Association. To have the wife of India's leading anti-Communist campaigning for her was too good a photo-opportunity to miss, and she leaked the story to the local press.

Father was already fighting a tough election campaign in his own constituency, where the news from Delhi came as a shock to his supporters. 'I hope you received my telegram regarding the press leakage,' Mother wrote to him. 'I thought it best to make a statement clarifying the issue. I have made it clear that I do not belong to any party and that I am going to work for you in Rajkot as well. I have had quite a few phone calls from friends expressing their admiration for you for being so tolerant and democratic.'

But the die was cast. Father wired back declining her offer to come and canvass for him on the grounds that her presence would only attract further negative media attention and keep the issue alive. Aware that she was being accused of political disloyalty, Mother wrote a circular letter defending her position and sent it to all their mutual friends. She began by attributing her support for Mrs Joshi to her secular values and her championship of Muslim minorities during communal riots, even when it meant risking her own life. 'In the last election,' she wrote, 'when she was contesting against a Jan Sangh candidate, her jeep was sabotaged and she met with a near-fatal "accident". Her head was crushed, and she had to undergo a series of operations. She has only half a skull, and if anything is thrown at her it could kill her. But this has not deterred her from fighting the Jan Sangh again this time.'

'I have great respect for Minoo,' she continued, 'and I admire his secular outlook. But I must confess that I was rather disillusioned that he was prepared to compromise his principles by joining hands with the Jan Sangh against his own better instincts. I have had strong feelings on the subject for some time, and knowing that this was going to be a crucial election for the country I felt I could not remain silent any longer.'

She went on to disown the press publicity she had attracted. 'It was certainly not of my choosing. I have avoided all public meetings and confined myself to door-to-door canvassing, which is the most exhausting and thankless part of a campaign.'

'I am facing enough criticism from my enemies,' she concluded, 'and I would be sad if close friends like you misunderstand me now.'

She also wrote to Father trying to soften the blow. 'I feel sad that I have been the cause of embarrassment to you, and I want you to know that I am most appreciative of your understanding. I admire and respect you for letting me have my own political convictions.' She concluded, with characteristic overstatement: 'I feel closer to you than I have ever been.'

Through all this, my own role was to encourage Mother to stop dithering and join the Congress. She might as well be hanged for a sheep as for a lamb, I argued; and I warned her that she would not be taken seriously by anyone if she sat on the fence. Eventually, she agreed to join the party the day after polling, when her action would not influence the election result in Father's constituency; nor could she be accused of opportunism because the election result would not yet be known for several days. None of us expected Mother's enrolment to get the publicity it did. It was front-page news in all the national papers, and the pro-Congress daily, the *National Herald*, ran it as its lead story with a huge, very glamorous picture of Mother on the front page.

In a press statement that day which was widely reported, Mother said her decision had grown out of her first-hand experience of door-to-door canvassing. 'My experience of the needs of the voters has convinced me that the policies of the Congress Party are essential at this moment . . . Secularism and democratic socialism are the only solution.' She ended with a public plea to Father. 'The essence of democracy is the coexistence of different points of view. In the 20th century, I see no reason why a wife must subscribe to the same political principles as her husband. My husband is a great democrat, and I am sure he will respect my right to my own opinions.'

She had also written a personal letter to Mrs Gandhi offering her support, and the response was warm.

Prime Minister's House,
New Delhi.

March 4, 1971.

Dear Shakuntala,

I hope I may call you this.

I have been deeply touched by your letter. If I may say so, your statement is dignified and restrained, yet firm. We need people like you in the Party.

I should like to meet you and your son when we are all less rushed.

With good wishes,
Yours sincerely,
Indira Gandhi

Closer to home, feelings were more divided about Mother's actions. I, of course, was delighted. Mother had at long last made a public declaration of independence from Father; she had claimed the attention of the whole country; and she had been congratulated by our charismatic leader herself.

The future looked inviting. There was talk of Mother being rewarded with a seat in the Rajya Sabha, the indirectly elected upper house of Parliament, and in time possibly even a junior ministerial post. Given her enormous success in the low-profile electioneering she had been doing in Delhi, there seemed no reason why she shouldn't shine in national politics. Everything seemed possible; and best of all, I would be free to return to Oxford with her financial backing.

Our euphoria was short-lived. One week after Mother joined the Congress with such a fanfare, the election results were announced. It was a landslide for Indira and a rout for the Opposition, many of whose leaders lost their own seats. Among them was Father, a result that none of us, including him, had thought conceivable. It was the first and last election he ever lost in the course of a forty-year political career.

Ironically, Father's defeat was more of a blow to Mother than to him. At one stroke, it wiped out her value for the Congress and Mrs Gandhi. She was no longer the political asset she had been as the principled wife of an even more principled and formidable Opposition leader. Instead, she began to look increasingly like a political turncoat who had served her purpose and was now dispensable.

Father was in Bombay licking his wounds. In his public statements, he made light of Mother and me joining the Congress; but in private his silence was deafening. 'I have not had a line from you,' Mother wrote reproachfully, 'and I am really sad that you are being so aloof. I only acted according to my convictions, and I do hope you will in time see my point of view and forgive me if my political views do not tally with yours. I have the greatest respect for you, and I was so happy to read your statement to the press. It was gentlemanly and sporting and worthy of you.'

A month after the general election, Father announced his resignation as President of the decimated Swatantra Party. He said that he wished to take responsibility for the party's election defeat. Mother had hoped he would return to Parliament in a by-election, but he made it clear that he had no desire to be part of an Opposition rump in a House dominated by Indira.

The immediate consequence of Father's decision was that we were expected to vacate the large Delhi mansion on Tughlak Road that had been his official residence as Leader of the Opposition. Mother was dismayed at the thought. She loved the large, rambling house, its huge garden and, most of all, the status it represented. She was also terrified by the prospect of returning to Bombay and the collective disapproval of her old circle there, most of whom saw her championship of Indira as an act of betrayal. While Father himself was so far not overtly hostile, she could hardly expect him to take up cudgels on her behalf. What had been planned as a declaration of independence would end in an ignominious rout if Mother and I skulked back to Bombay with our tails between our legs.

And so we conceived a plan to stay on in Delhi. Mother would canvass Mrs Gandhi and those around her for an official job, which would carry with it not just a salary, but the much coveted status symbol of official housing. We were still too politically naïve to realize that promises of loyalty meant as little as socialist rhetoric among the sycophantic courtiers with whom Indira was now surrounding herself.

The 27th of April 1971 was my parents' silver wedding anniversary, but they spent it apart. 'What a pity we will not be together for it,' Mother wrote to Father a week before. 'I suppose there is no possibility of your coming up to Delhi round about then.' She went on to complain bitterly about the financially straitened circumstances in which his meagre remittances had left her. 'I really do not know how I am going to manage unless you send me more money. I do feel you should not leave me in this economic plight . . . It makes me sad to think that you are so unconcerned. Surely you are not going to victimise me for my political convictions by putting economic pressure on me.'

Father responded with a generous anniversary gift and Mother, somewhat mollified, wrote happily: 'I shall save the money for a rainy day.' He maintained that there was no question of 'putting economic pressure' on her, but argued quite reasonably that he could hardly be expected to foot the bills for her and me to stay on in Delhi in Mrs Gandhi's service. I had just started work on a biography of her, at the suggestion of our good friend Yvonne Hamish Hamilton, wife of the publisher, who had been staying with us on a visit. Mother, meanwhile, had been canvassing for the Congress in the Delhi municipal elections and was also busy with voluntary work for the Prime Minister's Relief Fund for the refugees who were flooding across the border from what was still East Pakistan but soon to become Bangladesh.

We were in for a long, hot and very stressful summer. After much lobbying, Mother was offered the job of Member-Secretary of a new government Committee on the Status of Women. But it took several months to process the appointment through various official channels, and it was a period of constant anxiety and suspense. Meanwhile, she remained without an independent income and continued to harry Father for funds. She also continued, rather tactlessly, to extol Indira's virtues to him.

'You must admit that Mrs. Gandhi has been a master statesman in the way she has handled the Bangladesh problem. I do not want to irritate you, Minoo dear, but I wish I could convince you that she is the only leader who can keep the country together. Please do try and be objective about her. I admire her very much. She is so clear-thinking and a woman of action. These are qualities which I feel would also appeal to you.'

A month later, she was admonishing him again. 'I wish you would not continue to be so abusive of Indira. Firstly, it is in bad taste, and secondly, I happen to have great admiration for her. She has developed into a remarkable person in one year. Earlier she was inhibited and lacked self-confidence . . . I feel so sad that you have closed your mind about her . . . Can you imagine what would have happened to this country if the members of the Grand Alliance were in power? I am certain, with your high standards of integrity, you would have had no truck with them . . . I do believe that you have more in common with Indira than with Morarji Desai and that jing-bang lot.'

Given the depth of Father's personal and ideological aversion to Indira, such appeals could only have rubbed salt in his wounds, especially when they were coupled with requests for money. 'Since I have not got a job yet,' Mother wrote in June, 'I do feel that you should help me out. If I were in Bombay, Zareer and I would be costing you much more. I am sad that you should take such a tough attitude. To put such a squeeze on me financially when you know I have no money is not a very ethical attitude, and I am sure you will not do such a thing.'

'Zareer and I are trying to live as economically as possible,' she assured him, and added with characteristic exaggeration: 'We have cut out all luxury food items like chicken. I am also retrenching the staff. We can easily do without the cook, as in any case our food is eggs and vegetables for both meals.'

She was equally imaginative with the truth in begging him to pay for new tyres for the Delhi car. 'Today I escaped a very nasty accident,' she wrote. 'Both tyres on one side of the car burst and the car overturned ... I have decided that from tomorrow I shall travel by scooter [auto rickshaw]. It is far better than to risk one's life. Your attitude just defeats me.' Whether or not he swallowed this somewhat improbable accident, Father responded by paying for new tyres. 'You seem to be so harassed with money problems,' he wrote, 'that you are needlessly developing a persecution complex. I'm not being a bit "tough" with you. On the contrary, I have agreed to every request you have made. So please relax and don't do foolish things like sacking the cook or cutting out chicken! You'll have to pay much bigger doctors' bills later!'

Mother spent the summer of 1971 organizing a series of fundraising musical and dinner events at various foreign embassies in aid of the Bangladesh refugees. The funds she collected were not enormous but significant enough to justify visits to Mrs Gandhi to present her with the cheques. She also wrote to Father haranguing him about the fact that his party was the only one in the country not to condemn Pakistani genocide, allegedly because the Americans were still supporting Pakistan's military regime.

'I cannot tell you how disappointed I am that you have not yet said anything about Bangladesh. Surely your pro-American line should not make you inhuman. As for the USA, I don't think anyone has any use in this country for them. They have at last been exposed ... The world today is threatened by American imperialism and Chinese Communism. A plague on both their houses! ... My letters are nothing but politics,' she admitted in the same letter, 'but I have faith in your courage to do some re-thinking about the USA. Please say something about Bangladesh and condemn Pakistan. It would be a good idea if you broke away from the Swatantra Party on this issue. Don't let "the old man" [C. Rajagopalachari] drag you down with him in his insidious and unprincipled policies. If you had the guts to write *Socialism Reconsidered*, I am certain you will not be party to the unprincipled Swatantra stand on Bangladesh.'

In fact, Father's reluctance to jump on the Bangladesh bandwagon was far from unprincipled. He had consistently fought for better relations with Pakistan, even if it meant India giving up Kashmir; and he felt that Mrs Gandhi was being typically opportunist in riding a chauvinistic wave of jubilation over the break-up of Pakistan.

He was also somewhat alarmed by Mother's accounts of how she was labouring in the heat of a Delhi summer to collect funds and clothing for Bangladesh. 'I am sorry to hear that your kidney trouble has recurred,' he wrote. 'I wish you would appreciate that you have done more than enough for the refugees, and making your health suffer is no way of helping the cause. This is an international problem of a long-term nature, and no one human being whatever he does can change it.'

As the summer dragged on without Mother's job materializing, Father became increasingly concerned that he would be liable for her failure to vacate the Delhi house and for the large arrears of penalty rent that were accumulating. He urged her to pack up and return to Bombay, but she was convinced that it would be disastrous for her to go back empty-handed; she had to hold on till Mrs Gandhi rewarded her loyalty.

As the months went by, there were new strains on their relationship. Friends reported back to Father that Mother and I were constantly singing Indira's praises and running him down. More serious were two press reports about Mother's non-political activities. One was captioned 'Mrs Masani fears danger to life' and reported that Mother had asked for police protection against mafia bosses in the antiques trade who were gunning for her because of her support for new legislation to curb their activities. As I recall, the threats had less to do with the legislation than with the fact that Mother's successful 'treasure hunts' had annoyed some of the bigger dealers who were after the same antiques.

The other report, 'Masani's Wife in Land-Grab!', was about Mother and several other prominent Indira supporters having jumped the queue for land allocations at hugely concessional rates in one of Delhi's most exclusive residential areas. The allocations were cancelled, but the breath of scandal lingered. Father increasingly felt that we were an embarrassment to him. He was also strongly opposed to my returning to Oxford to do a doctorate, especially if it meant Mother had to foot the bill and would then badger him for more funds.

Mother was concerned about what she perceived as Father's growing coldness towards her. But with my encouragement, she made whatever political capital she could from it in Congress circles, complaining that she was being victimized by him for her loyalty to Mrs Gandhi. Among those she lobbied was D.P. Mishra, the powerful Congress boss of Madhya Pradesh, who volunteered to try and mediate with Father. 'Although our politics have come to differ,' he wrote to Father, 'yet I have brotherly feelings for you. Mrs. Masani has met me a number of times, and from her talk it seemed to me that she has even now not a trace of ill will against you. I know that I am treading on delicate ground, yet as an old friend I do feel that I may be of some help to both of you.' Father's reply was polite but noncommittal.

Mother's appointment as Secretary of the new Committee on the Status of Women came through at last in September after six months of suspense. Mrs Gandhi also arranged for me to get a small scholarship from one of her educational trusts, and that made it possible for me to take up my place at St Antony's College, Oxford. I was going to do my doctoral thesis on the Congress Socialist Party, of which Father had been a founder-leader in the 1930s. There was a deliberate irony in this decision of mine to explore the socialist past on which he had so vehemently turned his back.

Mother put a brave face on my departure, though she felt it keenly. Her estrangement from Father had coincided with a major breach with her own family. In her anxiety to secure an independent income, she had filed a lawsuit against her brothers-in-law as Executors of her mother's still undivided estate. Though almost a decade had passed since Nanna's death, her will was bogged down in a convoluted family stalemate. The problem stemmed as much from the complicated provisions of the will as from the fractious nature of the Srivastava offspring. The main sticking point was Nanna's bequest of her most valuable asset, the family's Kanpur home 'Kailash', named after her, to her two sons, provided they agreed to share it equally and provided they also jointly paid off all the death duties and liabilities of the estate, leaving the daughters to inherit the rest without encumbrance.

Nanna should have known her sons better than to expect them to cooperate with such a grudging gift; indeed, Father harshly maintained that it was a typically malign attempt on her part to divide and rule from beyond the grave. Certainly, both brothers felt aggrieved and made things as difficult as possible. The elder, Sonny, who was in occupation of the house, regarded it as his birthright and refused to allow his younger brother, Hari, to set foot in it. And both brothers balked at paying the liabilities of the estate. Mother maintained, with considerable legal and moral justification, that the brothers' failure to comply meant that the entire estate, including 'Kailash', should now be divided among the sisters; but the other sisters remained reluctant to force an open split in the family.

Relationships were further soured by Mother's quarrel with one of the Executors, Uncle Gogu, over his criticism of her political defection to Indira. Aunt Sarala's husband had been very critical of Mother's decision, egged on by me, to join Mrs Gandhi's election campaign, especially while Father was Leader of the Opposition. Mother retaliated with a vengeance; and amid the heat and dust of a scorching Delhi summer, the row blazed to epic proportions worthy of the Mahabharata.

To Mother's somewhat disingenuous surprise, her sister sided wholly with her husband; and she was a formidable adversary. At my behest, Mother wrote Sarala Mausi a conciliatory letter, but she couldn't bring herself to make a full apology, and her sister would accept nothing less.

'I have known for a long time now,' Sarala Mausi wrote in reply, 'that you do not like Gogu and have been maligning him. . . . I hope that this strange attitude of yours is only the result of a disturbed state of mind and . . . you will realise where the truth lies.'

She went on to twist her knife in another emotional wound: 'As you know, I have always wanted to be close to you and have on many occasions tried to help your relationship with Minoo, despite your telling me that he dislikes me. Let me add here that we hardly know each other, and whatever superficial contact I have with him is only through you, so it surprises me why he should have any animus against me.'

Mother was faced with the demand for an unqualified public apology or a sentence of excommunication. With characteristic bravado, she chose the latter and, as though relations weren't bad enough, filed a lawsuit against her brothers-in-law for maladministration of her mother's estate, of which they were Executors. In the months that followed, she did make sporadic attempts to break the ice, but Sarala Mausi would have none of it. 'It is not correct to say third parties have made mischief,' she replied curtly to one such overture. 'On the contrary, you have made serious and baseless allegations against us in your lawsuit and elsewhere. At the moment, I feel no purpose would be served in meeting.'

A few months later, Mother elicited an even more terse reply when she sent her sister a note requesting the return of an infant's weighing machine she claimed she had lent her two decades ago. 'I certainly do not have any weighing-machine of yours,' Sarala Mausi retorted. 'I also do not recollect your having lent me one for Bhartu [her younger son] nearly 22 years ago when he was born. For, even if you did, you most certainly would have taken it back, or I myself would have returned it to you, as I am not in the habit of keeping borrowed things.'

The dispute escalated into a public war of words waged across the drawing rooms of Delhi: Mother's sisters condemned her as financially greedy and mentally unbalanced, while she denounced them as jealous and deeply prejudiced by their hostility to Mrs Gandhi. Both sides were undoubtedly damaged by the feud. Alarmed by Mother's emotional isolation as my departure for Oxford approached, I pleaded with her not to fight a war on two fronts, taking on Father and her own family at the same time. But, flushed with the self-importance of her new job, she felt she was riding too high in Mrs Gandhi's favour to contemplate an abject surrender to her sister. And so the quarrel raged on for another decade.

Mother's initial response to her new job was full of enthusiasm and optimism. One of her first engagements was a seminar on women's rights organized in Kashmir by one of Father's voluntary organizations. She thoroughly enjoyed being the centre of attention there and sounded particularly pleased about having been more popular with the younger participants than Aunt Mehra, who was heckled when she delivered her paper.

It looked as though Mother's long-drawn campaign to hang on to her official bungalow would at last be successful. She was hoping to have half the house allocated as the committee's office, an ideal arrangement from her point of view. She had already received invitations to visit abroad from women's organizations in Belgium, East Germany and Yugoslavia. And in her initial euphoria she even seemed pleased with her committee Chairman, a Congress politician from West Bengal. 'Mrs. Guha seems a very nice person,' Mother wrote to me in Oxford. 'I think we should get on well. She said she would have no objection to converting half this house into an office.'

My life, too, seemed to have got off to an excellent start at St Antony's, which was a cosmopolitan, intellectual paradise after the grim isolation of my undergraduate years. 'My rooms are very nice,' I assured Mother, 'except for the fact that I have to share a bathroom with five others ... The college food is excellent and one has every facility – quite different from undergraduate life. One meets so many interesting people, all working on interesting projects.' With Mother's encouragement, I had also started psychoanalysis twice a week in London, arranged through a psychiatrist friend of the family. The idea was to try and overcome my shyness and strong sense of social inhibition.

Whether it was the analysis or the change of college, my social life blossomed at St Antony's. The five years I spent there were the happiest of my life. I made lots of friends, some very close. For the first time, I felt part of a community. Life was a round of parties or long, convivial evenings in the college buttery, followed by intimate, late-night conversations in our rooms. Although that 'special relationship' still eluded me, I was increasingly open about my sexuality. It was the decade of gay liberation and I joined in enthusiastically. My hair, carefully groomed, grew to shoulder length, and my wardrobe became increasingly flamboyant and androgynous.

Politically, my rebellion against Father found new channels. I threw myself into college politics, became JCR President and campaigned for St Antony's to disinvest in South Africa. I made myself the bête noire of the Warden, Raymond Carr, by fighting for student representation on the college governing body and then using it to expose his links with the Franco government in Spain. It was all very exciting and exhilarating; and the only cloud on my horizon was Mother's very precarious situation in Delhi.

Her early optimism about her new job did not last long. The honeymoon with her Chairman was over in a month. 'Dr. Guha is nice,' she wrote, 'but inclined to be a little dominating. I shall let her have all the publicity (which she is rather keen on), so long as I am free to do the work.' She complained in the next breath that the Chairman was overworking her. A month later, she added: 'She is very sly and distorts whatever is said to her. I think she is resentful that people make more of me than of her.' A fortnight later, relations had hit rock bottom. 'Dr. Guha is a disaster,' Mother wrote. 'She is very underhand and is I know trying to discredit me so that she can encroach on my duties. She made me write the minutes of the meeting four times before she allowed me to finalise them. Hence the delay for which I am now being blamed.'

Mother also complained bitterly about the 'inferior' secretarial staff she had been given by the Ministry for Social Welfare, under whose aegis the committee had been set up. 'Each letter I dictate takes an hour, as it is re-typed so many times. Eventually I give up and sign what comes.'

The committee's press launch proved a disaster because the Chairman refused to begin proceedings until the minister's arrival, and he was two hours late. 'I understand that Mrs. Gandhi and Haksar [P.N. Haksar, Indira Gandhi's powerful Principal Secretary] are both upset by the poor start we have made,' Mother worried. 'The Chairman is so clever and sly that she goes round saying that it was all my fault.'

Relations between Mother and her family were also going from bad to worse as her lawsuit dragged on. 'Please be careful of Malati [her younger sister in Bombay],' she wrote warning Father. 'A regular vilification campaign against me has been started by the family. Padmaja Naidu [a close friend of Mrs Gandhi's] is being fed with all kinds of stories about me, and she is spitting fire . . . The story is being spread that I am a secret agent of yours planted by you in the Congress Party!'

To me she wrote with even greater agitation. 'Padmaja is on the warpath, and it appears she has assured them that she will destroy me. What is even worse is that they are trying to get people to poison Mr. Haksar's mind against me. I feel very alone and vulnerable and really don't know how to counteract this vicious propaganda . . . I am afraid a number of women are annoyed at my appointment and are lapping up this filth . . . I miss you very much. It was so wonderful having you here to advise and restore my perspective.'

I wrote back reminding her that her post was secure for two years and advising that she concentrate on producing a good report to give the lie to all these aspersions against her. I also wrote enthusiastically about Mrs Gandhi's visit to Oxford to receive an honorary degree, describing how glamorous she looked out of her austere politicians' weeds. 'The ceremony was very impressive, in the 17th century Sheldonian Theatre, with beautiful organ music. She looked so beautiful and girlish. She has dyed her hair and was wearing a black silk sari with a cerise border and a cerise academic gown. I was surprised to see that she also wore two strings of beautiful pearls!'

The high point was my unexpected luck in meeting her. 'There was an "Aid for Indira" student demonstration outside, and as I was leaving I suddenly found myself face to face with her as she went to meet the demonstrators. I can't tell you how warm she was. She spotted me immediately in the crowd and stopped to ask how I was and whether everything was all right. She conveys more warmth with one smile than other people do in hours. She was a great success here – very poised and aristocratic and yet so natural and girlish. She was obviously far more at home with the demonstrators than at the solemn ceremony.'

My glowing report and Mother's delighted response are a reminder of how genuinely besotted we were by Indira's charms. The Prime Minister's visit was part of a whirlwind tour of Western capitals to drum up support for her hardening line against Pakistan over Bangladesh. Coping with the serious refugee crisis had given her and India the moral high ground, and she made the most of it in preparing for a military solution.

Driven partly by their political differences and even more by financial bickering, my parents' marriage was by now in serious difficulties. 'Daddy is being very aloof and tough about money matters,' Mother complained to me in November 1971. 'I think his attitude towards me is hardening, and I feel almost certain that we are heading for a divorce. I hear gossip that he is involved with X [the person he had wanted to marry as far back as 1960]. He has stopped writing altogether.' She wrote to him suggesting that she wanted to spend Christmas and the New Year with him in Bombay, but he replied that he had already made arrangements to be away for a seminar and that she should make her own plans.

She decided nevertheless to visit Bombay for a few days on committee work prior to Father's departure. 'When you are in Bombay, you must try and win him over,' I urged her. 'Avoid any political arguments with him. I think a divorce would be inadvisable at this stage, as it might damage your career.' It was obvious by then that the ex-wife of an ex-politician would have little to offer Mrs Gandhi. I reassured Mother that Father had spoken of her with great affection on a recent visit to London. 'He must be basically very lonely and frustrated in Bombay,' I wrote, 'but is too proud to admit that he needs you, which is why he is behaving in this cold way.'

I was also extremely anxious about Mother on her own in Delhi, now that the long-drawn confrontation with Pakistan had escalated into a full-scale war. 'I heard on the radio last night that Agra has been bombed . . . What worrying times we are living through. The Western press has become hysterically anti-Indian and brands Mrs. G as a warmonger! I'm glad she is ignoring them.' Two weeks later, Mrs Gandhi ended the war on her own terms with a unilateral ceasefire after the Pakistani army in East Bengal surrendered. She was at the zenith of her power and popularity, having given independent India its first ever military victory and decisively shattered the regional rival, Pakistan.

Mother ignored my advice about being conciliatory on her Bombay trip. 'I managed to see just a few people,' she wrote on her return to Delhi, 'and I had terrific arguments with all of them, as they were all being critical of Mrs. Gandhi, and it made my blood boil. I just cannot understand how stupid and blind they are. I am so glad I do not live in Bombay. I find the atmosphere suffocating and oppressive. I am afraid I cannot keep cool when people just indulge in abuse and do not argue intelligently. How can they deny the fact that Mrs. Gandhi has handled the [Bangladesh] situation brilliantly? I have developed such personal loyalty to her that I see red when I talk to this useless and decadent crowd.'

Father had been confined to bed during Mother's visit, as a rest-cure for his chronic sciatica. 'I cannot quite decipher his attitude,' Mother wrote. 'He is cold and aloof, and everything he says and does is very calculated . . . I wonder what he is plotting, for I have the uneasy feeling that he has got something up his sleeve.'

Soon after her return to Delhi, she fell seriously ill with a kidney infection followed by flu, and her illness coincided with an escalation of hostilities between her and the Chairman. She had convened a special meeting of the committee in the presence of the government ministers concerned, at which she had hoped to thrash out in the open her disagreements with the Chairman. She had been particularly hopeful about the backing of the senior minister, Siddharth Shankar Ray, a handsome, urbane and anglicized figure, with whom she had a particular rapport. But her illness was a major setback. 'As a result of my not being there,' she lamented, 'everything went wrong. The other members are so weak that Dr. Guha, the chairman, got her way and all the decisions I had earlier got taken were reversed.'

Her initial optimism about the committee producing a groundbreaking report had evaporated. 'It seems an effort in futility – nobody wants to work, and the way we are setting about preparing the report is so unimaginative. We are just collecting statistics and data from various institutions and compiling them. We did not really need to create a committee for this purpose . . . I would not mind relaxing and taking things easy, but I know that later I will be blamed for not being an effective secretary . . . I feel I am being asked to do a job with my hands and feet tied.' She was particularly incensed that the Chairman had been critical of her trip to Bombay and had got the committee to agree that all future travel should be only with the Chairman's permission.

'I am still under the influence of Saturn, and the future looks grim,' Mother complained, referring to the latest astrological prediction. She had hoped to get her lawsuit heard at the Delhi High Court, thus avoiding the notoriously corrupt courts in her home state of UP, where her brothers would have more influence. But the Executors had contested the jurisdiction of the Delhi court; and after four months of arguments, the judge in the case was replaced before deciding on this preliminary issue. The prospects of winning her long-awaited inheritance seemed as remote as ever, and that made her all the more dependent on the government job that was also under threat.

'I seem to be fighting on so many fronts,' she wrote despondently, 'that the will to fight is slowly being destroyed. Sometimes, at the end of an exhausting day, I begin to wonder if there is any point to all this. The only consolation is that you are well and happy, and I think that keeps me going.' It also left me racked with guilt about my carefree Oxford existence while she seemed to be battling against such odds.

It was becoming increasingly clear that she had neither the physical nor the emotional stamina for a career-politician. She took everything very personally and worried about it incessantly. Having her office in the house did not help, and she spent her evenings brooding on the day's problems. Ever since the sisterly rivalries of her childhood, she had got on far better with men than with women; and it was an unfortunate irony that her job involved working predominantly with her own sex.

With Mother now on the verge of a physical and nervous breakdown, I decided it was time to intervene. I wrote her a concerned but firm letter, strongly advising that if she could not take the heat of committee politics, she should resign and get out of it. 'It is folly,' I remonstrated, 'to overwork yourself to the point where you fall ill just when the most important meetings are due . . . There is no reason on earth why you should make yourself a martyr to this job.' I went on to advise a measure of detachment about the petty faction-fighting. 'Stand up for your rights,

The Masanis arrive in Brazil, 1948.

The Ambassador's residence, Brazil, 1948, lavishly decorated by Mother with Indian artefacts.

Mother posing with her children's book about Prime Minister Nehru, Rio de Janeiro, 1949.

Mother and I, Rio de Janeiro, 1949.

Father and Mother at a fancy dress ball, Rio de Janeiro, 1949.

A picnic near Bombay. From left to right: Father, Mother, Thelly and Jeh Tata.

Mother at a dinner party, flanked by Kishore Uncle (left) and Uncle John (Aunt Malati's partner), Bombay, 1956.

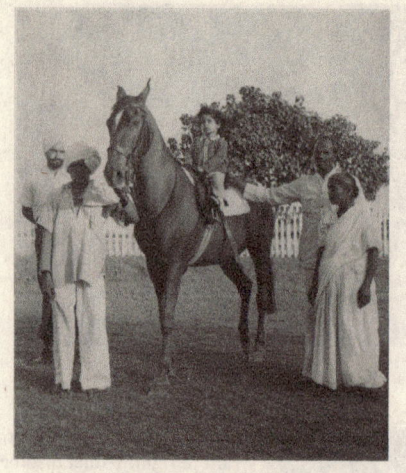

My first pony.

Me sulking with Father.

Nanna with all her grandchildren, Kanpur, 1960. Aunt Sarala and Mother on the left and Aunt Queenie on the right. I am the plump bespectacled boy standing second from right. Meera is on the mat, far right.

Mother on a Swatantra Party platform, seated beside one of the party's new stars, Ayesha of Jaipur (Maharani Gayatri Devi), 1960s.

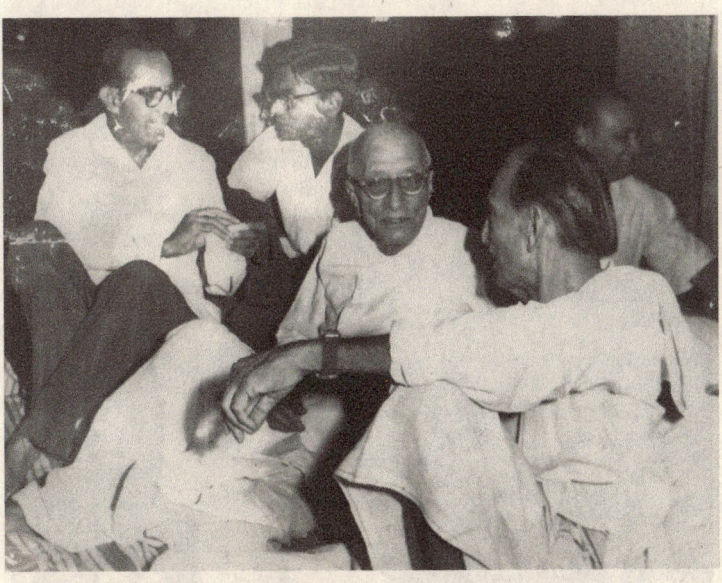

Minoo Masani (extreme left) at an election meeting in his Rajkot constituency with C. Rajagopalachari or Rajaji (centre) and Acharya J.B. Kripalani (right).

Mother in her Tughlak Road office as Member-Secretary of the Committee on the Status of Women, Delhi, 1973.

Mother in London, 1979, with David and me.

Mother at my London home, 1986, with my
dogs, Toffee and Elsa.

In my London garden with David, me and my
dog Sandy, 1998, the year before she died.

Two octogenarians: Father with his old friend J.R.D. Tata, 1986.

Father welcoming the liberal economic reforms of Dr Manmohan Singh (right), then India's Finance Minister, 1992.

but don't quarrel and don't take other people's attacks on you too seriously. Everyone in a responsible position has to put up with this kind of sniping – including Mrs. Gandhi . . . With your belief in *Vedanta*, it should not be too difficult to cultivate the necessary detachment. This is only one episode in your life, and you shouldn't give it undue importance, even if it doesn't work out.'

I also wrote to Father in an attempt to soften his attitude and prepare the ground for Mother's return to Bombay if she resigned her job. It was a difficult letter to write. I began with Mother's poor health, which I attributed to her 'working round the clock for the Committee'. 'This is basically because she is insecure,' I wrote, 'and feels very dependent on this job.' I went on to explain that her insecurity stemmed from Father's attitude to her 'becoming increasingly cool and indifferent'. 'She has a deep affection for you,' I assured him, 'and would like very much to be close to you. I feel that it would make an enormous difference to her if you were to show your concern for her and let her feel that there will always be a place for her in your life and home . . . After all, there is no reason why you both cannot have independent careers and yet give each other the understanding and companionship we all need'.

Lest this plea for a marriage of equals sound patronizing and disingenuous, I realized it was time to eat some humble pie. 'I know that there have been mistakes on both sides,' I assured Father, 'and that you have both hurt each other in different ways. I realise, too, that I myself may have contributed to your differences and, if so, I can only say that it was not intentional and that I sincerely regret it.'

Father's reply, though affectionate and candid, was not what I had hoped for. He referred at the outset to the distant marital crisis of 1960 when, according to him, Mother and he had agreed on a divorce, but she had 'changed her mind and resisted the thought in a highly emotional way'. 'Because of my concern for her health and state of mind, I gave in to her wishes,' he said, 'but it did not work out and we never got close to each other again.'

And then came the crunch. 'Things were drifting along fairly quietly till the 1971 parliamentary elections when Mummy and you publicly took up a posture which showed a complete lack of consideration for my feelings and my position and which has hurt me deeply. As you know, unlike many of our friends who have shown their annoyance, I have kept up, both in public and in private social life, an attitude of good-natured tolerance. But this does not mean that it does not matter . . .

'I frankly don't think that Mummy and I can really hit it off if we were to try to stay together again. The result may well be disastrous. For one thing, the gulf between our attitudes to things and people is much too wide. When Mummy was here for a week . . . it was impossible for her not to get emotional and excited the moment certain topics came up. She had an ugly row with a bedside visitor of mine, and she herself told me she would retire to her room as soon as any of my friends turned up.'

His conclusion justified Mother's worst fears. 'The sensible thing,' he urged, 'would be, if Mummy could take it cheerfully or philosophically, to make the separation formal . . . I do think it is time she built her own life along her own ideas.' And he went on to shift the responsibility for her future happiness on to my shoulders. 'I was sad for Mummy when you decided to return to Oxford . . . Considering how close she and you have always been, I have no doubt she would not be in this state of health or mind if you were with her in Delhi.'

Mother's troubles on the committee front were also coming to a head. I had advised her either to make peace with the Chairman or to confront her openly on a point of principle and make it a resigning issue. But now she complained that most of the other committee members were taking advantage of the situation to go their own way. They were abusing their position to clock up inflated allowances for travel and other expenses, especially for the sub-committees for which they were responsible. Mother's position was weakened by the fact that her chief ally, the senior minister Siddhartha Shankar Ray, was now busy masterminding the Congress election campaign in West Bengal.

Coming a couple of months after her military triumph over Bangladesh, the elections for state legislatures across the country ended in a landslide for Indira Gandhi, including in former Opposition strongholds like West Bengal. Ray relinquished his cabinet post to become the state's Chief Minister; and this left Mother at the mercy of the junior minister Dr Nurul Hasan, a left-wing academic, who she felt was determined to use the committee's funds and patronage to favour his own friends and associates.

As if all this were not enough, Mother added to her list of woes: 'The only male member of the committee is making a tremendous pass at me, and when he realises that I have no interest in him I am sure he will also turn against me.' I continued to counsel 'the maximum tact and diplomacy', pointing out that this was the only way to overcome a degree of natural envy and resentment among those who felt that she had been parachuted in as the PM's favourite.

In the midst of all this, Mother suddenly announced that there had been an attempt on her life, with somebody sabotaging her car. 'The driver walked out on me under very suspicious circumstances when I was about to go out to dinner,' she wrote, so she had decided to drive herself. 'I was returning home when the car blew up. Luckily for me, a couple of young people were in the car behind me. They saw my car swerve and hit the curb. I became unconscious. They pulled me out of the car and disconnected all the wires, so that the car did not catch fire. They took me home, and one of them later came to see me and told me that I should report this to the police as it was definitely a "cooked up job". The garage who checked up the car also confirmed this.'

The mystery of the exploding car, like so many others in Mother's life, was never solved. Her own theories oscillated wildly between blaming her estranged brother-in-law or a gangland boss from the antiques mafia. The far simpler explanation that it might have been a vengeful prank by a disgruntled driver was never considered; at a distance of thousands of miles I was unable to verify any of the facts. Mother had always been prone to exaggeration and conspiracy theories. From now on, these would sometimes verge on clinical paranoia, and I have no doubt this greatly damaged her relations with friends, family and colleagues.

At the time, however, I was still fairly credulous about most of what she told me, and I was beside myself with anxiety when I got her letter. 'Advise you immediately report car incident to police', I cabled her from Oxford. 'I cannot understand why you have not reported it to the police,' I exclaimed in a follow-up letter. 'I feel that you must have it investigated at the highest level and, if necessary, see Mirdha [Ramniwas Mirdha, a senior Minister for Home Affairs, with whom Mother was friendly] about it. Surely it shouldn't be difficult for the police to find the driver and question him. You *must* ask the police for protection. After all, you have witnesses and the testimony of the garage to bear out your case.'

As far as I know, she never reported it, and the incident was quietly forgotten, to be replaced by anger and alarm about Father's cool response to my overtures on her behalf. He had sent her a copy of his letter to me, and it confirmed all her previous suspicions that he was plotting against her. 'He is a very cold-blooded person,' she wrote, 'and we must never underestimate him. He never reacts on the spur of the moment. He waits for an opportunity.' She felt he was having it both ways by proclaiming in public that he had no objection to her having her own politics. 'This afternoon I addressed a meeting organised by all the women's organisations in Delhi. When introducing me, it was mentioned that I was the wife of the democratic leader, Minoo Masani, who had upheld the principles of a true democrat by allowing his wife and son to belong to another party. I could have laughed!'

She pointed out, correctly, that Father wanted me to pay the price for what had happened, and she insisted, generously, that there was no question of my having to rush back to help her. 'You must not worry about me. I am slowly coming to the conclusion that, apart from you, nothing else matters very much in this world to me, and it would make me very unhappy if you had to do something that affects your career and your studies... These are the best years of your life, and you must get the maximum out of them. If I know you are happy, half my troubles are over.'

Such assurances were magnanimous, but they could not fail to make me feel extremely guilty, when they arrived with a mounting catalogue of the disasters that were befalling her in my absence. 'I seem to be up against a sea of troubles,' she wrote a few days later. 'The influence of Saturn is very strong as far as my stars go. Last week, while going to a meeting with a girl from my office, the car met with an accident and was smashed up. We both had a miraculous escape. I got a head injury and she dislocated her arm. Yesterday I was in a hurry and went straight into a closed door and knocked out three front teeth! I wonder what is going to happen next.'

She assured me in the next breath that she was sorry to be such a source of worry to me and wanted me to enjoy myself at Oxford. I was beginning to grow a little sceptical about her never-ending tales of woe. 'I do feel that, Saturn notwithstanding, one makes one's own destiny and one should never despair,' I reminded her firmly, and went on to recommend a good dentist for her teeth and a good driver for her car. 'Life is full of ups and downs,' I concluded hopefully, 'and I'm sure things will improve soon.'

Father followed up his initial suggestion about a separation with a direct appeal to me to intercede with Mother to get her agreement. 'I should like to think you as a young and modern person will agree that the only civilised way . . . is to take a divorce by consent, without bitterness and throwing mud at one another. The alternatives are to separate and remain friends or to remain technically married and estranged . . . Now that Mummy and I have drifted apart to this extent, the right thing would be to face realities and bring formal relations in line with actual ones.' He referred to differences of temperament and to having 'a somewhat Western mind which is cut and dried and likes things neat and tidy'. Others, like the Srivastavas, he said, preferred 'to leave things vague, evade facing unpleasant issues and decisions and leave loose ends', leading to 'needless bitterness later'.

Mother's strategy was to resist at all costs a divorce by mutual consent and to put the onus on Father of being the guilty party if he really wanted to end the marriage. She suggested that he give her grounds to sue him for desertion or adultery or both, a course which he was not willing to consider because of the scandal and opprobrium attached to it. Otherwise, she proposed leaving the status quo undisturbed, unless he had a specific reason for wishing to alter it, namely, a desire to remarry. 'The impression you have given Zareer and me,' she wrote to him, 'is that the main reason for the rift between us is political. If, on the other hand, you are having a relationship with somebody else whom you now want to marry, out of fairness to me you should say so frankly.'

She seemed particularly offended by his reference to their relationship having lacked 'intimacy' since 1960. 'I really wonder how many marriages after 25 years are founded on "intimacies",' she wrote to him. 'And yet these marriages are very happy ones. After a while these "intimacies" are less and less important as one ages, and what really counts is understanding and friendship. Our marriage in a way has a better chance of surviving now that we are living apart and do not get in each other's hair ... I only wish we would not discuss politics when we are together, and this is very easily avoidable since we see so little of each other. If loving somebody and having different political views is being typically a Srivastava, I plead guilty to that charge.'

It was about this time that Aunt Mehra got involved in my parents' differences. She had thoroughly disapproved of Mother and me joining the Congress and tended to treat us as errant and rebellious children, which in some respects we were. We, for our part, viewed her as Father's spy in Delhi. She had recently been passed over for the post of Director-General of All India Radio because of the government's political bias against her; and she had opted for early retirement in protest. Mother was convinced that she was lonely, frustrated and determined to get her claws into her brother by breaking up his marriage.

As with so many of Mother's exaggerations, this had a kernel of truth. I later came across a bundle of letters between brother and sister, in which my parents' divorce was the main subject. 'Yesterday I went to see S,' Mehra wrote to Father in April 1972. 'We talked of various things including her doctor's verdict that unless she rests and takes things easy she will die of coronary thrombosis within two years.' Moving on to their marriage, she said she had advised Mother 'that there was no point in continuing as at present, and it was best to have things clear and well defined'. But Mother, she wrote, had demurred, insisting that 'there should be no need to break up something that had lasted for 25 years'.

'The only justification,' Mother had told her, 'would be if you [Father] wanted to get married again, and you had not said so. I got the impression that she had thought this out and would not budge ... I also got the feeling that your impatience in pressing for an early decision was unwise. It has given her the feeling that she holds the trump card, and there isn't anything you can do about it.'

As against Father's eagerness to clear the decks for a new marriage, Aunt Mehra advised caution. 'I think it would be extremely unwise to say that you want the break for the reason she suspects. There is no certainty that even if you did so she would cooperate. And it would make for talk which, apart from being unpleasant for you, would be more so for the third party. I think there is no alternative to waiting for a while and trying other means. Perhaps after a month or two you could say you couldn't send any more dough . . . You could also be quite aloof and have no more contact. I don't know whether that would affect her, but it might . . . She seemed very calm and composed and wasn't a bit excited, but said that you were so het up over this, and she couldn't understand why. It might be due to your frustration in politics!'

Father followed this sisterly advice. Much to Mother's chagrin, he ended his financial remittances to her, and he also wrote saying that he would prefer not to live under the same roof and would stay with Mehra on future trips to Delhi. Emotionally, their estrangement was now complete. Mother was indignant about his claim that he could not afford to go on financing her, but she made it clear that she would not be pressured into a divorce.

'You should try to subscribe to Gandhiji's philosophy of love, kindness and above all, tolerance,' she wrote with some sarcasm. 'This would cost you nothing! You may break me physically to a certain extent by putting financial strains on me, but you cannot break my spirit or make me change my political convictions and above all my deep admiration for Mrs. Gandhi. I think this is what irks you most. Every time a letter comes from you, I dread opening it, as I know it contains another bombshell. It would be rather nice if you could sometimes write a nice, normal letter saying how you are and what you have been doing . . . No matter what the provocation, I shall keep offering the other cheek, and really there is no fun in fighting somebody who refuses to fight back. So why don't you try to be friends for a change?'

On a more practical note, she insisted that she continued to regard the Breach Candy flat in Bombay as her matrimonial home and would exercise her right to live there on a forthcoming visit on committee work. It was a move that put Father on the spot, because he was reluctant to risk a public scandal by refusing her entry to the flat. 'I can't appreciate the legalistic attitude you are adopting about your "rights",' he complained. 'Thanks to your behaviour, the kind of relationship that justifies staying together no longer exists. I find your imposing yourself on me when I do not wish you to stay with me lacking in delicacy of feeling . . . Should you persist, I shall find myself compelled to move out, probably to some hotel, while you are here. You will be responsible for needlessly drawing attention to our separation, quite apart from the harassment and expense you will cause me.'

Meanwhile, Mother's troubles with her committee were also getting worse. The Chairman, she complained to me, 'is always putting up the members against me by suggesting that they should be getting allowances to which they are not entitled. When I say that the rules do not permit me to do this, she makes out that I am just being obstructive and difficult . . . Counteracting her intrigues seems to take up all my time'.

She was also worried by a sudden coolness towards her from Mrs Gandhi. 'This evening I went to a ladies' party thrown by her,' she wrote. 'I asked her if she could spare me a few minutes in private sometime. She said she would, but her whole attitude was aloof and far from as cordial as she used to be earlier. I fear she may be believing all the stories the Chairman is spreading about me.'

Beleaguered on all sides, Mother characteristically took refuge in the mystical. 'I have a dear, old Panditji, who is an excellent astrologer,' she wrote defiantly to Father. 'He keeps my morale up by saying that the fault is not in you but in your stars . . . My office staff have now tumbled to the havoc your letters cause, so as soon as one arrives Panditji is sent for. He chants some mantras, which chase away the evil spirits that accompany your letter, and I am chanted into a calm state of mind. So you see how futile it is to fight me!'

She had also revived an old friendship with Krishna Menon, formerly Nehru's pro-Communist eminence grise and Father's political arch enemy. He had aged gracefully, living in Delhi as an independent MP and the benign and avuncular elder statesman of the Indian left. Mother visited him often and confided in him about her marital problems, 'as he really is so kind and protective'. Menon had always had a soft corner for an attractive woman in distress; and he must, too, have relished this final round in an antagonism with Father which dated back half a century to their student years in London.

Mother was by now convinced that Aunt Mehra was fuelling Father's animosity. 'Mehra is up to a lot of mischief,' she complained to me, 'and I feel she is poisoning the entire atmosphere.' The tension spilled over into professional rivalries about another seminar Father was sponsoring in Kashmir on women's rights. Mother was furious that Aunt Mehra had been asked to lead the discussion on 'Women at Work'. 'I have refused to attend the seminar as a delegate,' she wrote to me, 'although I shall be touring in Kashmir then . . . They wanted our committee to prepare the basic papers etc. I have refused, as I will not give material for people like Mehra to write their papers on. I have insisted that the papers prepared by us will be presented at the time of discussion and not circulated earlier. Parvati Krishnan [a Communist MP with whom Mother was friendly] has been invited on my insistence, and she is preparing a paper which will knock Mehra into a cocked hat.'

Mother's unhappy relations with her Chairman and committee staggered along for another year; and then, in the summer of 1973, matters finally came to a head. The latest irritant was a notification from the ministry telling her she would be treated as a civil servant and therefore could not engage in political activities. 'I just do not know what is happening,' she wrote to me. 'Somebody in the Ministry is gunning for me, and to do this must be pretty high up. I have written to Mr. Haksar [the PM's Secretary] . . . pointing out the absurdity of this interpretation as it defeats the purpose for which I have made so many personal sacrifices.'

This question mark about her status as a political appointee coincided with a humiliating falling out between her and the Deputy Secretary Mrs Gupta, whom she had recently appointed as her assistant. Although the latter's attendance record was poor, she claimed that allowances should be made for the fact that she had a sick child; and when Mother tried to impose office discipline on her, she threatened to resign. 'She canvassed all the committee members on the quiet,' Mother complained, 'and they raised hell about her resignation and tried to make out that I was victimising her... Matters almost came to my having to resign... When I told the members about her working hours, she said that they had been cooked up and that her output was more than the whole office put together. The members all shouted me down when I tried to prove she was lying blatantly. Mrs. Gupta became the heroine of the day. I had a good mind to walk out, but I controlled myself and said that since they preferred to accept Mrs. Gupta's word against mine there was no point in arguing. Later, all the members went to Dr. Nurul Hasan [the minister] and were plotting their next move against me.'

The situation was complicated by Mother's desire to preserve her ex officio status as a political appointee. Technically that meant she could not exercise control of the committee's purse strings, which would have helped her to maintain office discipline and curb the members. The latter now suggested that these financial powers should go instead to Mother's rebellious deputy.

The question of her housing had also not been resolved, though she had hung on to her large bungalow as a stopgap arrangement. Here, too, she suspected a plot to humiliate her. 'I was allotted three rooms in a dilapidated and uninhabitable, semi-detached house. I cannot tell you how bad the condition of these rooms was and the locality they were in – right in the middle of a *dhobi* colony... Do you know, without exaggeration, the servants' quarters at 2 Tughlak Road are more habitable.'

Setbacks like these were quick to shatter her astrological illusions. 'How wrong Panditji was. I'm afraid he did raise false hopes.' But the worst was yet to come. Mother's opponents on the committee cleverly bided their time till she had left Delhi for a long-postponed summer holiday with me in Oxford. And then they struck. Four committee members led by the Chairman waited on Mrs Gandhi at her morning durbar and informed her that they could no longer work with Mother as Secretary: either she must go or they would. Indira, with a characteristic lack of loyalty to her now dispensable protégée, agreed to accommodate them. The result was a letter to Mother from the minister Nurul Hasan, advising her that it would not be possible to ask her to continue in her post because her insistence on her non-official status would lead to administrative difficulties.

The first inkling Mother had of this coup in her absence was a cable from her loyal office staff in Delhi begging her to cut short her trip and fly back immediately. But the battle was lost by the time she returned and the best she could hope for was a new assignment. While she waited for a crucial appointment she had requested with the Prime Minister, Indira's long-serving personal secretary N.K. Seshan sent word through a friend that she 'should not worry and would definitely get something else'. But she could do little other than worry as the weeks rolled by. 'I have tried my best to see Mrs. G through every source and contact, but with no success,' she wrote frantically to me. 'She is out touring all the time and is barely in Delhi. I am slowly sinking into despair.'

A week later, her spirits had revived with rumours that she was being considered for a diplomatic post as Ambassador to a West European country. Her source was Uma Shankar Dikshit, a senior Congress Party boss close to Mrs G. 'I have been seeing Dikshitji practically every day,' she wrote. 'He assures me that Mrs. G is very fond of me. He has spoken to Swaran Singh [the Foreign Minister] to tell him what my preferences are [for a diplomatic posting]. Since Swaran Singh feels there will be no difficulty, the matter should be settled within three to four days.'

She would have loved a comfortable foreign posting, close to me in England and far away from the intrigues of Delhi. But it never materialized, despite Dikshit's assurances, and the prospect gradually receded. Finally, a month after her return from England, Mother got her long-awaited interview with the PM.

'She was so sweet to me I cannot tell you,' she wrote ecstatically. 'She embraced me warmly, and when I broke down comforted me with tenderness. I am relieved to be reassured by her that she is very fond of me. She explained to me why she had to reconstitute the Committee. I did try to tell her about my side of the story, but she told me not to worry about the past and what was now over . . . Throughout the time I was with her, she was so warm and affectionate. I had about half an hour with her. She then had to hurry away for another engagement but insisted that I stay on with Amie Krishna [her social secretary] and have tea. She also personally supervised the packing of a large parcel of fruit, which was put into my car. She really is so wonderful and considerate. I cannot tell you how beautiful she looked too.'

Having thrown Mother's career to the wolves, it cost Mrs G. very little to be kind and solicitous on a personal level. A week later, she conferred another mark of her favour by inviting Mother to a dinner party for the anthropologist Margaret Mead. 'It was sweet of her,' Mother wrote, 'as it was an extremely select gathering of a handful of people. Mrs. G is being very sweet, but I am afraid nothing has materialised so far, and I am getting restless.' She was by this time in dire financial straits, since her salary had stopped, and she was being charged a penalty rent for the house, to which she was no longer entitled.

Her hopes of winning her inheritance were also dashed when the Delhi High Court, after three years of adjournments and three changes of judges, eventually refused to hear her lawsuit and transferred it to Lucknow, where she had little chance of success. Mother was convinced there had been foul play. 'The judgement was a very prejudiced one,' she complained, 'and it was obvious that the judge had been got at . . . I have lost all faith in justice and all self-confidence.'

And then came rumours of the new job she had been so anxiously awaiting. Far from being the glamorous diplomatic post she had been expecting, it was to be an adviser to the same Minister for Social Welfare who had made her life so difficult on the women's committee. 'Somebody has been up to tricks,' Mother lamented with what was becoming a persecution mania. 'I think it is Nurul Hasan. He wants me under him so that he can continue to harass me.'

A month later, she was more resigned to the post on offer, her hopes buoyed up by a new astrologer. 'I saw Sundaram, the famous palmist, and he predicted a glowing future – particularly for you. He seems to be much more accurate than Panditji.' Her faith in Sundaram was bolstered by an interview she had with the PM's new Principal Secretary P.N. Dhar, a charming and urbane civil servant, quite unlike his more ideologically driven predecessor, Haksar. He formally offered her the adviser's post she had been dreading.

'He was most warm and friendly,' Mother wrote the same day, 'and told me that Mrs. G was very fond of me and is worried about my present state ... So after all Sundaram's predictions are coming true. He told me over a month back that today I would hear some final news about a job which is far from satisfactory, but that I should accept it, as it is temporary, and in the summer I will change jobs.'

A week later, she was even more optimistic. 'I do not know what accommodation I shall be offered, but rumour has it that I shall stay on here [at her beloved Tughlak Road], and a part of the house will be my office. I hope this is true. Sundaram is proving right in all his predictions!'

I had been planning a trip to Delhi to help sort out her problems, but she was adamant that things were looking up now, and there was no need for me to come. 'I am keen you make the most of your time at Oxford ... I regret so much that when Daddy gave me the opportunity to go to Cambridge I refused, because I wanted to get married to Minoo.' I had recently had a brief but exhilarating holiday romance with a Dutch teacher in Amsterdam; and Mother as always had been solicitous and supportive.

Unfortunately, her astrological hopes were dashed yet again. The months rolled by and summer arrived, but the adviser's job had still not formally materialized, let alone a promotion to something more attractive. To her alarm, she also found herself denied access to the Prime Minister and wrote her a series of increasingly reproachful letters. Mrs Gandhi's reply was distinctly cool.

Prime Minister's House,
New Delhi.

April 15, 1974.

Dear Shrimati Masani,

I got your letter some time ago. I am surprised that you were turned back at the gate, as my instructions are that everyone should be allowed to come.

I had received several letters from you. Although I did not write a reply, I did ask Usha and Amie [her social secretaries] to talk to you to let you know that I had received your letters and we were trying to do our best regarding your house and other problems. The last few days have been exceptionally busy, even more so than I could myself have imagined. I hope this week will be a little better. Please do come and see me at any time.

With good wishes,
Yours sincerely,
Indira Gandhi

Mother continued in a state of perpetual suspense and anxiety, fearing yet another intrigue or plot to discredit her with the PM. 'I have heard some rather disturbing news,' she wrote in May 1974. 'It seems Mrs. G believes I am very rich and do not need money. I feel this story has been put across to her by my sisters through Padmaja Naidu. I got this information from Yunus [a close family friend of the Nehrus], who talked to her about me today and about the job not coming through. He now advises me to lie very low and not push the job. I feel absolutely defeated. What can one do when one is surrounded by enemies? . . . I am afraid all Sundaram's forecasts have gone wrong. Now I have become a complete disbeliever.'

When at last her letter of appointment arrived two months later, Mother, worn out by worry and the heat of yet another blistering Delhi summer, was ill with a severe kidney infection. Three years of political intrigue, financial uncertainty and emotional warfare had taken a heavy toll.

ELEVEN

EMERGENCY

By 1973 my parents' marriage was effectively over, and they never again cohabited under the same roof. But it was another sixteen years before they were legally divorced. The main obstacle was Mother's refusal to cooperate, except on terms that Father found unacceptable. I never entirely understood her reluctance. Her own rationalizations, that he must be made to honour his moral obligations to her, or that he must provide adequately for her financial support, were never wholly convincing. Father believed her real motivation was vindictive and malicious, a determination to deny him happiness with someone else. 'Hell hath no fury like a woman scorned,' he was fond of saying about her. Perhaps he was right; but in Mother's emotions love and hate were always very close, and she found it impossible to distance herself emotionally from him.

'I never believed that you could be so unkind,' she wrote to him on New Year's Day, 1973. 'Have I committed an unpardonable sin by having my own political views? . . . I have known about your affair with X . . . for nearly 15 years, but I had accepted this and have been completely reconciled to it. If I can accept this, which so few wives can, surely you can accept my political views? You can be with her as much as you want. I shall not object, but please do not break up our marriage. I love you very much and cannot face the ugliness of a divorce. What you are doing is so ungentlemanly.'

This mixture of emotionalism and self-righteous anger was becoming typical of her letters to Father. A month later, she was at it again. 'Minoo dear, what has happened to you? You have become so cruel. You refuse to stay under the same roof as me and are trying to humiliate and insult me in your letters.' In the next breath, her tone changed from sorrow to indignation. 'You have been married three times already and are now thinking of a fourth marriage at the age of 67! Does not the fact that we have been married for over 26 years and have a son 25 years old mean anything to you? Where is your heart, where are all the qualities which made me fall in love with you and marry you against stiff opposition from my family? . . . Please do not destroy the belief I and hundreds of others have in you.'

Such rhetorical appeals cut little ice with Father. In November 1973, he almost died from unexpected complications during a prostate operation. Sensing that this might be an opportunity for reconciliation, Mother wrote to him expressing great concern about his recovery and appealing to him to let her have one room in the Bombay flat. She proposed, somewhat impractically, that she would live, cook and eat in that one room and make no further demands on him. 'I have learnt to cut down my needs to the minimum and can do everything for myself. I shall not intrude on you in any way, for my expectations have long been shattered . . . We do not even have to see each other, for I shall strictly confine myself to that room.'

This plea was made just before her new job materialized, when it looked as though she might have no alternative but to pack up and leave Delhi. The official version of events she had put out, except to her inner circle of friends, was that she had resigned from the women's committee on matters of principle; the truth would have been far too humiliating. 'I write this to you in utter desperation,' she appealed to Father in that letter, 'and I do not ask for anything more than what one extends to a person in dire need and want, irrespective of any feeling for that person.'

Father politely declined the proposal, pointing out quite reasonably that the configuration of the flat, with a single entrance and only two bedrooms, did not permit the kind of separate use she had in mind. Her reaction was predictably angry. She now asserted that she had 'no feeling or respect' left for him and would like a divorce, provided he agreed to let her have the Bombay flat and a modest lump sum in alimony. But when I put the idea to him on her behalf, he was adamant that he could not surrender the flat to her, because he had nowhere else to go. Bombay property prices had been steadily rising; and controlled-rent flats of the kind we had were now at a premium.

Despite Father having turned down her demands, Mother—in one of her often unpredictable mood swings—suddenly became more compliant. 'I am wondering if it would not be a good idea if I accept Rs. 65,000 [his alimony offer] and call it a day,' she confided to me. 'I feel sorry for him, as I am told he is in very poor shape and has aged very much. I feel perhaps if he had a few years of a happy marriage with X . . . his health and state of mind might improve. Quite frankly, I have no feeling left for him, and I also feel no ill will. He cannot change at his age.'

Imbued with this new magnanimity, she urged me to keep up my own relationship with Father, because 'deep down he is a very lonely person and needs your love'. 'His life has been such a failure,' she concluded, 'and the sad part of it is that he was capable of great things, if only he had not been so uncompromising and rigid.' Though probably an accurate epitaph to his political career, this was a bewildering twist to her very volatile emotional state.

My own relationship with Father seemed to be improving in inverse proportion to Mother's. It was a measure of the change that, after a two-month-long research trip to Bombay in 1973, I wrote thanking him for 'all the consideration and warmth' he had shown me and saying how much I missed 'our evening chats on the balcony'.

Mother, meanwhile, continued to bombard him with what he euphemistically called 'reproachful' letters. A frequent theme was her own youthful folly in disregarding her parents' warnings about marrying him, and her even greater error in not divorcing him in 1961 when her mother was still alive and able to provide for her. She also dramatically exaggerated the financial privations she was undergoing as a consequence of his meanness towards her: 'I have one servant. I do my own cooking. I live on vegetables from the garden and cannot afford the luxury of chicken and fish.' 'The only luxury I do indulge in,' she confessed, 'is that I play golf three times a week, as exercise is very important for my health.' But she added in mitigation: 'Even that does not cost anything, as

I do not take a caddy and carry my own clubs in a trolley.' She concluded this largely imaginary catalogue of woes by assuring him that she had 'given up entertaining since the last two years, and it is nearly a year since I even went to a film'. Whether Father took any of this seriously is doubtful: the relevant sections of her letter to him had been marked with red exclamation marks when I found it thirty years later.

When she failed to move or shame him into abandoning the idea of divorce, she returned to the offensive, countering his plea for a divorce by mutual consent with the demand that he must give her grounds to sue him for desertion or adultery, and preferably both. This, she insisted, would give her 'a sure standing should he try and back out of payments, etc.'. Her main adviser and confidante in these matters was Krishna Menon, despite his now rapidly failing health. 'He is so very soft and kind,' Mother wrote after one of her visits to his sickbed. 'How different from Daddy! I fear he will not live for very long, and it makes me very sad.'

Her rejection of a 'no-fault' divorce owed as much to political as to emotional considerations. 'It would damage my reputation,' she argued to me, 'and we must not lose sight of the general election due in 1976.' Probably for similar reasons, Father was just as adamant that he was not interested in a divorce that made him the guilty party. With his public reputation in mind, Aunt Mehra also urged him to avoid an acrimonious public scandal, even if that meant giving up the idea of remarrying. She corresponded regularly with Father throughout this period, reporting to him on her various conversations with Mother in Delhi.

'If you would take a decision not to marry it would be helpful,' Mehra advised him early in 1974. 'I do think it would be a great mistake. Ignoring the public ridicule of elderly men marrying girls young enough to be their daughters, and the loss of esteem on the part of your good friends and admirers, such as JP [Jayaprakash Narayan, his closest friend], JRD [Tata] and anyone you can think of, there are all the difficulties that can easily be anticipated between you both [Father and his intended wife-to-be]. X is used to being extravagant about clothes, etc.; she likes a gay life; she would find your irritability, impatience and critical attitudes hard to take; and on your part you would be much better off free and untrammelled.'

Mother, of course, knew nothing of this sisterly advice, but she always maintained, cynically but accurately, that the existing stalemate suited Aunt Mehra admirably, with her brother single and herself the most important woman in his life. Whether or not her motives were selfish, Mehra's moderating influence prevailed, and Father drew back from a public and open break.

Mother's new job was far less glamorous than she had hoped, but less stressful in the long run. She had hoped to function as a ministerial special adviser, overseeing the work of the entire Ministry for Social Welfare and its state-level boards. Instead, she found herself sidelined into a research role, asked to produce reports on esoteric subjects like prostitution and the relevance to India of British race equality legislation. She was refused an office near the minister's in the departmental building and expected to work from home with a small secretarial staff.

She attributed all these vexations to the petty jealousy of the minister, her old adversary Nurul Hasan, and his senior civil servants. But there was a silver lining. At least she was relatively insulated from office politics and intrigue and left in peace to get on with her reports. She was also, at long last, allocated suitable alternative accommodation to the large official mansion where she had overstayed for almost four years. Her new bungalow, in the quiet, residential government area around the lovely Lodi Gardens, was half the size of Number Two Tughlak Road, but very charming and compact with a nice garden. Most important of all, it put her on an equal footing with the senior officials and politicians who were her neighbours.

Her life seemed to be entering a more tranquil phase and she even began to contemplate remarriage. For some years she had had a close relationship with the Canadian High Commissioner; but it had foundered when his wife was diagnosed with cancer, making divorce unthinkable. A new and more glamorous prospect was a visiting American from Los Angeles, whose main distinction, from what I could gather, was having been married before to the Greek millionairess Christina Onassis. Mother wrote describing him as 'very charming and intelligent'. 'He took quite a fancy to me,' she confided, 'and is keen I marry him. I have said "no", but he insists on coming back and spending a month here to convince me to accept him. He is a quiet person and does not drink or smoke. He is also good-looking in a rather distinguished way and fabulously rich.'

It all sounded too good to be true and I strongly urged her to accept. I had realized by now that she could not survive on her own without day-to-day guidance and emotional support, not to mention generous financial backing. A second marriage which gave her these props seemed my only hope of absolution from the guilt and responsibility I felt for her predicament. But I was too far away to intervene directly; and Mother, for reasons best known to her, decided to turn down her new suitor. When I pressed her, she replied that she was too old (at fifty-four) to start a new life, based predominantly in America, with someone so different from herself in culture and background.

By the end of 1974, a new challenge had emerged to what many saw as Mrs Gandhi's growing despotism. Secure in her triumphant victory over Pakistan in the Bangladesh War, she had ditched her left-wing populism and turned on the trade unionists and socialists who had backed her against the Congress old guard. Her increasingly imperial court in Delhi was as rife with nepotism, corruption and intrigue as any of the feudal principalities she had abolished. And her own dynasticism was becoming blatant with the corrupt political and business dealings of her favourite son Sanjay.

Indira's political nemesis was the septuagenarian Jayaprakash Narayan, who had assumed the mantle of Mahatma Gandhi. He was my father's oldest friend and together they had founded the Indian Socialist Party way back in the 1930s. Unlike Father, JP had expressed his disillusionment with socialism by retiring from party politics altogether and devoting himself to Mahatma Gandhi's social and charitable campaigns at the village level. Through the 1950s and '60s, he had been the voice of India's liberal conscience, speaking out forcefully and impartially against Nehru and his daughter on issues like the right of Kashmir and Tibet to self-determination and the immorality of condoning Soviet repression in Hungary and Czechoslovakia.

Now, as Indira's popularity declined, JP emerged as the charismatic head of a mass movement against corruption. Starting as a student campaign in his home state of Bihar, it spread across the country in a tidal wave, drawing in all sections of society and most political parties ranging from socialists to Hindu nationalists. The one common plank in the JP movement, as it came to be called, was to hold the Congress Party and the Prime Minister herself responsible for the ills of the country.

My own assessment of Indira had been evolving in the course of the three years during which I had been writing her biography. My increasingly doctrinaire Marxism saw her pragmatic handling of the Indian economy as a betrayal of the socialist promises on which she had been elected. Along with others on the left, I was appalled by her ruthless suppression of a railway workers' strike in 1974 and by her increasing contempt for civil liberties generally. I had begun to agree with the critics who accused her of aiming at a personal, dynastic dictatorship. And although the JP movement was by no means a socialist alternative, I was willing, like many other Indian Marxists, to see it as a *Front Populaire* against Indira's budding fascism.

My misgivings about Indira's authoritarian regime were reflected in the final chapter of my biography, which went to press in November 1974. Although most of the book had been a balanced but generally sympathetic portrayal of her rise to power, the conclusion warned about the consequences of her attempts to purge opposition and impose absolute control. What I had not anticipated was that the showdown between Mrs Gandhi and her opponents would coincide with the publication of my book, confirming my worst predictions, but also putting Mother and me on the horns of a grave dilemma.

Mother had initially been dismissive of JP and his movement. She had known him intimately since her marriage and though personally fond of him, had always considered his politics rather woolly if idealistic, an assessment shared by Father. Now she felt he was being led astray by unscrupulous Opposition leaders who were using him for their own ends. But by January 1975 she recognized that JP was becoming a serious danger to Mrs Gandhi. Her good friend, the senior journalist Khushwant Singh had travelled with JP for four days and reported to Mother that his popularity was 'tremendous'. 'He feels Mrs. G is being misled,' she wrote to me, 'and asked me to see her to give her a correct picture.' Mother duly turned up at the PM's morning durbar to warn her of the gathering storm. 'She was sweet and kind, and I understand from T.K. [another courtier] that she was very touched by my concern.'

A fortnight later, she visited Mrs G again to warn her of Opposition plots. She also took the opportunity to revive her request for a diplomatic posting. But the PM was noncommittal and the tête-à-tête was rudely interrupted. Mother's friend and house guest, the ageing dancer Ram Gopal, had been waiting outside to see Mrs G after Mother. A flamboyant and androgynous figure with his silk turban, heavily made-up face and sparkling jewels, he decided to barge in unannounced, and his histrionic entry and camp humour quickly put an end to any serious talk.

Nevertheless, Mother's loyalty to Mrs G seemed to be paying off. Early in June 1975, she wrote to me cheerfully with the news that a new job was being processed for her as chairman of a government-sponsored Institute of Mass Communications. 'It is extremely prestigious and will have a high status,' she announced. 'It involves a lot of travelling all over the country and to various places abroad. Please keep this very secret, as there is many a slip between the cup and the lip. I have not mentioned it to a soul.'

Her good news coincided with the publication of my biography of Indira in the UK. Mother was delighted with the advance copies of the book I had sent her, especially as it was dedicated to her. She showed it off to all her friends and went round personally to present it to Mrs Gandhi herself. And then, only a week later, a political thunderstorm hit the country and our own lives with an impact that would be felt for years to come.

Ever since the March 1971 general election, an election petition filed by one of Mrs Gandhi's opponents had been slowly making its way unnoticed through the Indian judicial system. Suddenly, in June 1975, it hit the headlines when the Allahabad High Court found the PM guilty of corrupt election practices, set aside her election to Parliament and disqualified her from office. The Opposition could not believe its luck. Huge demonstrations across the country demanded her immediate resignation, culminating in a vast rally in the capital addressed by JP, who endorsed the call and appealed to the police and armed forces not to carry out 'illegal' orders if they were asked to suppress opposition.

Indira was stunned by the news and at first considered stepping down pending an appeal to the Supreme Court. But the hawks in her camp, led by her son Sanjay, had their way and she decided to tough it out, while appealing to the Supreme Court to overturn the verdict. Mother was among the loyal band of courtiers who continued to turn up at her morning durbars, assuring her of their continued loyalty and begging her not to contemplate resignation.

'We suspect the hand of a foreign power in bringing about this crisis,' Mother wrote to me just after the high court judgement, in a typed letter dictated to her secretary and therefore intended for official consumption. 'You can well imagine who it could be,' she continued, in an obvious allusion to the hidden hand of American imperialism. 'We are however confident that the stay order in the Supreme Court will be absolute, and eventually we will also win the case. There is a general feeling that Mrs. Gandhi should not resign, and I am in full agreement. Daddy, of course, informed me on the phone that we have no leg to stand on, but I feel his views are very prejudiced.'

Mother had been due to arrive in London, but decided to put off her trip to be near the centre of events. 'We are still reeling from the blow,' she confided in a handwritten letter the next day. 'I rushed to her [Mrs Gandhi's] place yesterday and spent the better part of the morning there. She was magnificent in her dignity and self-control. She was smiling and chided me for having such a long face. The position is still very tense and undecided, but I am sure she will not have to resign . . . I think if she comes out of this crisis, her stature will go up.'

On a more personal note, she added: 'I have established fairly close touch with her, and only day before yesterday, before this news burst on us, she told me that she intended to have a long chat with me and iron out all my difficulties. She was so sweet and affectionate.'

The shattering high court verdict coincided to the day with the launch of my biography in London. Early that morning, I found myself whisked out of bed in Oxford and on my way to a series of television, radio and press interviews in London. It was a very welcome if unexpected publicity coup, and I made the most of it. The book was widely, prominently and generally very favourably reviewed in all the national papers, with captions like 'The Leopard's Timing!'.

Mother wrote congratulating me and seemed optimistic that the political crisis would resolve itself. She expected Mrs Gandhi to take advantage of the Supreme Court stay order to call a snap election and put her opponents on the defensive. But faced with rebellion inside her own party and mounting pressure from the Opposition, she decided on more drastic action. On the 26th of June, in the early hours while Delhi slept, she proclaimed a state of Emergency and had the entire Opposition leadership, including JP, dragged out of their beds and carted off to prison.

My own response to these events, expressed in a major front-page lead story for the *Observer*, was that Mrs Gandhi had turned a personal emergency into an unnecessary and undemocratic political crackdown which would have serious consequences for India's future. I was worried about the impact my criticisms might have on Mother's situation, but she did not seem too bothered about it. 'There is nothing to worry about,' she reassured me. 'I am sure Mrs. G is big enough. I'm glad I stayed back, as I have been rather useful, and I think she has become quite fond of me. I see her every couple of days.'

Mother was complacent about the political climate. 'Everything is peaceful and quiet here. It was necessary to declare an emergency, as J.P. and others were inciting civil war, and the situation would have got out of control. J.P. was inciting a mutiny, and no government can tolerate that. I think the common man is very relieved as he feels there is law and order now. Prices are also coming down rapidly. This emergency should have come a year back.' It was the official Congress line, claiming that the Emergency powers were being used for the benefit of the poor to crack down on hoarders and foodgrain speculators.

Mother was just completing her own children's biography of the PM, *The Story of Indira*, intended as a sequel to the very popular lives of Gandhi and Nehru she had written in her youth. Indira herself was taking a benevolent interest in it, giving Mother long interviews, and so she decided to cancel her trip abroad and concentrate on finishing the book. Despite my more critical approach to the Emergency, she was also very optimistic about the sales of my book in India. She said that the PM and her office thought it the best of the many biographies about her and that there would be large orders for several thousands of copies from the foreign ministry and the Congress Party for the Indian edition, to be published by Oxford University Press.

My own feelings about the Indian edition were more complicated. Though happy at the prospect of extra publicity and sales, I was worried about the book being used by the government to promote the image of the woman I was now coming to regard as an evil dictator. And then Mrs Gandhi herself relieved me of this unpleasant moral dilemma. Under OUP's arrangement with Hamish Hamilton, the printed page proofs of my book were to be imported from Britain and bound in India. When they arrived in Bombay a fortnight after the British launch, they were impounded by customs under Emergency censorship regulations. OUP immediately asked Mother to intercede with the PM's office. When she did, she was assured that the book would be released for publication on one condition: I would have to 'eliminate' the final chapter, which had concluded with a bleak and fairly accurate assessment of my subject's growing intolerance of dissent.

Mother was eager I accepted this proposal, as were my British publishers, who stood to lose their royalty from OUP if the Indian edition could not appear. Under pressure, I agreed, provided there was a clear statement after the penultimate chapter, stating that it had been written in April 1974 and that the final one had been 'deleted in view of subsequent developments including the proclamation of Emergency'. I wanted to make it clear that the book had been censored, a point I considered important because the government had been preventing the censored Indian press from carrying blank or blacked-out columns to indicate what had been cut out.

Mother wrote triumphantly to say that the PM's office had accepted my condition and that the book could now appear. But then came a rider: my desired announcement should say 'omitted', rather than 'deleted'. I was already uncomfortable about the original compromise, and this new hair-splitting by the censors gave me an opportunity to back out. I refused to budge from 'deleted', and there the matter rested for the next two years while the book mouldered unpublished in a Bombay Customs warehouse.

While I felt I could cock a snook at Mrs Gandhi from the safety of Oxford, returning to India was another matter while her critics were being arrested at random and detained without trial. Opinions were divided as to whether I should risk coming out for my Christmas vacation in 1975. The climate of fear was such that Mother and I even suspected our letters might be intercepted and used a primitive code to disguise political news. Mrs G was 'Bhai', Mother's name for her elder brother Sonny, and the Opposition leader JP was 'Russet', my long-deceased and much-loved spaniel.

At first, Mother felt that the risks were being exaggerated. 'The general impression is that Bhai will never take action against you if you come,' she wrote in October, 'and that you should not delay it too long. I have asked for an appointment with Bhai and shall let you know what you should do after seeing him.' She also contradicted rumours that JP had died in captivity, the victim of callous medical neglect or even worse. 'Russet has not been put to sleep and is very much alive, but not at all well. He is being treated for his illness and is slowly improving.'

The truth was that JP was suffering from kidney failure, brought on by the overly strong antibiotics with which he had been dosed by a prison doctor. Contrary to Opposition propaganda, this appeared to have happened more by accident than design, and Indira had no desire to make a martyr of him. When Father wired her, warning that JP was critically ill and might die in custody, she agreed to release him on compassionate grounds. Father immediately flew up to Chandigarh in Punjab, where JP was in hospital, and fetched him back to the Jaslok Hospital in Bombay, which had the most advanced renal unit in the country.

For two weeks, JP hovered between life and death, despite being put on a dialysis machine. Father later wrote that his anxiety 'was heightened by an awful thought. Suppose J.P. were suddenly to collapse, what was there to stop the Prime Minister rushing down to Bombay, becoming the principal mourner at his funeral and claiming that J.P. had realised his errors and had intended to give her his cooperation?'.

Father decided to discuss this possibility with JP himself and suggested he wrote a short political testament to guard against such misrepresentation if the worst were to happen. To Father's relief, JP nodded his agreement and asked him to draft a statement. 'J.P.'s habit of asking me to draft statements and resolutions for him was one I had known since the 1930s, when we were co-secretaries of the Congress Socialist Party,' Father later reminisced. 'Rather anticipating such a request, I had already prepared a short draft of what I imagined J.P. would like to say; so I produced it from my pocket. "Just like you!" he quipped happily. When I asked if he would sign it right then as a holding operation, until we could get the final document properly attested and authenticated, he did so, but only after making a change which showed that he was by no means signing it without applying his mind.'

The document was again signed and sealed and notarized a few days later by Soli Sorabji, the prominent lawyer who later served as Attorney-General of India. It read:

> Today is the 5th of December 1975, and I am undergoing treatment . . . for my kidneys, which have been very badly damaged during the four and a half months of solitary confinement . . . from which I have just emerged. Just in case I am removed from the scene, I would like to state for the information of my friends . . . and the Indian people in general that my views about the situation in India are precisely what they were on the 25th June 1975 . . . Indeed, all the ugly things that have happened since have only confirmed my apprehensions. I am making this clear just in case there should be any attempt to misrepresent the position when I am no longer there to correct any such misstatements. I hope the people of India will be able before long to liberate themselves non-violently from the present tyranny.

Fearing that the tightly censored Indian press would not be allowed to publish this document, Father secretly arranged for copies to be smuggled out to the London *Times* and *Daily Telegraph* and also to his contacts in New York, to be used only in the event of JP's demise.

Despite preparing for the worst, he was balanced enough to write and warn me against exaggerating the extent of government repression. 'You young folk in England seem to be carried away by a lot of somewhat silly rumours about people being picked up in coffee-shops for indiscreet conversation. Things are bad, but not *that* bad! I have not been able to verify a single one of these rumours, and I have come to the conclusion that there are a lot of cowardly people who seek to justify their own cowardice by these cock-and-bull stories.'

Father's own strategy for opposing the Emergency was to push the parameters of political activity within the legal limits allowed. He challenged a censorship order against his small, liberal journal *Freedom First*, and won in the Bombay High Court. He also helped organize an All India Civil Liberties Conference presided over by a former Chief Justice of India, and moved the main resolution urging restoration of democracy. 'It was a magnificent show,' he wrote, 'with over a thousand people packed into a college auditorium. Of course, not a single word appeared in the press the following morning, thanks to the censorship!'

Mother, meanwhile, was paying the price for my recalcitrance about the biography. 'He was rather cold when I met him briefly,' she wrote, after an interview with 'Bhai', 'and not too friendly about you. So please do not come just now. I shall follow up my talks with him, and if his attitude improves I shall let you know.' But on two subsequent visits to the PM, she continued to find her 'aloof but polite'. 'I agree with you that he is vindictive,' she conceded. 'I do not expect him to do anything for me and am now making plans to return to Bombay by March 1976.'

I was mortified by the adverse effect my political activities were having on Mother's prospects. But to her credit, she took this reversal in her fortunes philosophically and did not try and pressure me into softening my criticisms of the Emergency—which became more strident in the articles I was writing for the British press and in public talks I gave at venues like the Cambridge India Society. She was desperately keen I came out to visit her that winter, but was adamant that I must take no risk of being arrested. A close friend of hers had discussed my return with no less a person than Sanjay Gandhi himself. Sanjay had said: 'You should come out, and so long as you meet the right people there would be no harm.' But others took a more alarmist view and thought I might be prevented from returning to Oxford. 'Since there is this danger, it would be wiser to finish your thesis, and by that time things will be more normal,' Mother counselled. 'I feel sad and disappointed, but I would like you to play safe.'

In a letter hand-carried by a friend, she was more open about Mrs Gandhi's ominous attitude towards me. 'When I saw her and we talked about you, she said that you were old enough to stand on your own feet and must take the consequences of your actions. I was a little worried.' Mother was unusually stoical about her own fall from prime ministerial favour. 'I shall have to fend for myself. Loyalty and devotion don't seem to count for anything. I am not upset any more by this attitude. I am glad I know where I stand. I have been so loyal and devoted, and if that was not good enough there is nothing more to be said or done.'

Mother warned that my unpopularity with 'the powers that be' would be further compounded by the impending publication of the American edition of my book, to which I had added an even more critical postscript about the Emergency. 'How complicated life has become,' she lamented. 'I cannot tell you how very sad I am that you will not be coming out. I was hoping against hope that it could be managed and have left no stone unturned to bring it about. But I assure you that this decision is in your interest, darling, and both of us have to bear the disappointment.'

Early in 1976 she wrote that the prospects for a trip out still looked 'pretty dim'. 'The weather is not at all good,' she confided, 'and if anything it has got worse.' But to her surprise, Mrs Gandhi had invited her to 'a very select' dinner party for the French Prime Minister, 'a good sign' she thought of a possible thaw in relations.

The enticing new job that Mrs Gandhi had dangled before Mother, as head of a new Institute of Mass Communications, had disappeared without trace. No doubt, Mother's connection with someone as critical as me made her an unsuitable choice at a time when the government was closely managing the media. Indeed, she was rapped on the knuckles by Mohammed Yunus, the PM's loyal media supremo, when I published a scathing assessment of the Indian situation in the London *Observer* on the first anniversary of the Emergency. I received a letter from Mother, no doubt intended for the censor's eyes, couched in language worthy of a Stalinist show trial, praising Mrs G to the skies and pleading with me not to be misled by Western propaganda.

As the winter of 1976 approached, it became clear that it was still unsafe for me to visit India. Mother now began to plan a holiday in Nepal, where we could meet without fear of Mrs Gandhi's reprisals. She was planning to rent a house in Kathmandu and to move up there for the spring of 1977 with her servants and dogs. And then, quite suddenly, in January 1977 Mrs Gandhi confounded all expectations. She announced the general election that she had postponed a year ago, ostensibly because of the Opposition's bad behaviour. Press censorship was lifted and the prisons opened their gates to thousands of Opposition activists.

The immediate reaction was that it would be a rigged election, necessitated by Indira's desire to legitimize and formalize her Emergency rule. Why else would she submit herself to a popular vote? The Congress Party controlled all the machinery of government and would have no compunctions about abusing it for electoral purposes. The Opposition parties, with their organization and finances disrupted by eighteen months of repression, would be unable to rally their forces in time. The outcome seemed a foregone conclusion.

Nevertheless, Mrs Gandhi's desire to convince the world that she was a democrat meant a window of free access and reporting for the Western media; and it was an unexpected opportunity for me to return from what was becoming a painful exile. I had managed to get freelance commissions from the *Guardian* and the *Economist* to cover the elections for them. This was both a financial help and some kind of insurance against rough treatment from the authorities.

Mother was still worried about possible risks and wrote repeatedly emphasizing that I must come armed with a return ticket, preferably not on the government-owned Air India, with a confirmed return date and flight. 'There is no reason to worry about your return,' she added, 'but I want to take no risks and am erring on the cautious side.' She was also worried about the fallout of the resignation of Indira's wily Deputy Prime Minister, Jagjivan Ram, who had gone over to the Opposition. 'It was a carefully planned move and is a terrific feather in the cap of the Opposition,' she concluded, speculating that it might cost Mrs Gandhi the crucial Hindi-speaking heartlands of Bihar and Uttar Pradesh.

Little did we foresee at that stage that Indira would lose the election by a landslide, suffering a crushing defeat in her own parliamentary constituency, which she had inherited from her father. It was an explosion of popular anger and frustration which eighteen months of repression had only intensified. As I travelled from Delhi, through Bihar and UP to Calcutta, I saw for myself the huge crowds the Opposition was drawing, and by contrast the apathetic Congress meetings at which the PM was heckled and booed despite the best efforts of her cheerleaders and bully boys.

On election night Mother and I congregated with many others outside the press offices on Bahadur Shah Zafar Road, where—in an era before televized results—we saw the latest election tally going up on huge, cricket-style hoardings. The atmosphere was one of euphoria, tinged with near disbelief. By midnight, the Congress rout was well established. We went to bed fearful that Mrs G would not respect the popular verdict and that we might awake to a military coup. But wiser counsels apparently prevailed and she announced her resignation in a dignified statement on All India Radio the next morning.

Mother loyally went to her house to commiserate. She found the once-proud would-be-dictator stunned into an expressionless and stony silence, greeting her small band of sympathizers with no more than a sombre namaste. Indians love a good disaster, congregating with gruesome delight at road accidents and other scenes of carnage. Many who came to condole with the stricken Prime Minister on that post-election morning had come to see the death throes, or so they thought, of a fatally wounded tigress.

TWELVE

LOOSE ENDS

Along with most other Indians, we celebrated Mrs Gandhi's defeat and the end of the Emergency; but I did not realize at the time what a watershed it would be in Mother's life and my own. Her job in Delhi, for all its vicissitudes and intrigues, had given some structure to her life and an external focus. She had enjoyed the research, the contacts with voluntary organizations and the writing of the reports she did on subjects like prostitution, destitute women and race relations.

As a political appointee, she could not expect to remain in the post under the new Janata government formed by the coalition of Opposition parties that had ousted Indira. Bereft of her job and what little independence it had afforded her, she now desperately needed a new source of income, and that made her increasingly vulnerable to the carrot-and-stick approach Father applied in his campaign to get her to agree to a divorce. The saga was to drag on for the next twelve years, dominating Mother's emotional life, poisoning what goodwill remained between Father and her and putting me in the invidious position of having to mediate between them. It was the position of power I had dreamt of as a child, but an onerous burden to carry as an adult keen to get on with my own life. A month after the election I had returned to London, where I had just bought a flat of my own.

Back in Delhi, Mother's immediate concern was to try and hold on to her much-loved official house for as long as possible; and she was nothing if not resourceful in such matters. She had known the new Prime Minister

Morarji Desai quite well way back in the late 1940s when he had been Chief Minister of Bombay. A remarkably sprightly octogenarian, he had a soft corner for attractive women in distress, and Mother appealed to his sense of chivalry. By now a practised courtier, she became a frequent visitor at his morning durbars and enlisted his sympathy with tales of Father's mistreatment of her and his refusal to support her financially.

Relations between my parents had improved during the Emergency, partly because of their shared concern about my future. To my surprise, in mid-1976 I had received a curious letter from Mother filled with foreboding because no less than three astrologers she had recently consulted had unanimously forecast that she would be a widow in a couple of years. 'This has upset me very much,' she had confided to me. 'I am planning to observe a Santoshi Ma fast every Friday for three months, which has to be done with great devotion. I know you do not believe in all this, but I have faith, and I shall ask for Daddy to live on for many years.'

A year later, Father was still very much alive, and Mother was hopeful that the new democratic dawn might be an opportunity for a marital reconciliation, now that her contentious support for Indira was a thing of the past. Her hopes were buoyed by rumours that Father was about to make a political comeback with the patronage of his close friend Jayaprakash Narayan, the uncrowned head of the new government. She calculated that Father would not want the scandal of a contested divorce to cloud his prospects of public office.

At first it was rumoured that he was about to be parachuted into the Cabinet as JP's personal representative and would soon be contesting a by-election in his old constituency of Rajkot. When that failed to materialize, he was expected to become India's new Ambassador to Washington. But the sceptics maintained that that would be tantamount to appointing an American to represent India; and sure enough, the Washington post went to someone else. The next and most persistent rumour was that Father would go as High Commissioner to London. Mother dropped broad hints to the new PM that she expected him to honour her status as Father's wife and to see that he took her abroad with him as his official hostess.

To me, she rationalized these manoeuvres by maintaining that she wanted to find herself a new job abroad, after which she would give Father his freedom. She also insisted that Morarji had far more use for her than for Father. 'He told me to sue Minoo in front of 10 or 15 people,' she wrote to me. 'He did not say it once but several times, and everybody in the room heard it. He seems to make it clear that he thinks Minoo is an unscrupulous person with no morality or conscience.'

While she made sure Father heard of this exchange through Aunt Mehra, she also wrote to him saying she would soon be homeless and appealing for his 'forgiveness'. 'I am not trying to make any excuses for myself,' she pleaded, 'but try and understand how humiliated I felt for all these years. My mother was still alive when you told me that you were in love with X . . . My mother advised me not to give you a divorce and patch it up somehow or other. My pride was shattered over the years that followed when we continued to live together, but not as husband and wife. I was still young and considered fairly attractive. Deep inside me I was terribly hurt.'

This reproachful account of Father's past behaviour was followed by a melodramatic prediction that she would not live more than a couple of years, given her mental and physical state. 'I am not trying to cadge for sympathy, but my life has become an absolute nightmare. Thank God, it will come to an end soon—the sooner the better.' In the meanwhile, however, she asked on a more practical note if he would do her the favour of getting her Delhi house allotted to himself if he returned to Parliament, so that she could stay on there in the time remaining to her.

She ended with a surprisingly emotional appeal. She referred to the very eligible American who had courted her recently, with 'wealth, good looks and a high position', said she had turned him down flat and confided: 'I have never been able to find an explanation for what I did, except that somewhere I must still care for you.' This was proof, she claimed, that her motives in resisting a divorce were not 'vindictive and mercenary'.

On a more altruistic note, she concluded this appeal with a request to Father not to press me to move back to India to look after her. 'For certain emotional reasons which I would not like to mention,' she wrote, hinting at my homosexuality, 'it is necessary for him to be in England for a couple of years. I can assure you that he has been a wonderful son. My life is now almost over, and I would never permit his young life to be ruined because of my mistakes and failures.'

Mother was in the habit of jotting down the predictions of her latest astrologer. About this time, one of these notes forecast that 'the bad time will leave soon'. 'After 7 months,' it continued, 'another relationship for me. From '79 a happy life, another marriage till age 80.' At first it did seem that her luck was turning. Prime Minister Morarji Desai extended her job, and therefore her right to the house, till the end of the year. 'The extension came out of the blue when I had abandoned all hope,' Mother wrote euphorically. 'I cannot tell you how relieved I feel. Life had become a nightmare. I know you do not believe in *puja* and the magical impact of the chanting of *mantras,* but I went daily to a temple for 4 days to do Shivji *puja.* On the first day the *pandit* told me that my problems would resolve within these four days, and they did.' She went on to extol the virtues of the new Prime Minister: 'He is so kind and has given me a longer extension than Mrs. G ever did. What a difference between the two!'

Mrs Gandhi, by this time, was facing various commissions of inquiry that had been set up by the new government to investigate the corrupt practices of her son and her own abuse of power. 'I am keeping clear of her,' Mother wrote, 'as I doubt very much if she will help me in any way. I feel she is very selfish.' She also passed on with some relish a story she had heard about Indira gatecrashing a dinner party at the British High Commission and causing general embarrassment all round.

Mother's hopes that Father was about to get a major diplomatic post were receding, especially after he published a series of characteristically critical articles in his monthly magazine, attacking the opportunism and factional intrigues of the Janata government. Mother's own attempts to court favour with the new regime also suffered a major setback when she saw Kanti Desai, Morarji's son and closest aide, about getting her a controlled-rent flat in Bombay. 'He was aggressive and obnoxious,' she complained. 'I wish I had not seen him. He was quite critical of Daddy and you as well.'

Mother was by now convinced that Delhi, with its superficial emphasis on official status, held no future for her and that she would be happier in Bombay. I agreed with her and came out to India in the spring of 1978 to help her move. The plan was to sell a bungalow in Kanpur, which her mother had left her, and buy a flat in Bombay with the proceeds. The problem was that no sooner was this decision taken than Mother began to vacillate like a donkey between two haystacks, clutching at straws that might enable her to stay on in Delhi. I found her mood swings and indecision infuriating and intensely frustrating, especially because it put me in a limbo where I was unable to do what I'd come for and move her, but felt guilty about leaving her in a mess and returning to London. Years later, one of her sisters told me she was convinced that Mother was clinically bipolar or a manic depressive and couldn't help herself. She may well have been right, but I wonder if the knowledge of it would have made me more tolerant at the time.

My closest friend, then in London, wrote advising me to stick it out at any cost: 'If you leave before you've settled her, then you are not doing your duty at a time when she genuinely needs it, even if she in fact makes it difficult to actually do your duty . . . Her plight is very real. She must feel entirely marginalized and bereft in a way in which it is *not possible* for us to be or feel. Middle-aged, jobless, family-less, almost interest-less. I can't quite imagine what goes on in her head but if it is, as you say, pretty weird, then really no wonder!'

As my friend had implied, doing my duty by Mother meant grappling as much with her unbalanced mental state as with the practical difficulties of her situation. Often enough I would lose my temper with her, only to be consumed by guilt, especially when as so often she swung from truculence to abject remorse and self-abasement. A note she wrote me after one such quarrel sums up the emotional pressure she could apply.

Zareer darling,

I know you are going through a trying time emotionally, and I feel terrible burdening you with my problems. I seem to be heading for a complete nervous breakdown. It is due to an accumulation of all the trials and tribulations of the past few years. I find it difficult to talk to you about it, but at this moment I need your help desperately.

Something inside me is breaking, and I am absolutely panic-stricken. *Please, please* help. You are the person I love most, and I need your understanding and love now. I may sound irrational and confused, but Zareer I am fighting a fast-losing battle to retain my sanity. I go through the motions of everyday living, but there is an all-consuming despair within.

God has been good to send you to me at this time. I have never needed you more.

Mummy

Unfortunately for Mother, I tended increasingly to see such appeals as emotional blackmail; and if anything they hardened my heart against her. Eventually I was able to prevail on her to go ahead with her original plan and managed, through a good friend in Bombay, to find her a pleasant flat there at a price she could afford. I was free to return to London, and Mother wrote assuring me that 'an enormous load has lifted off my shoulders now that the decision to buy the flat has been taken'.

Father, meanwhile, had been appointed Chairman of a new Minorities Commission set up by the government, modelled on the British Commission for Racial Equality. The post at first seemed an attractive opportunity, carrying with it the status of a cabinet minister; but it soon became apparent that the Janata government, for all its democratic pretensions, would not allow the commission the independence it had been promised. The Janata Party was essentially a coalition of former Opposition parties, of which the Hindu nationalist Jan Sangh was an important component; and inevitably this put political constraints on the rights of minorities. Within six months of accepting the post of Chairman, Father resigned with a public statement castigating the government for interfering in the commission and trying to clip its wings. It was the last public post he ever held.

Mother's return to Bombay revived her suspended divorce negotiations with Father: he was keen to avoid the embarrassment of having an estranged wife living nearby, and she was persuaded by me and her sisters that she needed the extra income an alimony settlement would provide. Unfortunately, she was far from emotionally reconciled to the break. For the next decade, she treated the divorce negotiations as a kind of sparring contest with Father, a substitute for the intimacy she had hoped to revive. In a bizarre parody of some courtship ritual, every now and then she would approach him with an apparently friendly handshake, offering to set him free, only to back off at the last moment with new demands that he was bound to refuse. It was a process that inevitably increased his hostility and bitterness towards her. And it also soured Mother's relations with me, since I had the thankless task of mediating between them and trying to impose some semblance of consistency on her.

The first round took place in my absence, shortly before Mother made the traumatic move from Delhi to Bombay. Father had offered her an attractive lump sum of Rs 2 lakh as alimony, with an advance of a quarter of that amount to help her with her down payment on her new Bombay flat, and the right to all the antiques and other movables in his own Breach Candy flat. But he was prudent enough to insert a clause for good behaviour: if Mother changed her mind and withdrew the petition for divorce by mutual consent, she would forfeit her right to the movables and to any future alimony.

Reluctant to abandon the possibility of a last-minute change of mind, Mother balked at the penalty clause. When Father flew up to Delhi to obtain her signature to the draft petition agreed by their lawyers, she threatened not to sign unless he dropped that clause. He refused to budge, and there followed an ugly scene at her lawyer's office, at the end of which Mother gave in and signed.

As usual, I received diametrically opposite versions from them of what transpired. Mother wrote two indignant letters saying she had been browbeaten into signing by financial blackmail. 'He has driven a very hard bargain,' she complained, 'and behaved in a most horrible way, calling me a "bloody bitch" and referring to you as "her son", implying that you are illegitimate . . . After this, everybody is convinced that it is better I cut off all contact with him like one cuts out a cancer and close the chapter . . . I never want to see Minoo again or have anything to do with him. I am sorry for you, as you will now have to decide which parent you would like to keep up a relationship with. You are old enough to take the decision, and I am not going to try and push you. If you see him when he comes to London, please drop me a line, and I shall cut myself off from you . . . I am afraid, Zareer, this is a point I am going to be very firm on.'

Her next letter three days later was even more distraught, and it was clear she was channelling all her anxiety and sorrow about the divorce, which now seemed irreversible, into self-righteous anger against Father. 'He has shattered my entire nervous system,' she wrote, 'and tried to destroy me in a most ruthless manner . . . I am still reeling from the shock of what happened, and I think it will take me some time before I feel a complete person again.' Nevertheless, she withdrew her ultimatum to me to choose between them: 'This is a decision you must make on your own, and please remember that, as far as you and I are concerned, it will not affect our relationship, which I hope will always be a very close one. My love for you is so deep that, no matter what happens, it will always be there.'

Two days later, she added: 'I really do not want to come between you and Minoo, but I would like to tell you that he has no feeling for you and made it clear that he did not mind if he did not see you again . . . What really upset me is the total rejection of you and his implication that you were not his son. Vohra [her lawyer] still does not believe that Minoo is your father. What a horrible thing to do to your own son!'

Father's account of that stormy meeting and the alleged aspersions on my legitimacy was predictably rather different. 'When I told her that she had previously agreed to give security against going back on her commitment to see the divorce through, she asked me to prove that. I then read out the relevant passage from your letter to me, where you said: "She is willing to provide any guarantee or security", and having read it out, I said: "This is from your son on your instructions", my only point being to prove that she was a party to the assurances given by you on her behalf. She replied: "And *your* son too." I laughed and said: "Of course", but this does not seem to have mollified her!' He went on to refer to Mother's ultimatum about my having to choose between them and generously assured me: 'I am very keen that your relations with Mummy, who has done so much for you, should not be impaired in any way, and I certainly will not be touchy about any attitude you adopt as a result of this pressure.' It was this latter assurance that had prompted Mother's remark that he did not care whether or not I saw him.

Mother's main reason for going ahead with the divorce was to obtain the financial advance that enabled her to make the move to Bombay. But no sooner was she installed in her new flat, five minutes' walk from Father's, than she started upping the ante. The divorce by mutual consent would not be final unless she joined with Father in moving the court for a decree six months later. She now threatened not to do so unless Father improved on the financial terms to take account of the fact that he had just sold his management consultancy firm for a handsome amount.

Father, for his part, maintained that his retirement income would be no greater than what he had been earning, so there was no question of revising the terms already agreed to. To show his good faith, he offered to put half his capital in trust for me, with the income to go to him for life; but Mother insisted it must be an outright gift. 'We have already won half the battle,' she wrote to me, 'and it would be a pity to let go at this stage.'

I wrote to Father appealing to him to make some concessions and citing Mother's very disturbed state of mind. But he was adamant that he would not give in to her pressure tactics: 'The impression you have about Mummy's state of mind is not correct. I find her extremely cool and collected. She plays golf at the Willingdon Club and leads an active social life, being seen at concerts, dinners and other functions, mostly in the company of Hirji Jehangir.'

The picture Mother painted to me of her life in Bombay was rather different. Always quick to find the grass on the other side greener, she was now as eager to return to Delhi as she had been to leave it only a year ago. 'The job prospects here are practically nil,' she complained, 'and I feel after the divorce I would like to move back to Delhi, where I am close to the family and can live more economically. This flat is so noisy that I just cannot sleep. I don't see the point of making myself so miserable.'

Mother's flat, which she had acquired at a bargain price thanks to a friend of mine, lacked the sea view and spaciousness of Father's; but it was undoubtedly a catch by Bombay standards. She saw only its drawbacks and magnified them a hundredfold in her letters to me. 'It has no privacy whatsoever,' she lamented, 'and one is literally living on the road . . . I cannot use the basement garage, as after dark it becomes a gambling and drinking den . . . All kinds of riff-raff sleep in the foyer and on the stairs. It really is a slum . . . I was not happy in Delhi, but I have never been as miserable as I have been here.' Even her servants, she claimed, were threatening to leave because they found the living conditions so intolerable.

Proceeding with the divorce would have eased Mother's financial worries, which—as I never tired of reminding her—was the reason she had agreed to it. But as the deadline approached, she seemed determined to wriggle out of it. When Father refused to agree to her new financial demands, she seized on this to withdraw her consent and spoke instead of selling her Bombay flat to raise the funds to move back to Delhi.

The flat now became a symbol of all that was wrong with her life, especially as she blamed the decision to buy it for the divorce she now dreaded. 'I have made up my mind to return to the north,' Mother announced to my dismay. 'It was a terrible mistake to come here in the first place. These four months have been the bleakest I have ever known. The Parsi community hate me, and the dice is too heavily loaded against me. Apart from the pressure from Minoo, the Parsis are gunning for me for seeing Hirji, who has been so kind to me. I am so exposed, so vulnerable, and I stand absolutely alone . . . There are times when I long to crawl into a hole and die—life has become unbearable, and I am really very weary.'

Her paranoia about 'the Parsi community' having united against her sounded particularly fanciful when some of her closest friends in Bombay, like JRD Tata, were Parsis. One could not predict from one week to the next what new quixotic scheme she would come up with next. At times she spoke of giving it all up and withdrawing to an ashram for the few years remaining to her; a couple of days later she would be busy thinking up new ruses to increase her alimony.

In the midst of the most acrimonious financial wrangling between her lawyer and Father's, she suddenly phoned him to ask if she could drop in for a chat. Father's account of her visit was more ironical than angry:

'She started by putting forward the amazing proposition that we should give up the idea of a divorce and that she should come and live with me here. I can't imagine how she could think of this after all she has done recently. Anyway, this posture did not last long, for within a few minutes she started calling me ruthless and someone she could not trust [to abide by the divorce terms]. How such lack of elementary trust is compatible with the desire to live with a man is frankly beyond my comprehension.'

I too was growing weary of Mother's litany of woes and her refusal to be practical or to see through any agreed course of action. I had recently, for the first time, started living in a long-term, monogamous relationship, which had its own emotional stresses and adjustments. I was also busy trying to find a congenial full-time job as a journalist in London. I found the burden of sole responsibility for Mother's wayward and self-destructive behaviour increasingly irksome, and it began to show in my attitude to her. My tone towards her became unmistakeably short-tempered and exasperated, and I began to dread her letters and visits to London.

In the spring of 1980, there at last appears to be a breakthrough in the divorce negotiations. Uncle Jeh, who has the respect and affection of both parties, persuades Father to agree to an additional payment of Rs 75,000 to be made two years later, when the funds are released from a tax-exempt investment he has made after the sale of his business. Mother at first appears to accept this concession, but then insists she has been misled into expecting the additional amount immediately. Father refuses; and there the matter rests, with considerable ill will on both sides.

'I am being subjected to visits by him,' Mother complains. 'He rings the doorbell, storms in and abuses me in the most foul language and creates such awful scenes. I am a little worried about him, as I think he is slowly losing his sanity.' 'I feel very serene and calm,' she assures me about her own state of mind. 'I have been reading the *Bhagwad Gita*, and my faith is unshakeable ... I feel no rancour or bitterness against Minoo, and if the divorce had gone through I would have been only too happy to be good friends.'

Now that she can expect no financial pay-off from the divorce, Mother begins to try and sell her Bombay flat with a view to moving back to Delhi with the proceeds. It has been a sound investment, having doubled in value in one year; but it makes no sense to have spent as much as she has on the move from Delhi, and what she euphemistically calls 'doing up' the new flat, only to sell it and repeat the whole process six months later. When I try to remonstrate with her, she pleads in typically melodramatic fashion that her very life will be in danger if she stays on.

'The flat is surrounded by smugglers,' she writes. 'Haji Mastaan [a prominent Bombay crime baron] lives just opposite, and there are various other smugglers living all around it. As a result, it is most unsafe and also very noisy at nights when the gambling and drinking starts and goes on till the early hours.' To add to her troubles, the children of her upstairs neighbours 'collect all the children from other buildings and play football, cricket and badminton in the foyer near our lift. There is a perpetual din, and it is often not possible to hear one's own voice'.

A couple of months later, she is claiming that the tide of smugglers has invaded her own building and turned the empty ground-floor flat into 'a den of gambling and prostitution', so much so that she is afraid to use the foyer or the lift after dark. The other residents, she says, are too frightened to complain to the police for fear of 'having their throats slit'.

She also maintains that the general stress and Bombay climate are destroying her health, complaining of 'terrible pains' in the heart, chest and kidneys. I am tempted to ascribe these to her imagination, especially when she writes that a Delhi faith-healer has cured her of the heart condition, while a herbal treatment has done her kidneys 'a world of good'. At other times, she complains of 'wildly fluctuating' blood pressure. 'I go into a state of coma,' she announces, 'which lasts for a couple of hours sometimes, and I have to be brought round by coramine injections.'

When I decide to visit India that winter with my new partner David, Mother transfers her health worries to us and advises that we bring plenty of soup-cubes, chocolate, Bovril and cheese, in case we find the food on our travels inedible. 'Find out what those tablets are that disinfect water,' she also advises, 'and bring those, and also certain medicines like good painkillers and stomach-settlers.'

When we arrive, we find that her apartment-house, far from being the den of thieves she has described, is a charming building in one of Bombay's few remaining leafy and quiet lanes. But David falls seriously ill with a rectal abscess he has brought with him from London and has to have an emergency operation in Bombay. Both my parents are very supportive and sympathetic, spending long hours at the hospital and using all their contacts to ensure he gets the best medical care. I am particularly touched by Father's concern, since the subject of my sexuality has never been discussed with him; and one consequence is that I see a good deal of him and his partner, with whom my relations are now friendly and relaxed.

Unfortunately, Mother chooses to see this as a sign of disloyalty. 'I want you to know that there is a hole in my heart,' she writes to me some months after my trip. 'I cannot understand what I have done that you should abandon me. Perhaps to avoid further suffering I should keep my distance from all three of you . . . You love your father, and I hope he will deserve it. As far as I am concerned, write me off.'

Fortunately, as is so often the way with her tantrums, the storm passes and she quietly forgets her ultimatum. But distancing herself from Father now becomes her new pretext for leaving Bombay and returning to Delhi. Bombay property prices are just beginning the runaway spiral which will put them among the highest in the world in a decade. Within a year of buying the Bombay flat, and despite all her complaints about it, Mother has an offer of twice the price she paid for it. With unnecessary haste, she accepts an advance from a prospective buyer, spends the money and then decides to back out because she has a higher offer. The legal wrangles that result drag on for the next three years and become her second-most important occupation, the first of course still being the divorce.

Every few months, when financial constraints are pressing on her, Mother revives the divorce negotiations, only to back out again at the eleventh hour. This cat-and-mouse game understandably embitters Father, who finds his hopes raised only to be dashed yet again. It also exasperates me, because I am usually the main channel of communication she uses; and I begin to see her behaviour as a calculated and perverse attempt to stir up trouble and maintain some kind of contact, however acrimonious, with Father.

A typical incident in 1982 is a note she sends over to Father, five minutes down the hill from her, asking if she can come over for a chat. He phones her instantly to ask when she would like to come and is 'a little taken aback to be told that she was suffering from malaria and kidney trouble and could not come for some three or four days'. She clearly hopes that this news will bring him over to visit her; and when he does not rise to the bait, he hears nothing further from her.

A few weeks later she suddenly writes again, inviting him over to dinner with some mutual friends who are visiting. He politely declines, explaining 'that this kind of friendly relationship would be possible only after a divorce, but that unfortunately she had thwarted and twice back-tracked on this'.

Against his better judgement, Father agrees to a third divorce attempt a few months later. He maintains that Mother has begged him to re-open the matter because she is desperate for money. 'She came to my place and started sobbing her heart out, pleading with me to agree to her request as she was very hard up, and I was foolish enough to fall for it. It is quite clear to me now that . . . her malice and vindictiveness far outweigh even her greed for money.'

What happens is that two days before the final divorce decree is due, Mother makes a new demand that he must hand over to her all the contents of his Breach Candy flat. She forfeited her claim to these two years ago when she defaulted on the first divorce petition and failed to return the advance on alimony. Father could no doubt give in in the interest of winning his freedom, but he stubbornly digs in his toes, insisting 'that this is blackmail to which I am not prepared to yield'. He proposes instead that he will make an irrevocable bequest in his will, leaving the disputed movables to me.

My own overriding concern through all this is somehow to persuade Mother that it is in her own financial interests to go through with the divorce, which will give her an alimony she badly needs and enable her to stay on in Bombay without having to sell her flat. But it is a lost cause, because she is quite prepared to cut off her nose to spite her face. Since she also expects me to share the consequences and take her side unquestioningly, the strain on our own relationship becomes intolerable. Although I defend her to Father, in private I warn her forcefully that her behaviour is self-destructive, and we quarrel often and fiercely.

One symptom of Mother's growing emotional isolation is her intense involvement with her domestic servants. Her relationships with staff have always been volatile to say the least. She oscillates from euphoria about their excellence to fury about their ingratitude or dishonesty. Now she is convinced that her maidservant Susheela, whose energy and intelligence she has so far been praising to the skies, is stealing her silver and crystal. 'When I asked her to return them,' she reports, 'she turned very abusive and threatened to set her *goonda* boyfriends on me.' Mother hands her over to the police, though with injunctions 'not to hurt her or beat her up', as is their wont with the lower classes. But she never gets anything back. Her conviction that she is being robbed often borders on paranoia, especially as she often forgets that she has sold some of her valuables or stored them away.

Susheela's arrest coincides with our loyal, old manservant Bhula being diagnosed with terminal throat cancer while he is on home leave in his village in Gujarat. He has been with us for three decades, apart from brief interludes when Mother has quarrelled with him and sent him packing, only to re-engage him a few months later. Now she is distraught at the prospect of losing him for good. She wires funds to his family to have him treated at the nearest cancer hospital, phones daily to the doctors there and speaks of making a trip to visit him as soon as her own health permits.

Unfortunately, Bhula dies soon after, and Mother's grief does not last long. A few weeks later, she is ecstatic about his successor, another Gujarati called Jairam, whom she describes as 'a younger edition of Bhula'. 'I have become very fond of him,' she assures me, 'as he is so good and hardworking. He is already devoted to me, as I look after him so well.'

Never one to despair for long, Mother once again started cultivating Mrs Gandhi, who had made a spectacular comeback in an election landslide in January 1980, after the Janata government disintegrated in faction-fighting. 'I know how you will feel about this,' she wrote about the election results, 'but I must admit to you that I cannot help but feel a sense of elation. I think I must care for her very much deep down in my heart.'

Nevertheless, she had studiously avoided any association with Indira while she was in the political wilderness; and three years had gone by since she last saw Mrs Gandhi on the morning after her catastrophic election defeat. Now Mother prepared the way back into her favour by cultivating the Prime Minister's yoga teacher Swami Dhirendra Brahmachari, a strikingly good-looking man who was fond of posing for cameras with very few clothes on and had a reputation as a ladies' man and an influential political fixer.

Be that as it may, the Swami's Rasputin-like influence ensured Mother a friendly reception when she called on Mrs Gandhi; and there was talk again of a job and house in Delhi working for the Congress Party. But, as before, months went by without any formal offer, and Mother sensibly decided to drop the idea. Her plan now was to move back to Delhi and live in rented accommodation on the proceeds of the sale of her Bombay flat.

I had recently begun a demanding full-time job with BBC Radio Current Affairs in London and had little time for Mother's many problems. But I flew out to see her in Delhi in the winter of 1983, in the nick of time to stop her running through all the money she had received from the sale of her Bombay flat. She had rented an expensive flat in one of Delhi's posher areas, Defence Colony, and seemed happily resigned to living on her capital till it ran out.

With the utmost difficulty I eventually convinced her that she must buy a flat within her means and invest the rest of her capital to give herself a regular income. I dragged her kicking and screaming around Delhi building sites and apartment blocks; but the only flat she would consider was a third-floor penthouse near the leafy Mughal ruins of Hauz Khas. She loved its open aspect, surrounded by greenery, with a large roof-terrace, and refused to consider more practical objections such as the prospect of having to climb three floors without a lift in her advancing years. 'My doctors insist that stairs are the best thing for me,' she asserted cheerfully and also airily brushed aside the fact that terrace flats were heat-traps in the merciless Delhi summer sun. Ground floors, she maintained, were dark and depressing and also very unsafe for a woman living alone.

We bought the flat, and it was to be her home for the next fourteen years, the scene of very little joy and a great many disasters. She had barely moved into it when I got a call from her saying that all her jewellery had been stolen by Jairam, the wonder-servant she had brought with her from Bombay. Despite my best efforts, I never got to the bottom of what actually transpired. Mother had a choice collection of very pretty, antique Mughal jewellery, some of it inherited from Nanna and the rest bought for her at the time of her wedding. As the years advanced, she tended to wear less of it, preferring the simpler elegance of pearls; so she decided to sell most of it to a Delhi jeweller.

According to her version of events, she took all the jewellery out of her safe-deposit locker at the local bank and kept it in her cupboard at home in an overnight bag. She then fell ill with severe gastroenteritis and forgot all about the jewellery; but when she looked for it a couple of weeks later it was all gone, and so was Jairam, who had just left for Bombay on home leave because his wife was dying of cancer. Mother phoned Hirji Jehangir, whose chauffeur was Jairam's cousin, and Hirji got Jairam to return to Delhi post-haste. When he turned up, Mother handed him over to the police, but there was no sign of her jewellery, and he denied all knowledge of it. Mother insisted that she did not want the police to beat a confession out of him (their usual tactic), so he was released without charge.

The whole affair was so bizarre that I couldn't make head or tail of it. Could even Mother be so careless as to leave a bagful of jewellery lying in an unlocked bedroom cupboard after having stored it in a bank all these years? And if Jairam had stolen it, would he really be foolhardy enough to return to Delhi when summoned, knowing that the police might torture him into a confession if Mother pressed charges? The plot became even more murky when Mother embellished her conspiracy theory with suspicions that Jairam was in league with the jeweller to whom she was about to sell, and even that he had seduced a female clerk at her bank into giving him a duplicate key to her locker there.

My own best guess is that Mother might have imagined or invented the heist herself, in order to account for the fact that she had already sold the jewellery and spent the proceeds. I suspect that she seized upon Jairam's departure, possibly against her wishes, to kill two birds with one stone by pinning the blame on him. Whatever the truth, that was the last we saw of Jairam and of Mother's jewels.

As the years passed, the theme of theft, conspiracy and loss was a familiar one in her life, and it became difficult to judge when she was crying wolf. Her sisters were convinced that she actively hallucinated, and a close friend of mine speculated that she might have a drug addiction, which would also account for her financial straits. The less credibility we attached to her crises and catastrophes, the more melodramatic they seemed to become.

On a trip to London in 1986, Mother insisted that she must buy a state-of-the-art television and video player to take back with her to Delhi to keep her company in her lonely existence. As I'd predicted, she had to pay a hefty customs duty on them when she arrived back in India. With a logic peculiar to herself, she then decided to sell them to recoup her losses. Against all advice, she advertised them in the Delhi papers and allowed complete strangers into her flat to examine them. After one such visit, I got an alarming call from her to say that a prospective buyer had drugged her with a handkerchief of chloroform and absconded with the VCR. All she remembered was showing it to him, after which she blacked out and came to on the floor with a scent of chloroform in the room.

A year later, she was complaining of yet another servant crisis. Aunt Sheela had found her a new, Christian maidservant called Millie, who had worked for twelve years for her in-laws and came highly recommended. At first, Mother was ecstatic about her: she was an excellent cook and kept the flat spotless. But then came trouble: 'She has one big fault—a frightening temper. She is also a T.V. addict and must watch it every day. She is threatening to leave if I do not hire a set for her, which she can turn on whenever she wants.'

A week later, events took a more dramatic turn, with Mother claiming that Millie had threatened her life. 'She attacked me with the kitchen knife unless I let her use my VCR and television whenever she wanted to . . . It is a pity that she has these maniacal tendencies, as in her sane moments she is an excellent cook and a hard worker.' According to Mother's account, she called in the police, and they evicted Millie. But a day later she returned and confronted Mother, whose two menservants also took Millie's side. The three of them demanded large amounts of cash from her, and when Mother refused 'they all walked out, threatening to return with a gang of *goondas* to beat me up'. Mother then locked up the flat and fled to Aunt Sheela's, taking her dog Madhav, a large and very unruly greyhound cross-breed, with her.

Two days later, she returned home with police protection and a new servant, and life seemed to be returning to normal. But then disaster struck again: the dog Madhav disappeared unaccountably. For three days and nights, Mother and a loyal band of friends scoured the neighbourhood for him, with no success. On the fourth day, the dreaded Millie appeared and begged Mother to take her back. 'I was so broken and exhausted that I let her come back,' Mother explained. 'I could not carry on doing all the house-work and looking for Madhav in this terrible heat. The next morning Madhav appeared just out of the blue.' Mother now suspected that his disappearance had been staged by the servants in order to get her to reinstate Millie, but she seemed unaccountably resigned to such blackmail. 'Millie is in a chastened mood,' she assured me, 'and is doing all the work. There is no denying that she is an excellent servant. Madhav gets on very well with her, so for the time being I can relax.'

But a week later, she was describing Millie as a *rakshin* (she-devil) and had again given her notice to leave. 'She started her old tricks and almost made me a captive. My fear is that she will do something to Madhav before she goes, so I am being very kind to her. Yesterday she put on an act of having a heart-attack, but the moment the doctor came she was up and about. She is the devil incarnate.'

The drama did not end with Millie's second and final departure. 'I have just discovered that she had been for two years an inmate of the asylum for the insane in Ranchi [the Indian equivalent of Bedlam].

Unfortunately, she was not just a loony but a big thief. I found that all my suitcases locked and put away in the box-room had been slit underneath and everything of any value taken. With great glee, she told me before she left of all the things that had been stolen or wrecked. The damage is something awful. Things went so far that my car was wrecked at night by some hoodlums. I am now without any transport.'

It was becoming increasingly hard to separate fact from fiction in Mother's tales of woe and the conspiracy theories to which she was so prone. Crises like these made her a Calamity Jane among her family and circle of friends, not least because her own mood swings were so extreme and dramatic. She seemed blissfully unaware of how inconsistent it might appear to be calling in the police to evict a maid who was threatening her life, only to re-employ her a few days later, and then accuse her of robbery and criminal damage a week later.

'When troubles come, they come not single' was one of Mother's favourite aphorisms; and she certainly seemed to have the knack of attracting them. About this time, she became the accused in a criminal trial that was to drag on for fourteen years, something of a record even by Indian judicial standards. It all began with an antique medieval bronze figure she had bought from one of her dealer contacts and then resold at a profit to a friend. Sporadic antique dealing had for some time been both a hobby of hers and a welcome source of additional income. But on this occasion, it all went horribly wrong.

On a hot and dusty summer day in 1986, a posse of policemen turned up at Mother's front door, with the dealer who had sold her the bronze in tow. They were from a small town called Rajgarh in Rajasthan, about a hundred miles from Delhi. The dealer, it turned out, had been arrested for stealing the statue of the deity from a local temple, where it had been the resident idol. Now he led the police to Mother, in return for a promise of more lenient treatment if the idol was recovered.

Since the object was no longer with her, she could have denied all knowledge of it and invited the police to search the premises. It would have been her word against the dealer's, and it's unlikely that the matter would have gone any further. Unfortunately, she decided to tell the truth, admitting that she had bought the piece without knowing it was stolen.

The police inspector in charge seemed understanding and assured her that all would be well if she retrieved it and returned it to him; so she rushed over to the friend who had bought it, refunded her money and handed the bronze over to the police.

But then came the sting in the tail: the inspector demanded a bribe for his trouble, threatening that she could be charged with receiving stolen goods if she did not pay. At this point, Mother unwisely dug in her heels and flatly refused to pay. The police left, but a week later they were back with a warrant for her arrest from the district magistrate in Rajgarh. They had orders to take her back with them to Rajasthan, but she managed to persuade them to take her first to the nearby local police station, where she was well known from her various confrontations with rebellious servants. There the station sergeant allowed her to phone her sisters, whereupon Uncle Gogu gallantly rushed to her rescue and managed to get her bail from a Delhi judge.

All this took several hours, during which she had to sit it out at the police station; but she seems to have taken it all with remarkable sangfroid, prompting her other brother-in-law to remark on her brazenness in such a humiliating situation. Although the Rajgarh police had to return home empty-handed, they made sure that Mother paid dearly for her refusal to bribe them. They insisted on pressing charges against her, and she had to appear in the local district court to present her defence. That involved hiring a local lawyer, and the arduous four-hour journey there, on poor and dusty roads, became a dreaded act of penance she had to perform three or four times a year for the rest of her life. It was hugely expensive, because in typically Indian fashion everyone from the judge to the court clerk expected to be bribed. And because Mother looked like such a promising meal ticket in this small, run-down town, everyone there, including her own lawyer, had a stake in prolonging the proceedings indefinitely.

Every time she appeared, the case would be unaccountably adjourned because vital witnesses were absent or the judge himself was taken ill. Two successive district magistrates heard the case and were on the point of delivering judgement when they were transferred and the case had to be heard all over again by their successor. At each stage, money changed hands in return for promises of a quick and friendly verdict, which were broken with monotonous regularity. It would have been farcical had it not been for the very real threat of two years' rigorous imprisonment—the maximum penalty for the offence.

'The Case', as it came to be known in Mother's circle of family and friends, replaced the earlier long-running civil suit about Nanna's estate as the centre of her existence; but this time there was no promise of a crock of gold at the end of the rainbow. A succession of Delhi lawyers were drafted in to help bring it to a close, officials were approached, and even the MP for the area was lobbied to apply political pressure. But to no avail; the case dragged on till Mother's death eventually deprived the town of Rajgarh of this lucrative source of income.

Adversity and the passing of the years do not make Mother any more consistent in her relationships with friends or family, and she veers between extremes of euphoric attachment and bitter reproachfulness. The long-running quarrel with her sister Sarala has at last been laid to rest and normal relations restored. Now that she is back in Delhi, Mother sees a great deal of aunts Sarala and Sheela; but there is a constant undercurrent of resentment about what she perceives as their treating her like a poor relation, and they alternate regularly in her favour. One month Sarala is very affectionate and Sheela very 'casual', the next, Sarala offhanded and Sheela 'sweet and caring'. And it is the same with her friends, whose loyalty and motives she is quick to suspect. It does not occur to Mother that people's behaviour towards her might have something to do with her own erratic mood swings.

It never ceases to amaze and annoy me how violently some minor event can cause her to turn against people who have given her years of loyalty and affection. Often I find myself dragged in to mediate, as in the case of Mr Dogra, who was her loyal PA on the women's committee in the early 1970s, and has run errands for her ever since in his spare time. Early in 1986, he writes me a pained letter about Mother refusing to settle the bill for repairs to her car, which he oversaw at her behest during her absence abroad. 'All these years you have seen and known,' he writes, 'how loyal and sincere I had been to Madam, and doing all the jobs at all times, day and night, waiting at the airports even at the dead of night, receiving her, and at every time of difficulty I was available to her.'

Mother's version is that the cost of the repairs has been inflated by Mr Dogra in league with the garage. Under pressure from me, she agrees to pay; but sadly that is the end of her fifteen-year friendship with Mr Dogra.

As Mother lurched from one crisis to another, Aunt Sarala decided it was time to intervene and put her life into some kind of order. She urged Mother to take a more practical view of the advantages of a divorce if the alimony gave her a regular source of income; and her arguments prevailed where mine had failed. She undertook to negotiate fresh terms with Father, but on one condition: that there would be no going back this time. She made it clear to Mother that if she did back out again, the price would be her own friendship, which had been retrieved with so much difficulty after a decade.

Although Mother agreed to go ahead, it was with a heavy heart. 'I have such an overwhelming sense of sadness,' she wrote to me. 'Everything has come to an end—all the things I believed in and people I trusted. There is nothing really to look forward to.' The new divorce negotiations went smoothly, mercifully not requiring my involvement this time, and Aunt Sarala was able to get both sides committed to a reasonable alimony settlement.

In the summer of 1988 a new divorce petition, the fourth in this long-running saga, was filed in the courts; but Father, thrice bitten, did not trust his luck. He wrote to enlist my help in ensuring that Mother went through with it this time. He began by admitting how difficult it was for him temperamentally to open his heart to me. He had recently had a second prostate operation, which he said had left him rather weak. He was eighty-three, he wrote, and 'living on borrowed time', facing 'almost complete blindness in a year or two' due to macular degeneration. Since his retirement he had been living on a shoe-string budget and doing without many of the comforts of life: 'I cannot afford to invite friends to dinner. But this means that I do not get invited out, and almost all my evenings have to be spent at home. Quite often, I am on my own from 2 p.m. to bedtime, and since I cannot read, which was my main pleasure, all I can do is listen to music, which I cannot do for eight hours running.'

Apart from what he called 'prolonged loneliness', he cited the fact that he could no longer afford foreign travel and had to stint on all sorts of things ranging from food and clothes to razor blades. And then came a curious ultimatum. If the divorce went through as scheduled that autumn, he was 'prepared to carry on in this manner, because I can then have the consolation of someone staying with me and looking after me and giving me the necessary companionship and security'. If, however, there was any further hitch or delay, he would negotiate with the landlord of Breach Candy House to sell the valuable tenancy of his flat back to him 'for certain compensation which will make it possible for me to live in comfort'. The loser, he pointed out, would be me, since I would not inherit the valuable tenancy; but I would have only Mother to blame for this misfortune.

He suggested I show her his letter to 'convey the message to her that the divorce means you getting the flat, and no divorce means everybody losing it. I do not expect her to back out for the fourth time, but it is just as well she and you should know the implications in good time'. Her response was truculent: 'I am quite happy that you have feeling for him, for I agree that you are very much a Masani, but I do not see Minoo showing much love for you.'

In Mother's vocabulary, being a Masani meant being a bully and rather lacking in feeling, if not entirely heartless; in mine it meant consistency and rationality, as against the fickle and volatile Srivastava way. The battle lines were drawn, and for the rest of Mother's life we coexisted, despite our close bonds, like two somewhat hostile species, almost like a dog and cat forced to live together in a confined space.

As Father had feared, Mother again tried to back out of the divorce as the court deadline approached. As before, her tactic was to make new demands, this time for furniture that she claimed had been given by her mother. Father retaliated by reiterating that he would return the tenancy of his flat as threatened. When I remonstrated that he was penalizing me for Mother's bad behaviour, he insisted that he did not want her to profit from her legal status as his wife by living in the flat after his death.

Despite pressure from Aunt Sarala not to let her down, Mother prevaricated till the bitter end, threatening first to withdraw her consent and then, after the divorce decree was issued, to appeal against it. As luck would have it, her telegram to her Bombay lawyer to file an appeal reached him just after the court's deadline had expired. Two days later, Father had remarried.

Mother's response seemed resigned, if elegiac. 'It is a sad end,' she wrote, 'to a marriage which gave nothing but pain to my parents. The past 40 years have left me with a taste of ashes—so many promises broken and so many dreams shattered. My life with Minoo was empty and lacking in lasting values. On the surface it seemed a pleasant one, but it never went very deep. Everything I had cherished as a young girl was destroyed over the years. You were the only good thing that happened . . . I made so many others unhappy, and now the end has come. It was all to no purpose.'

We had all hoped that once the suspense and uncertainty were over, Mother would recover emotionally and take a more positive view of the opportunity to open a new chapter. But her state of mind was going from bad to worse. Although Father and she had lived apart for seventeen years, the finality of the divorce and his remarriage was an emotional blow that seemed to tip her fragile sanity over the edge.

In the month after the divorce, three separate and familiar strands of anxiety in her life—servants, money and illness—converged into a single catastrophe. She had just succeeded in selling a plot of her ancestral land in Kanpur. Early one morning in London, I was woken by a call from Father in Bombay to say that he was very alarmed about Mother's condition and state of mind. He had just heard from her sisters that she had been mugged in the street and robbed of a large sum of Rs 50,000 in cash, which she had just withdrawn from the bank. He thought I might need to fly out to help her through the crisis.

Mother, when I called her, was adamant that there was no need for me to come. The circumstances of how she was robbed remained mysterious, and I never ascertained the truth of it. Had she just spent the money and found a melodramatic way to account for it? I had had similar doubts five years earlier about the theft of all her jewellery. Much later, when

I asked her servants about it, they had no recollection of her coming home from the bank and reporting the mugging to them or anyone else.

The plot thickened a week later when her driver, who had been escorting her on that fateful visit to the bank, died in mysterious circumstances. He had gone home to his village on leave and was killed when he fell off the roof of a crowded state transport bus on his way back. Mother insisted that he had been murdered by the same people who had robbed her. She became obsessive about this and spoke of nothing else to her sisters and friends.

By now she was clearly in the throes of a deep depression, and the symptoms included incessant talking and a stream of paranoia in which fact and fiction became impossible to distinguish. At the same time, her physical state began to deteriorate alarmingly. She developed acute gastroenteritis, stopped eating, grew weak and had repeated falls, one worse than the other. The last of these resulted in a broken rib, whereupon she was taken to hospital by one of her nephews. The doctors diagnosed severe dehydration and damage to her kidney function, which had raised her blood urea to dangerous levels and induced delirium.

Mother's condition was now officially critical, and I flew out to Delhi filled with foreboding. By the time I arrived she was out of danger and responding to treatment, though mentally still far from normal. Her mood alternated between extremes of gratitude for the concern shown by all around her, including myself, to irrational rages and tantrums with her nurses and carers. The main focus of her anger, however, was Father. Whether driven by guilt or affection, he had flown up to Delhi in the hope of seeing her and giving me some moral support. While he hovered outside her hospital room, I did my best to persuade her to let him in, but she became tearful and emotional, and we decided not to risk distressing her. She was adamant that she would never set eyes on Father again as long as she lived, and for once she was as good as her word.

'An anger arising from the deepest depths within one,' Mother wrote in her diary a year later, in a reference to how Father had destroyed her very being by insisting on a divorce. 'Has any human being the right to destroy another so effectively that there is not even a spark left to quicken a new birth? I am slowly dying, but not because of age. Something deeper has been destroyed. It has gone right down to my roots. I have turned to the philosophy of *Vedanta*, which up to now had withstood the vicissitudes of fortune, but it brings me no comfort today. My philosophy can no longer stand up to the vagaries of fortune. I am more in tune with the *Rubaiyat* of Omar Khayyam. *Vedanta* is a dangerous philosophy which, in the hands of an unscrupulous person, can play havoc.'

Her condemnation of Vedanta is puzzling, because Father certainly had no time for it. Perhaps she meant that one should live in the moment like Omar Khayyam, seizing life's pleasures, rather than submitting to karma. I can only guess, and perhaps she was confused about her own emotions.

'When I left Minoo, I gave up a husband who was more precious than a thousand sons,' she wrote in the same diary entry.

Now, when it is too late, this has become so clear. If only I had had someone whom I trusted to guide me at the time I made this decision. But I always did what I wanted. Mummy said I was headstrong—that was putting it gently!

Minoo always paid me such compliments! There was no one like me in the family. I was the best of the 'Silly Sisters'. 'Oh, she's different,' he would insist. 'She does everything so well. She dances beautifully, is the best-looking, the most talented. There's nothing that she puts her hand to that she doesn't do with excellence. When she goes down the golf-course, everyone remarks that she plays golf better than all these other women. Everyone wants to play with her. The men watch her with admiration. Oh, indeed I'm a lucky man. I sometimes find myself attracted physically to another woman because I'm jealous of my lovely wife. Sometimes ordinary, wholesome food can be more satisfying than such beauty and elegance. But then I know they can come nowhere near her.'

Absurd words! They destroyed my life and warped my values. When I think of all those compliments men paid me, I wish there had been someone to give me a tight smack and say: 'Come to your senses.'

The idea that Father turned to other women as an antidote to his wife's beauty is a little disingenuous. Even so, Mother's lament for the loss of a husband 'worth more than a thousand sons' was clearly sincere and heartfelt, though it hurt me to read it after her death. In life, she had reproached me often enough—whenever we quarrelled—for persuading her to leave Father, and then turning my back on her. 'Minoo would never have treated me the way you do.' But what's plain in her sad reminiscence is that, more than any external intervention, she blames her own hubris and naïveté for the end of their marriage.

THIRTEEN

LITTLE PROBLEMS

Mother had a predilection for jokey birthday cards, usually about the pains of ageing. One she sent me in 1985 demonstrated that her humour could be self-deprecating. It showed a small dog chasing a postman, with the caption: 'Everybody has their little problems . . . Happy birthday from one of yours!'

Jokes apart, there is little doubt that by then I regard her as the major problem in my life, and my responses range from a cold tolerance to unconcealed resentment and even rage. During her breakdown in 1989, it becomes clear, even to her critical sisters, that she cannot really be held responsible for her capricious and erratic behaviour. But while I accept this intellectually, it does not make her any easier to cope with.

In the long run, Aunt Sarala is right about the divorce clearing out the emotional cobwebs and helping Mother to move on. Father now ceases to be the focus of her discontent, and in time she overcomes her bitterness towards him. The divorce undoubtedly triggered the physical and mental crisis she suffered soon after, and her health never fully recovered from it. But emotionally she seems to have arrived at a kind of acceptance of old age and of making the best of the years remaining to her.

Despite, or perhaps because of, her own mistakes, she is full of emotional wisdom in her advice to me. My twelve-year relationship with David is grinding towards a break, hastened by our temperamental differences and my reluctance to be more accommodating. 'It is a pity that you and Dave have drifted so far apart,' Mother writes to me in 1990. 'He is a very fine person and highly intelligent. It would have been wonderful if you both could have been close to each other. Basically, he is a lonely person, and since his mother died he feels even more alone. Try and be understanding and kind to him. He has a number of acquaintances, but no real friends, and he is not close to his family. Also, I assure you that you will not find anyone as congenial to live with.'

At the time, I take no notice, especially as David leads a far busier social life than I and seems anything but lonely. But with hindsight I realize that Mother was more perceptive than I gave her credit for about what went on beneath the surface. Two years later, the relationship finally breaks up, and David moves out to a flat of his own. He and Mother remain as close as before, and largely due to her we stay good friends. He drops in often to see her and takes her out on drives to the country and antique-hunting expeditions to Portobello market. He confides in her and introduces her to his new lovers, and she gets on well with most of them, always happy to be at the centre of a group of men, gay or otherwise. Perhaps they have the kind of intimacy that he could not achieve with his own mother, who was unaware of his sexuality, or that Mother, for her part, feels denied by me.

Now that the divorce is over and done with, the main cause for concern are Mother's failing kidneys, which seem to deteriorate with every Delhi summer and the bouts of gastroenteritis, urinary infection and dehydration to which she is so prone. She also has a range of other complaints, such as high blood pressure, arthritis, an underactive thyroid, diverticuli or pouches in the colon, and a prolapsed uterus that requires surgery.

For two decades now, Mother has referred tragically to these being her 'last few years'; so it seems something of an achievement that she is well into her seventies and still around, bouncing back up from even the most severe illnesses. Other, sturdier relations have already fallen by the wayside, notably Aunt Mehra, to whom I have come very close in her later years. After seventy years of perfect health, she is suddenly struck down by crippling arthritis, which kills her in 1990 after a series of severe falls and fractures.

Father, too, has been ageing rapidly since his fourth and final marriage. He is now almost completely blind (due to macular degeneration), and with his sight he seems to have lost his mental acumen and zest for life. Since his retirement from politics, his pet cause has been the legalization of euthanasia, or the right to die with dignity, as he puts it. But he grows increasingly fearful of his own death the closer it approaches. He becomes restless and obsessively anxious, constantly getting up to check that the front door is properly shut and that his keys are in a safe place. Unable to read, he now stops listening even to the radio or to music and descends gradually into the oblivion of dementia.

The last time I see Father is in January 1998, soon after his ninety-second birthday. He is completely bedridden, following a fall in which he has fractured his hip, and he has lost the power of speech. He is as frail and helpless as a newborn babe, and with our roles reversed it is hard to imagine that this was the martinet I feared as a child. He still responds to visitors who take his hand, but it is impossible to tell whether he recognizes anyone. It has been an undignified, two-year descent into the vegetative state he feared so much. Five months later, he slips away altogether.

Mother's decline is less dramatic: certainly she remains mentally lucid till the very end, or at least as lucid as she has ever been. Her mood swings are still frequent, but now they centre on the relative merits of her various consultants and hospital wards, and on lesser mortals like the nurses and carers on whom she is dependent. In view of her tendency to fall critically ill in the Delhi summer, it is generally agreed between her sisters and myself that she should spend the six hot months of the year with me in London.

She becomes a familiar and popular figure in my local neighbourhood at Tufnell Park. Despite her physical frailty, she still spends hours of the day grooming herself and her immense wardrobe, which overflows from the ample cupboard space I give her and is ranged around her room in various suitcases. Despite her illnesses, age has been kind to her appearance. Her skin is as glowing and unwrinkled as ever, her figure trim and her hair a fine and burnished silver, which she spends many hours touching up out of a bottle. She cuts an undeniably elegant and exotic figure as she walks my dogs in the local park or shops for antique bargains in the Nags Head flea market. But the isolation in London from her own friends and family makes her overdependent on me and encourages her to manufacture emotional crises to attract my attention.

There are frequent ups and downs in her relationship with my neurotic but priceless Polish cleaning lady, Krystyna. Having lived through what must have been traumatic times as a young girl—captured, raped and deported by Soviet Russian occupation forces—she is prone to take fright or umbrage on the slightest pretext. She worships Mother and insists on running all sorts of unpaid errands for her. But when Mother fails to reciprocate her devotion and takes it all for granted, Krystyna responds with the fury of a woman scorned and hands in her notice. I am distraught to lose her after twelve years of sparkling and unstinted service, and I angrily blame Mother for it.

Her failing health requires constant medical attention, which I would not be able to afford without the National Health Service. I managed to register her with my local G.P. practice and, though not strictly entitled, she is referred on to consultants and hospitals as her condition deteriorates. Mother herself always loves a bargain and is delighted to be getting free treatment. But she is less enthusiastic about being an inpatient in NHS hospitals, which she scornfully dubs 'working-class medicine'.

Her first admission is in the summer of 1997, when she goes into the Whittington Hospital with a suspected heart attack, but is eventually diagnosed with severe anaemia arising from her progressive kidney failure. A month later she is back in with a chest infection. She hates the Whittington with a passion, not least because she is in a mixed ward and is treated to the spectacle of working-class men wandering around in their pyjamas. Every visit to her bedside produces a new tale of woe, often surreal in its complexity. The ward is far too full and noisy, she complains, and she is never allowed to rest; she would be far better off at home. The place is overrun with unruly visitors: the children who visit the woman in the next bed throw sweets at Mother when she dozes off. A younger Cypriot man farther down has dozens of rowdy, late night visitors who bring in food and drink and turn the ward into a noisy party, with the nurses turning a blind eye or joining in.

There is usually a grain of truth somewhere in Mother's horror stories; but, to borrow one of Father's favourite mixed metaphors, one has to take her cock-and-bull with a large pinch of salt. And the more sceptical I sound, the more outrageous her embellishments become. Although I preserve a façade of calmness and even indifference, I find her decline deeply unsettling, not least because it is so difficult to judge the severity of her symptoms. She is often at her most stoical and courageous when her illness is at its worst; but the moment she feels better, she exaggerates her discomfort to manipulate those around her.

Her sisters, too, find this combination of helpless dependence and aggressive demands difficult to reconcile. Secure in their own comfortable marriages, aunts Sarala and Sheela feel sympathy for Mother's predicament and help her out financially with a regular monthly subsidy; but they are not prepared to disrupt the comfort of their own lives to cope with her illnesses and emotional crises, and this in turn makes them feel guilty and uncomfortable around her.

After yet another serious illness in the summer of 1998, when Mother again has to be hospitalized in Delhi, the aunts pack her off to London as soon as she can travel, and they are adamant that she must not return. 'In this last stage of her life,' Aunt Sarala writes to me, 'the love and care you can give her is her only source of joy.' 'London suits her,' Aunt Sheela adds in the same letter. 'Perhaps it is possible for her to get residence there and come out to India for the winter. She has nobody who can take care of her in Delhi. Sarala and I are too old and too sick ourselves to take on that responsibility.'

The decision is effectively clinched by the deterioration of Mother's kidneys to the point where she needs regular dialysis. She is in London at the time, and it makes sense for her to stay on there and have the dialysis on the NHS. The alternative would mean my having to give up my job to take her back to India and live with her there. Mother still hopes and plans for a return to Delhi in the winter, to be with her beloved dogs and servants and visit her sisters. But her growing frailty and the risks of infection associated with dialysis make any travel increasingly remote.

For the last ten months of Mother's life, I am officially her sole carer, a role I have dreaded for most of my adult life. At a practical level, it involves a demanding range of daily duties. First thing in the morning, I have to disconnect her from her automatic, overnight dialysis machine, which sits by her bedside huffing and puffing mysteriously as it pumps various bags of saline and other solutions in and out of her. I then have to lay out her vast array of medications, too complex for her to remember, and bring her breakfast. Later, a home help from Social Services comes to help her bathe and dress. Mother would not tolerate meals-on-wheels, so I am also responsible for giving her lunch and dinner, usually on a tray. And then comes the most onerous and physically intimate duty of all: connecting her to her bedside dialysis machine before she turns in for the night.

The machine and its rituals dominate our lives with a near-religious power of life and death. It works by pumping several litres of saline in and out of Mother's diaphragm area through a small catheter permanently embedded in her abdomen. The fluid draws out the toxins that would normally be expelled by her kidneys, thereby partially compensating for kidney failure. The alternative and more conventional form of dialysis, which works on purifying the blood supply, requires attendance at a hospital for most of the day every alternate day; so the machine is designed to make life easier by dialysing you in the privacy of your own home while you sleep at night.

That is the theory, but in practice it is all much more complicated. The machine is designed to be operable by the patient without any assistance. But in Mother's case, it soon becomes apparent that her arthritic hands, general frailty and absent-mindedness require someone else to do it for her. The machine carries with it a high risk of infection, which can lead to peritonitis and death; so the process of setting it up and connecting it to the patient involves repeated antiseptic washing and scrubbing of the hands by the carer responsible and takes a good half hour to set up. It needs to run uninterrupted for ten hours, which means starting it around nine-thirty at night, so that Mother can be disconnected from it when she wakes at eight in the morning.

All this means that I have to be home every night to connect Mother to her machine. It also means dropping anything else I am doing, like cooking dinner or watching television to go through the half-hour ritual at the appointed time. To make matters worse, the computerized machine has a mind of its own; it emits a loud, beeping alarm signal if Mother turns over in bed and twists the supply tube, interrupting the dialysis. Since she often sleeps through these alarms, I have to remain vigilant through the night and, if necessary, wake her and reset the machine.

This routine only lasts for about nine months, but at the time it seems like a life sentence. While Mother accepts it all quite stoically, my own reaction is one of desperate anger and frustration, which I vent on her. The half hour spent connecting her to the machine assumes the status of a nightly penance, during which I bristle with ill-concealed resentment, snapping at her for being too slow or uncooperative and even on occasion shaking her with anger. And those nightly sessions, when I am compelled to wrestle with her and the machine, become our only contact. For the rest of the day, I avoid her as much as I can, performing my various duties with the ruthless efficiency of a reluctant prison guard, silently presenting her with trays of food and various doses of medication.

Mother and I no longer speak, unless it is to discuss the logistics of her next hospital appointment or her latest complaint about one of her home helps. As her mobility deteriorates, all this becomes increasingly problematic. It begins with a fall in February 1999, in which she fractures one wrist, followed with an unfortunate symmetry two months later by an almost identical fracture of the other wrist. She is also suffering from advanced osteoporosis, which is collapsing her spine and making it increasingly difficult for her to walk, let alone climb the stairs in my house.

Despite her physical decline, Mother still exercises considerable charm on those around her. She has a very sympathetic social worker from Islington Council, who makes sure she gets the maximum hours of home help available, especially after Mother confides in her about my irritability and impatience with her needs. She has an NHS physiotherapist who visits her twice a week (quite an achievement in itself) and who is full of admiration for Mother's spirit and determination.

By the summer of 1999 she is virtually immobile and needs help even to walk the few steps from her bedroom to adjacent bathroom. There is now a rota of home helps who come in morning, noon and night to dress and 'toilet' her. Since she is unable to open the front door to them while I am at work, they each have keys to the house. Thanks to the vagaries of the agencies whence they come, there are frequent problems when a particular carer fails to show up or her replacement turns up without the keys.

Mother has her favourites among the carers and complains bitterly when they are off sick or on leave and some green and inexperienced locum replaces them. For my part, I live in constant anxiety that no one will show up at all, leaving me with the dreaded task of 'toileting' Mother and dressing or undressing her. In the event, I always make sure that someone does turn up, but only by dint of constantly chasing the agencies on the phone and threatening or cajoling them into action.

Much of Mother's last nine months are spent at the Middlesex Hospital, where she is periodically admitted to readjust her dialysis regime. For me, these periods of hospitalization are a longed-for respite, freeing me from the nightly ritual, and I dread her return home. Her own feelings about hospital are mixed. She much prefers the Middlesex to the Whittington, gets on well with her young and charming consultant and strikes up friendships with some of the regular nurses on the renal ward. In some respects, she feels safer and less isolated in hospital, as against the long hours she has to spend alone at home. But while she enjoys the bustle and chatter of life on a ward, she is never satisfied with the level of service she gets on the NHS. She is also prone to muddle times and dates and to imagine neglect where there has been none.

During one of her spells in hospital, in August 1999, the ward sister decides to carry out a forty-eight-hour written assessment to determine how much care Mother will need when she goes back home. When I look at the log now, in one of Mother's medical files, the entries are a pathetic record of a life narrowed down to the barest essentials.

15.30   Wanted to be prepared for bed. Slightly confused. Reassured that it was too early to go to bed.
16.40   Not happy with position of bed. Rectified by moving to bed by window.
19.10   Mrs. Masani feels claustrophobic. Reassurance given.
19.50   Not happy with bed change. Reassurance given and alternative offered.
21.00   Complaining about bed space. Says she has no leverage! Told she can move around in bed if she wants.
21.10   Complaining about bed, and again says she has no leverage! Reassurance given.

The catalogue of complaints and reassurance continues unabated the next day.

9.00   Assist patient with wash. Needs encouragement to be more independent.
10.00   Mrs. Masani's chair moved from the corner to the side of her bed to make her less claustrophobic. Patient is happy with this arrangement.
14.20   Called to discuss bed status and whether she could be moved. Explanation given.
15.00   Mrs. Masani had her hair washed and her nails cut. Enjoyed her hair being washed.

5.8.99, 3.00 am: The dialysis machine was bleeping and Mrs. Masani was trying to disconnect herself, believing that the cycles were finished.
   Reassured and re-connected. Some vagueness in her speech and report of situation not always actually happened.

10.00 am: Wanted to swap beds with patient opposite. Explained that we didn't have time. She wanted to make room for her birthday party tomorrow, as she is expecting a lot of visitors. Told her that only 2 visitors allowed per bed.

10.30 am: Ditto. Said she would fax Mr. Woolfson (the consultant) about her bed.

Unsure as to whether patient opposite really wishes to swap beds as she doesn't speak English.

~

19.20   I took Mrs. Masani to the bathroom. She was regularly checked to see if she had finished her toilet, but complained that she had been ignored.

19.45   Mrs. Masani transferred to chair. Again comment that she'd been ignored.

~

Mother still hopes and plans for a return to Delhi, with a homing instinct that grows stronger as she approaches the end of her life. With a callousness I will regret, I pooh-pooh the idea, ruthlessly reminding her of the impossibility of undertaking even the long air journey in her current condition, let alone the question of who would look after her there.

Her sisters, now confident that the offer will not be taken up, both invite her to come and live with them in Delhi if she so desires. She toys with the idea, though she knows in her heart that it is impractical. 'I could divide my time between Sheela and Sarala,' she says; to which I protest: 'You know perfectly well that you'd fall out with them in a matter of days if you were living under the same roof. And what would happen when they leave Delhi, as they do during the summer? Who would look after you then?'

'I could go next year, by which time I'll be better. And by then they will have slowed down too. Sheela will soon be too old to travel.'

'And what makes you think you'll be better next year?' I ask with a relentless logic. The only justification for such cruelty is that I am reaching the end of my own tether, and I see her fantasies as an attempt to evade the real decisions that have to be made. Foremost among these is the question of how long she can be cared for at home and whether it might be better for her and me if she were to go into residential care.

Social Services give us the opportunity for a trial run when a vacancy comes up for a two-week respite at one of their nicer nursing homes in a green and leafy corner of Highgate. It is a relatively bright and cheerful place with a nice garden; and Mother has the luxury of a large room to herself. Nevertheless, her move there, which has to be arranged by ambulance, proves traumatic. She bursts into tears as soon as she is wheeled in and starts howling and wailing like a wounded animal, much to the excitement of other 'inmates' and the distress of her designated nurse, who dissolves into tears herself.

My own reaction is one of studied indifference, covering up a combination of guilt for ridding myself of Mother and irritation with her for making such a scene. The pattern is set for the rest of the fortnight's so-called respite, with Mother phoning me twice or thrice a day with a string of largely imaginary complaints about her ill-treatment at the home. The staff have forgotten to give her her medication; they have starved her all day; they have ignored her requests to be 'toileted'; the food has upset her delicate stomach; the other 'inmates' are senile and demented; and so on. Each time I ring the nurses' station to complain on her behalf, it soon becomes apparent that Mother's grievances are little more than a cry for my attention.

Hence my astonishment, when it is time for her to return home two weeks later, and she is every bit as reluctant to come out of the nursing home as she was about going in. She has been very well looked after, she insists, with constant attention through the night; the food has been excellent; and she has enjoyed being surrounded by other people, rather than being on her own all day at home. She weeps copiously when the ambulance arrives to bring her home and begs me to try and arrange an extension of her stay, which proves impossible.

And so she comes home for the last time. Three days later, she is struck down by the dreaded peritonitis, the great hazard of her method of dialysis. Weary of the daily demands of the implacable machine, I have delegated the task to two of her more conscientious carers, whom I have trained in the various sterilizing rituals. But in the weeks and months to come I will often wonder if her final illness is due to a lapse in hygiene and therefore indirectly the result of my neglect. And sometimes, in the early hours between sleep and waking, I even blame myself for having unconsciously willed it so.

Mother goes back to the familiar ward at the Middlesex, her bed this time mercifully near a window, so that she does not complain of claustrophobia. In fact, she complains of very little, although the infection is painful and makes her permanently nauseous. The antibiotics she is given are having little effect, and there is not much else the hospital can do. They warn me that there is a fifty-fifty chance she might not recover; but the prospect of her dying still seems unreal.

I visit her in hospital every day, and for the first time in years I chat to her and allow myself to show her signs of tenderness like a kiss on the forehead and a pat on the shoulder. She seems remarkably composed and unafraid of the approaching end; but each time I leave her and turn for a final glimpse, I see her eyes following me intently as I disappear down the corridor from the ward.

The last time she speaks to me is on a Saturday afternoon five days after her admission. I tell her that she will soon be back home and that I am planning to buy her a special orthopaedic chair with some money her sisters have sent as a Diwali gift for her. 'I don't know why you're prolonging my life,' she says quite firmly with a hint of exasperation. 'I'm seventy-nine, and that's a good age to die. Please let me go now.'

I respond with the usual protests: it is only an infection, which the antibiotics will soon cure. But I am struck by her calmness, dignity and composure: she has looked death in the face and found its oblivion preferable to the painful physical decline that her life has now become.

The next morning I am woken by a phone call from the ward Sister. Mother has had a bad night and is growing weaker; septicaemia or blood poisoning is setting in: we should spend as much time with her as possible. Half an hour later, while I am shaving, the ward rings again. Mother has choked on her own vomit, a sign of the approaching end, and is now unconscious: I should come at once. I phone David, who has been a constant visitor at her bedside, as concerned as I am.

By the time I dress and drive down to the hospital, he is already there before me, weeping uncontrollably as he holds Mother's hand. She is still breathing but unconscious with her eyes fixed. 'The hearing is the last thing to go,' says Sister, 'so go on talking to her.' I've no idea what I say, but I clutch Mother's free hand and talk to her through my own tears and sobs. Her breathing grows slower, and twenty minutes later it ceases altogether.

Mother's passing has affected me more profoundly than I could ever have anticipated. In the immediate aftermath, I am remarkably cheerful, kept busy by the funeral arrangements, the calls to friends and family and the daunting task of sorting through her immense wardrobes in London and Delhi and distributing her personal effects among those who knew her. Later, there comes a sense of freedom and even relief: for the first time in years, my life is my own and I have only myself to worry about.

It is much later, perhaps two years on, that I really feel her absence. 'When I'm gone, you'll be sorry' has been one of her favourite reproaches when I am being harsh or censorious. 'I have no reason to,' I counter, refusing to be guilt-tripped. 'I've done more for you than any other son I know.' And so I have. But what I have failed to recognize as I cope with Mother's needs is just how much I too need her. Her departure has left an immense emptiness at the heart of me, which may never be filled.

Now that Mother and Father are both gone, neither can confirm or deny truths that were often stranger than fiction. He lived long enough to see his free-market, pro-Western political values triumph, not only in Eastern Europe but in India too. From being a voice in the wilderness of opposition to Nehru and his daughter, he had the satisfaction of being asked to bless the economic liberalization policies of India's current Prime Minister, Dr Manmohan Singh (Finance Minister in the early 1990s). Mother died without any such vindication: I was her sole achievement. I hope that by telling her story I have afforded her some of the tragic dignity she never quite achieved in life.